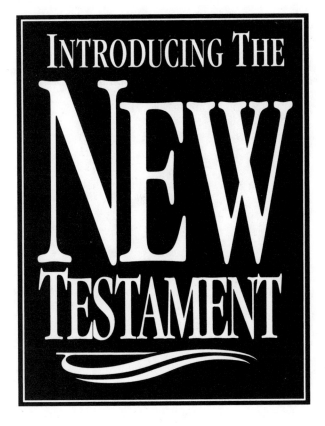

INTRODUCING THE NEW TESTAMENT

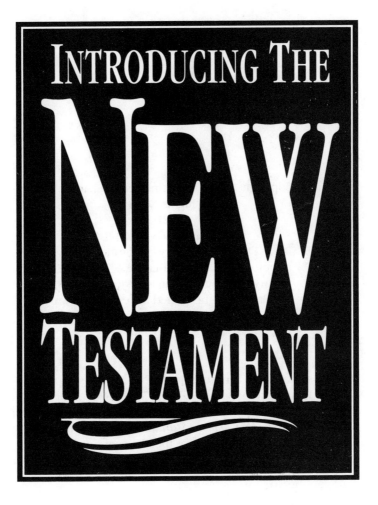

INTRODUCING THE NEW TESTAMENT

JOE BLAIR

BROADMAN
& HOLMAN
PUBLISHERS

Nashville, Tennessee

Unless otherwise noted, all Scripture quotations are taken from the Holy Bible, *New International Version*, copyright © 1973, 1978, 1984 by International Bible Society. Scripture quotations marked (KJV) are taken from the *King James Version* of the Bible; (NRSV) are taken from the *New Revised Standard Version* of the Bible, copyright © 1989 by the Division of Christian Education of the National Council of Churches of Christ in the United States of America, used by permission, all rights reserved.

Library of Congress Cataloging–in–Publication Data

Blair, Joe, 1941- .
  Introducing the New Testament / Joe Blair.
      p.   cm.
  Includes bibliographical references and index.
  ISBN 0-8054-2123-8
  1. Bible.   N.T.—Introductions.   2. Bible.   N.T.—Textbooks.
  I. Title
BS2330.2.B535   1994
225.6'1—dc20

93-33581
CIP

List of Illustrations

List of Tables

List of Maps

Preface

This book is a nontechnical survey of the New Testament and its background. Its purpose is to give students of the New Testament some basic perspectives and the information necessary for making responsible interpretations and applications of the New Testament Scriptures.

A book of this size cannot deal adequately with critical issues. However, the reading lists at the ends of the chapters and the books listed in the endnotes indicate authors who, by their critical scholarship, have contributed in some way to my thinking and writing. Colleagues have encouraged me by their interest and confidence. Randall Bush, David Capes, Wayne Day, Curtis Freeman, George Guthrie, Randy Hatchett, Kelvin Moore, Alvin Reid, and Gene Wofford either read portions of the manuscript and made numerous suggestions. The editors, Trent Butler, Forrest Jackson, and John Landers, have been patient and helpful with their suggestions. Denise Brown, Nancy Garst, Becky Greer, and Karen Martin have assisted at different phases of the preparation of the manuscript.

Biblical Illustrator has supplied all photographs. My friend James McLemore, editor of *Biblical Illustrator,* has given counsel and resources to make this book more attractive and helpful.

A special expression of gratitude is afforded my wife, Carrie, whose encouragement, perceptive suggestions, and constructive criticism were invaluable. My son, Brad, has read the text from a student's perspective and has added insight as well as occasional doses of wit to the whole process. My prayer is that students searching for truth will find directions that lead them more fully into God's revelation in Jesus Christ.

Introduction

William Barclay wrote of a man in India who read the Gospel of Luke. So impressed was he with the witness to Jesus Christ that he became a Christian. At first he thought that being a Christian was a private matter. Then, by chance, he received a copy of the Acts of the Apostles. After reading the Acts, he sought out and implored a local pastor to allow him to become a member of the church, because, he said, "I felt I must become a member of that church *which carries on the life of Christ.*"[1]

This man's story demonstrates the vital relationship between Christ and the New Testament. The New Testament gives witness to Christ, what He was about in His public ministry, and what He continues to be about through the church. Therefore, we approach the New Testament as the supremely important witness to Jesus Christ.

Important information about the early witness to Christ can be gleaned from first- and second-century sources outside the New Testament, but these are very limited. Careful interpretation of the Old Testament can inform us about the Messiah, or Christ, that the people expected. In addition, church history, church teaching, and the personal experiences of many people can add vital information. For both the curious and the earnest seeker of information, the reading and study of the New

Testament is a primary step to knowing who Jesus is and what He is about.

This book is a guide in taking that necessary step. While almost anyone with some reading ability can understand and appreciate the New Testament, much more light awaits those who search into background and introductory information. Part 1 of this book gives information about the New Testament itself and introduces various helps and methodologies in reading and interpreting the New Testament. Part 2 deals with some basic background which can be of significant help in understanding the New Testament and, therefore, understanding Christ. The remaining three major parts of the book introduce and survey the New Testament documents, stressing the unique witness which each gives to Jesus Christ or to His work through the church. The book includes a glossary and an index to make the content more accessible to the reader.

The New Testament documents are introduced in terms of writer, readers, and message. The writer and reader sections are pivotal for understanding the meaning of the writing. In this regard the documents are approached as they are, noting in a limited way some of the interpretative questions important to writer and readers. Generally, the traditional positions on authorship and readers and their situations are followed. Allowance is made for some adjustment to authorship in terms of a secretary's input, such as Silas serving as secretary to Peter (1 Pet. 5:12), or a close associate or disciples who wrote in relationship to stated authors, such as a school of disciples contributing to the Johannine literature under the tutelage of the apostle John. Such allowances still give the direct authority of the apostolic witness and legitimately claim the authorship as indicated by the writing itself or by long-standing tradition, such as the tradition that Luke, physician and companion of Paul, wrote the Gospel of Luke and Acts. Of course, with some documents we can only draw reasonable but uncertain conclusions as to the writers.

Christians and non-Christians alike should approach and interact with the New Testament in a responsible manner. Some persons have manipulated the New Testament—misappropriating, misapplying, or distorting it—for their own selfish goals. We certainly would not want to treat the New Testament witness in that way. We would not want to promote Jesus Christ for our own financial gain or the enhancement of our status and prestige, for example. Neither would we want to disregard the poor or homeless or justify racism in the name of Christ or the New Testament witness. Nor would we want to follow and support someone who did. Having a sound basis for understanding the New Testament will help us to be responsible in interpretation and application.

But why study the New Testament specifically? H. I. Hester's answer to that question is appropriate still.[2] The study is important because of the greatness of Jesus Christ. The New Testament focuses upon God's ultimate revelation of Himself in His Son. The New Testament, then, is about a person. Without Him, who He was and all that He did and said, no New Testament would exist. Christianity is not so much a religion as it is a relationship to God as we encounter Him and know Him in Jesus Christ.

Also, the study is important because of the significance of the Christian movement and its effects upon history. Literature, art, and science in various cultures have the stamp of the Christian religion upon them. The political and educational domains of humanity have been greatly influenced by the Christian movement, especially in the West. The Judeo-Christian ethic significantly impacts our ethical base. An influence so basic in our Western culture should be given special study, even by those who may be unsympathetic to the Christian movement at this point. Although books about Christianity may be helpful in understanding the movement, the primary source and beginning point for understanding is the New Testament.

A third reason for studying the New Testament is simply for what the New Testament can mean to the student. If the New Testament reveals God's ultimate act of revelation in Jesus Christ, which it does; and if God's revelation is the revelation of truth for human beings, and it is; then intellectual honesty and personal integrity should lead persons to study the New Testament.

In the various parts of this book, an effort has been made always to keep Christ the focus for interpretation. From the background materials, which emphasize formative influences upon the times of Christ, to the witness of the New Testament materials themselves, Christ is the key to understanding who God is and what He is about with humanity and this world.

ENDNOTES

1. William Barclay, *The All-Sufficient Christ* (London: SCM Press, 1963), 111–12.

2. H. I. Hester, *The Heart of the New Testament* (Nashville: Broadman Press, 1963), 5–13.

The New Testament Canon

The collection of books that we call the New Testament is the New Testament canon. The word *canon* comes from the Greek word for "reed." In the development of the usage of the word, *canon* came to mean a standard of measurement. Then *canon* developed to mean an official standard by which other things are measured. In terms of the New Testament, the books of the New Testament are the standard list of books, those accepted as distinctive and authoritative by the church in relationship to other Christian writings. They are officially reserved as the revelation of God in and through Jesus Christ and His church. The development of the canon to official status may be considered in three major stages.

The First Stage: Oral Transmission and Literary Activity (A.D. 30–90)

Basically, the written Scriptures for Christians of New Testament times were those of the Old Testament. The New Testament was in the process of being written. Until the writing down and collecting of the New Testament, the apostles' teachings of and about Jesus were authoritative for the Way of Christ (Acts 9:2). Apostles, teachers, missionaries, and others passed these teachings along orally. This oral communication is often referred to as the oral transmission of the text. After a time, independent units of Jesus' activity or teachings were written down and circulated.

The New Testament does not make direct reference to "oral transmission" as a term, but some statements indicate the reality and importance of the oral transmission of the gospel. Paul wrote of having received the oral gospel: "For what I received I passed on to you as of first importance: that Christ died for our sins according to the Scriptures, that he was buried, that he was raised on the third day according to the Scriptures, and that he appeared to Peter, and then to the Twelve" (1 Cor. 15:3–5).

Paul's farewell speech to the Ephesian elders, recorded in Acts, gives some insight into the oral gospel, also. In Acts 20:35 he encouraged his listeners to remember that Jesus said, " 'It is more blessed to give than to receive.' " These words do not appear in the gospels, so it is likely that they came from a line of oral transmission which may have been written down eventually as part of a document we no longer have.

The literary activity which produced the New Testament began with Paul. Paul's earliest written work probably was 1 Thessalo-

5

nians, penned around A.D. 49 or 50. Paul wrote many letters after that, and a number of different authors later wrote the Gospels and the rest of the books of the New Testament. By the end of the first century, however, some evidence indicates that individual writings were being collected into groups.

The Second Stage: Collection (A.D. 90–180)

A collection of Paul's letters possibly was completed by the end of the first century . A quote from 2 Peter tells about Paul's letters: "He writes the same way in all his letters, speaking in them of these matters. His letters contain some things that are hard to understand, which ignorant and unstable people distort, as they do the other Scriptures, to their own destruction" (3:16).

This statement points to two probabilities. First, the reference "in all his letters" indicates that Paul's letters were known as a group. Second, the reference to people twisting the meaning of Paul's letters suggests that they abused them as a collected body of materials.

A witness outside the New Testament is Clement of Rome, who wrote to the Corinthian church around A.D. 95. He quoted the Old Testament as Scripture, revealed a knowledge of the teachings of Jesus, made mention of 1 Corinthians, and revealed that the book of Hebrews was known.[1] Again, such reference to various parts of the New Testament writings demonstrates that a group of materials was available for use. But it is impossible to tell how formal such a collection was. By the end of the first century, Christians depended upon a collection of Paul's letters and perhaps a greater collection of New Testament Scripture as they taught and lived the Way of Christ.

A papyrus manuscript of the Greek New Testament. The Chester Beatty Biblical Papyri. *Biblical Illustrator* Photo/David Rogers/Kelsey Museum, Ann Arbor, Mich.

By the middle of the second century, collections of New Testament writings were vital to the church, as is evident in at least three collections. First, Marcion put together a collection of writings around A.D. 145, which became known, appropriately, as *Marcion's Canon*. Marcion rejected the Old Testament; he wanted to separate Christianity from Judaism, and he considered the God of the Old Testament to be evil. Marcion was an ardent follower of Paul, so his canon included about ten of Paul's letters. He rejected the Gospels, except for portions of Luke having no Old Testament references. The church at Rome, where Marcion was a member, excluded him from the church because of his rejection of the Old Testament and other Christian writings.

Second, the *Muratorian Canon*, used by the church at Rome by at least A.D. 170, may have been a response to Marcion's Canon. Included in the Muratorian Canon were the four Gospels, Acts, two and perhaps three letters of John, thirteen Epistles of Paul, Jude, and Revelation.

A third collection was of the Gospels, composed before A.D. 170. Tatian wove the four Gospels into one account called a *Diatessaron*, which refers to an "interweaving" of the Gospels.[2]

These various documents indicate a growing awareness on the part of Christian leaders that the church needed to separate those Christian writings uniquely authoritative and inspired from other writings which could have been considered on the same level. Other writings during the second and third century vied for a place in the New Testament canon. Christians in the Egyptian city of Alexandria accepted the Epistle of Barnabas, which discusses Christians and Jews in relationship to the Old Testament and teaches a way of light and a way of darkness. Those in Carthage used the Shepherd of Hermas, a document teaching that Christians have a second chance if they repent of their sins. The Apocalypse of Peter became important to Christians in Rome. It contains certain visions, including one of people in torment in the afterlife. These writings all date from the second century and were read in some Christian churches. Other churches refused to allow them to be read.[3]

The Third Stage: An Accepted Canon (A.D. 180–400)

Quite early Christian leaders began to discuss what should and should not be considered as writings of divine revelation. Records are not available to trace every discussion or every stage of development, but enough extant evidence exists to give us a sufficient idea. For example, Irenaeus, toward the end of the second century, relates instruction he received from Polycarp, who considered the Gospels and other writings as of God. Polycarp's ministry occurred in the first part of the second century.[4]

Origen, in the middle of the third century, recognized that the New Testament canon had limits, and he revealed a knowledge of all the books presently in our New Testament.[5] Around A.D. 325, Eusebius surveyed the prevailing views of the canon in his Ecclesiastical History.[6] He listed books in three categories: those universally accepted as Scripture, those accepted by the majority, and those considered unacceptable.

A significant event occurred at Easter in A.D. 367. Athanasius, bishop of Alexandria, wrote an Easter letter to his parishioners in which he spelled out a canon, the first in a writing of an official nature. The list corresponded exactly with the twenty-seven books we have today as our New Testament canon. Although some debate would continue, the New Testament canon was set rather securely by A.D. 400.

Noteworthy to this discussion is the fact that Christians used the New Testament writings as authoritative and divinely inspired long before the completion of the process of canonization described above. Nevertheless, the process helped many Christians, who came after the eyewitnesses to Jesus were no longer present, to understand better the nature of divine revelation. The official collection of Scriptures enabled others to avoid giving authority to writings which may have been mistaken to have the same authority and inspiration of the New Testament canon. Also, the process of canonization is a witness to how God worked through the church to effect His will in the writing and collecting of the New Testament.

FOR STUDY AND REVIEW

IDENTIFY:

Canon
Eusebius
Marcion
Athanasius
Muratorian Canon
Diatessaron
Tatian

QUESTIONS FOR CONSIDERATION

1. What are the names, dates, and characteristics of the three stages in the development of the New Testament canon?

2. Did some Christian groups depend upon other works as authoritative Scripture? Explain.

FOR FURTHER READING

Brooks, James A. "The Text and Canon of the New Testament." *The Broadman Bible Commentary*. Vol. 8. Edited by Clifton J. Allen. Nashville: Broadman Press, 1969: 15–21.

Carson, D. A., Douglas J. Moo, and Leon Morris. *An Introduction to the New Testament.* Grand Rapids: Zondervan Publishing House; 1992, 492–499.

Harrison, Everett F. *Introduction to the New Testament.* Rev. ed. Grand Rapids: Eerdmans, 1982: 97–133.

Harris, Stephen L. *The New Testament: A Student's Introduction.* Mountain View, Calif.: Mayfield, 1988: 6–10.

ENDNOTES

1. See Everett F. Harrison, *Introduction to the New Testament,* rev. ed. (Grand Rapids: Wm. B. Eerdmans Publishing Company, 1982), 99.

2. Ibid., 103.

3. Glenn W. Barker, William L. Lane, J. Ramsey Michaels, *The New Testament Speaks* (New York: Harper & Row, 1969), 27.

4. Eusebius, *The Ecclesiastical History*, V, xx, 6, *Loeb Classical Library*, vol I, trans. Kirsopp Lake, ed. G. P. Goold (Cambridge: Harvard University Press, n.d.), 499.

5. Ibid., VI, xxv, 4.

6. Ibid., 1–10.

1) ① ORAL & TRANSMISSION & LITERACY (AD. 30-90)

② COLLECTION (AD 90-180)

③ ARE accepted canon (AD 180-400)

2)

The Inspiration of Scripture

By *Scripture* Christians usually mean the sacred literature composing the Old and New Testaments. These writings are sacred because in them and by them God reveals who He is, what He has done in and through His people, and what He expects His people to become, be, and do.

Not all people approach the Bible from this point of view. Some people view it as writings from long ago which have no relevance to today's world. Others may consider the Bible with hostility, thinking that it is superstitious nonsense used by narrow-minded people to force their opinions upon society in general and upon their neighbors and friends in particular. Still others approach it as literature of a certain group of people belonging to a certain period of time, valuable as a study in literature but having no present religious value.

Christians have a positive attitude toward the Bible, viewing it as a body of material that is available to us because God Himself wills it to be so. They believe that God's revelation of Himself is a valid form of knowledge, of knowing. They also believe that this revelation has taken shape in a written form, the Bible. In viewing the Bible as God's revelation, Christians use various ideas and words to express their respect for and belief in the revelation of Scripture as the inspired Word of God.

Divine and Human

Generally, as Christians begin to talk about Scripture, they will agree that both the divine and human activity in the producing of Scripture must be kept in proper balance. Some people have not thought much about, or pursued information concerning, how the Bible came to be. The fact that so much humanness was involved in the development of the New Testament canon may disturb them. We must remember, however, that God, as the biblical account reveals, often worked His will through human beings. He chose to do that in relationship to the biblical text as well. Luke 1:1–4 is an example of how human authors wrote some New Testament books.

Accepting the New Testament Books

Recognition of a New Testament canon did not develop until the fourth century. The church gradually made decisions that a canon of specific books did exist as an exclusive body of Scripture. But churches used the same writings as authoritative much earlier. For example, the church at Rome rejected Marcion's Canon and used the Muratorian

Canon, indicating that they already had a commitment to a body of authoritative Scripture. Therefore, Christians used writings as Scripture long before they officially became Scripture.

Factors Influencing the Canon

Growing out of the process of canonization and subsequent discussion about the canon is a strong witness to the inspiration and authority of Scripture.[1] The *principle of apostolicity* was uppermost in the minds of followers of Christ as they thought about which books should be authoritative for the church's guidance and instruction. A writing possessed apostolicity if written by an apostle or if influenced substantially in its content by an apostle. Above all, the writing had to conform to apostolic teaching. A traditional belief that Simon Peter influenced the content of the Book of Mark attributed apostolicity to that account of the gospel. Likewise, the writer of the Book of Luke was associated with the apostle Paul. While other writings may not have been considered directly influenced by an apostle, they nonetheless were in the stream of the authoritative teachings of the apostles, as was also true with Mark and Luke.

Another factor of influence in forming a canon of Scripture was that of *use by the church*. The writings that the earliest churches used as their guides for living and teaching became Scripture for them. Yet even this factor grew out of the principle of apostolicity. In addition, a writing had to express *unity of doctrine* with the earliest accepted apostolic teaching as well as with Old Testament revelation in order to be viewed as authoritative Scripture.

Relationship of the Divine and Human Activity

Balancing and explaining the relationship of the divine and human in Scripture have been a challenge to Christians. Reformation leaders, for example, struggled with some books of the New Testament and their importance for the canon. Martin Luther, the great German Reformation leader, had reservations about Hebrews, James, Luke, and Revelation while 2 and 3 John and Revelation posed some problems for Calvin.[2] Yet both of these leaders looked upon the New Testament as God's Word.

Modern theologians have made contributions toward explaining the divine and human in the formation of the Scriptures. B. F. Westcott, a New Testament scholar, stressed the superintending providence of God in guiding the church to a conclusion about the New Testament canon.[3] Karl Barth, a major theological influence in this century, emphasized that the church cannot give the canon to itself. "The church cannot 'form' it, as historians have occasionally said, without being aware of the theological implications. The church can only confirm or establish it as something which has already been formed and given."[4] Both Westcott and Barth stressed divine influence and guidance, but also they stressed the role of the church. Again, history attests to the role of the church in the formation of the New Testament canon; God chose to use the church to accomplish His purpose.[5]

Everett Harrison stressed the divine and human elements in inspiration as he considered the principle of canonicity from the standpoint of authority. The authority is ultimately traceable to God. The writings of the New Testament are traceable to human writers. The authority of the human writers is traceable to the apostolic witness. The apostolic witness is traceable to the apostles, whose authority for conveying the revelation of God is traceable to Jesus. Jesus is God's expression of Himself in revelation. Christ, as the revelation of God, authenticates and completes the Old Testament revelation and promises the guidance of the Holy Spirit for all truth after His death. Harrison, therefore, believed that Christ is the key to canonicity. According to him, it was inevitable that New Testament Christians would eventually regard the New Testament as having the same authority as the Old Testament as it enclosed the completed revelation of God.[6]

Christians refer to the Bible as God's Word. That the words are human words expressed in human concepts, influenced by the culture of the time, cannot be discounted. The human side must be accepted. God chose to work through human beings, and in the process their humanness was not set aside. Therefore, as Christians talk about the Bible, other words become important in expressing the relationship of the human and divine in the formation of Scripture.

Inspired

The witness of Scripture about itself is that it is *inspired*. Indeed, this is the only word, in comparision with those discussed below, which the Bible uses about itself. Second Timothy 3:16 often is cited in this regard: "All scripture is given by inspiration of God" (KJV). "Scripture" in this quote referred to the Hebrew Scripture, roughly corresponding to what today we call the Old Testament, but Christians generally take the statement to apply to the New Testament documents as well. *Inspiration* comes from a Latin word meaning "to breathe in." The Greek word

behind the English word means "God-breathed," a word that occurs only in the New Testament in the verse just quoted. The words for *breath* and *spirit* are the same in Greek. So 2 Timothy 3:16 carries the idea that God "in-Spirited" the writers of Scripture. The basic idea is that God guided human beings in the writing and preservation of the Bible.

Other writings are sometimes identified as being inspired, particularly poetry and prose that provide special insight into something or lift people's spirits and urge them to positive living. However, there is a difference. In reference to the Bible as inspired, *who* inspired it is the central issue. God inspired the writing of the Bible. This means that God's will and guidance are stamped upon it. In the idea of Westcott, God superintended the church in the process. Or in the terms of Barth, the church did not create the canon; the church received it.

Authoritative

Christians also prefer the word authoritative to be added to the word *inspired*. The Bible is the writing of supreme authority among all the words and writings of this world. The Bible is authoritative above every writing about the way that people find relationship to God in Jesus Christ and about the way people are to be and live in obedience to Christ as Lord and Savior.

Infallible

Still other people join the word *infallible* with the words *inspired* and *authoritative* to explain their view of the Bible. While subject to interpretation, as all of these words are, *infallible* primarily refers to the message conveyed by the Bible, in which regard it is incapable of error. The words, sentences, paragraphs, and books of the Bible give the message in all its variety of meaning and applications, including the message of salvation, the message of how to be and to live, and numerous other messages ultimately traceable to God Himself about daily living and life's meaning. To say that the Bible is infallible means that it will not fail to give persons the ultimate truth which it intends to give, to guide them to salvation, and to teach them how to live. While interpretations of the words, sentences, paragraphs, chapters, and books may be fallible, the Bible in its properly interpreted, understood, and applied reality is not fallible.

Inerrant

In recent times, *inerrant* has become a favorite word for some in describing the Bible. The reason for use of this word, in its broadest sense, is to affirm the eternal and ultimate trustworthiness of the Bible. Some feel that the word is strong and needs to be used in relationship to the Bible as a means to state the high regard in which Scripture should be held. A widely accepted statement among conservative scholars is contained in the "Chicago Statement on Biblical Inerrancy."[7] The document explains and qualifies the meaning of inerrancy. The qualifications are given in order to protect the strength of the word and to indicate the ways in which the word *inerrancy* does not apply. Some Christians feel that the word cannot apply because it conveys ideas not applicable to the Scripture since inerrant must be qualified before it can be used in discussion.[8]

Simple Biblicism

Many Christians, after all the discussion is done, hold to a position described as "simple biblicism."[9] The position has nothing to do with simple-mindedness but with both knowledge and experience. People may know something of the debates about the positions taken in relationship to the Bible, and they may know some of the questions raised and the difficulties of interpretation and explanation. But they also know that the Bible describes their experience, or they find their experience mirrored in the Bible. They find that the Bible guides them into right thinking and right living. They believe that God has led them, in and through the revelation of the Bible, into truth, and He continues to do so.

The statement of this position is simply, "I believe the Bible." They do not make the Bible an end in itself, for this would be bibliolatry; the Bible is a means to an end. They believe the Bible to be God''s revelation of Himself and His will as He meets humanity in life and in history in and through Israel in the Old Covenant and in and through Jesus Christ in the New Covenant.

Donald Potts, after an excellent discussion of the various views of inspiration, points out that all of the views have elements of truth and weaknesses:

This might be indicative of the fact that the whole process of developing a theory of inspiration is quite difficult. Phrasing a theory is really secondary to the more important fact that the Bible is the authoritative Word of God and to the calling of obeying that Word. The Bible, itself, takes this position because it has no theory of inspiration. Nevertheless, it emphatically declares itself to be the authoritative record of God's revelation.[10]

FOR STUDY AND REVIEW

IDENTIFY:

Apostolicity
Infallible
Inspired
Inerrant
Authoritative

QUESTIONS FOR CONSIDERATION

1. What are factors to consider in the divine-human aspects of the Bible?
2. What have some modern scholars said about the canon?
3. What is meant by "simple biblicism"?

FOR FURTHER READING

Achtemeier, Paul J. *The Inspiration of Scripture: Problems and Proposals.* Philadelphia: The Westminster Press, 1980.
Dockery, David S. *The Doctrine of the Bible.* Nashville: convention Press, 1991.

ENDNOTES

1. Everett Harrison has an excellent survey of views expressed throughout history in *Introduction to the New Testament*, rev. ed. (Grand Rapids: Wm. B. Eerdmans Publishing Company, 1982), 109–21.

2. Ibid., 112–13.

3. *A General Survey of the History of the Canon of the New Testament*, 4th ed. (London: Macmillan, 1875), 496.

4. *The Doctrine of the Word of God*, I, 2, *Church Dogmatics*, ed. G. W. Bromiley and T. F. Torrance (London: T & T Clark, 1956), 473.

5. A discussion of the church's part in the doctrine of inspiration of Scripture is treated ably by Paul J. Achtemeier, *The Inspiration of Scripture: Problems and Proposals* (Philadelphia: Westminster, 1980), 114–36.

6. Harrison, 118.

7. See Carl F. H. Henry, *God, Revelation and Authority*, vol. 4 (Waco, TX: Word, 1979), 211–19, for the document, "The Chicago Statement on Biblical Inerrancy"; also, see Henry's discussion on inerrancy, 162–210.

8. See Achtemeier, *The Inspiration of Scripture:* 41–75; Robison B. James, ed., *The Unfettered Word: Southern Baptists Confront the Authority-Inerrancy Question* (Waco, TX: Word Books, 1987), 47–60.

9. "What Is Biblical Inerrancy," *The Proceedings of the Conference on Biblical Inerrancy*, ed. Michael A. Smith (Nashville: Broadman, 1987), 75–77.

10. "Inspiration of Scripture," *Holman Bible Dictionary*, ed. Trent Butler (Nashville: Holman Bible Publishers, 1991), 704.

❖3❖

The Interpretation of the New Testament

Understanding the New Testament is not usually difficult. We read texts and learn about God, Christ, and the church, as well as what we should be and do. Fortunately, certain helps in interpretation aid us and give us confidence that as we read the Bible, we are treating the Scripture with respect and our understanding is consistent with the revelation of Scripture. We shall now consider types of literature and their arrangement in the New Testament, literary helps, technical terminology and processes of intrepretation, and reliance upon God's guidance as several means to enhanced understanding and application of the New Testament.

Types of Literature in the New Testament

The *Gospels* are distinctively Christian forms of literature. At first the message about Jesus Christ was circulated by means of oral communication. However, in response to the increasing dearth of eyewitnesses to Jesus, to the challenges of competing religions and philosophies, to persecutions, and to questions, concerns, and needs of Christians, Matthew, Mark, Luke, and John emerged. The writers penned the Gospels at different times and under different circumstances; conse-quently, each writer compiled and wrote from a different perspective and purpose. They are not exactly history or biography, although they contain historical and biographical infor-mation. Rather, they are proclamations about Jesus Christ.

The other writings of the New Testament materialized for many of the same reasons as the Gospels. *Letters* of the New Testament are sometimes referred to as occasional writings, because some occasion (problem, need, question, etc.) evoked the writer to put his thoughts, message, information, or instruc-tions into a letter. The letter was a common form of communication in New Testament times. Letters of the New Testament generally follow the Greek letter-writing form. The components are (1) the name of the sender, (2) the readers, (3) the greetings, (4) the body of the letter, and (5) a closing. Not all writings in the New Testament have every element of this form. First John, referred to as a letter, does not have the name of the sender or readers nor does it have a greeting. Yet it reads like a letter.

A few writings of the New Testament are sometimes called *homilies*; they are more like sermons than letters. The Books of James and 1 John fall into that category, although they have characteristics of a letter as well. In addi-tion, a few books, such as Romans and

Hebrews, read more like theological treatises than letters. They give extended treatments of several major theological themes, such as particular aspects of salvation or a specific understanding of God and Christ.

While the New Testament contains historical information throughout, no work had as its sole purpose to present a history. The Book of Acts comes close to that, however, and is sometimes designated as a history of the Christian church covering the period from the ascension of Christ to Paul's imprisonment. Acts is especially concerned with the movement of the gospel through all kinds of barriers as different kinds of people in different places accepted Christ as Lord.[1]

Another unique literary form in the New Testament is the body of *apocalyptic* materials. The Book of Revelation is the only fully apocalyptic writing of the New Testament. But Mark 13 is referred to as the Little Apocalypse because it is written in apocalyptic style. Apocalyptic writing was a particular literary style arising in Judaism and used by Christian writers. This style used symbols, images, visions, numbers, and other expressions to vividly convey a message.

In addition, certain types of literature within the larger types should be noted. *Hyperbole* is sometimes used. Jesus' statement in Matthew 5:29, "If your right eye causes you to sin, tear it out and throw it away . . ." (NRSV), is hyerbole used to drive home the point of the seriousness of sin. *Confessional formulas* are also present in the text, confession of faith which Christians repeated from memory. "Jesus is Lord" (1 Cor. 12:3) was probably one of the earliest confessional formulas of the church. First Corinthians 15:3–5 is an early confessional outline of the church's belief about the death and resurrection of Christ. Even *hymns* are present in the text, Colossians 1:15–20 contains a "Christ-

hymn," which gives a number of affirmations about Christ. Obviously, as a person interprets, understanding the type of materials being interpreted is helpful.

The New Testament Books

Another prominent factor in the formation of the structure of the New Testament was the use of the books by the church. Probably Matthew stands first in the canon because the church could easily use it in teaching new converts and in giving witness to Christ as the fulfillment of God's revelation.

Box 1: A Listing of the New Testament Books

Gospels
    Matthew
    Mark
    Luke
    John
Acts
Letters of Paul
    Romans
    1, 2 Corinthians
    Galatians
    Ephesians
    Philippians
    Colossians
    1, 2 Thessalonians
    1, 2 Timothy
    Titus
    Philemon
Hebrews
General Letters
    James
    1, 2 Peter
    1, 2, 3 John
    Jude
Revelation

The church saved letters and other writings, arranged them in collections, and used them to instruct the church and to witness to outsiders. Romans was the longest work of Paul, in which he gave instruction and theological development to a number of Christian concerns. In the New Testament the Letter to the Romans stands first in the collection of Paul's letters. Yet Romans was not the first letter Paul wrote; that distinction likely belongs to 1 Thessalonians. Shorter or personal writings among the letters tend to follow longer writings. In the present arrangement of the New Testament canon, Philemon stands at the end of the Pauline collection. Paul wrote Philemon from prison, which would place it chronologcally with Ephesians, Philippians, and Colossians.

Box 2: Chronological Listing of the Books of the New Testament

1, 2 Thessalonians
1, 2 Corinthians
Galatians
Romans
Ephesians
Philippians
Colossians
Philemon
1, 2 Timothy
Titus
James
Hebrews
1, 2 Peter
Jude
Mark
Luke
Acts
Matthew
John
1, 2, 3 John
Revelation

The arrangement of the writings of the New Testament rarely follows a chronological order. One of the best ways to grasp the structure of the New Testament is to perceive the writings in their group arrangements. In the grouping of the New Testament books found in box 1, Acts, Hebrews, and Revelation stand apart from the other groups. Acts forms a transition between the Gospels and Paul's letters; Hebrews stands between Paul's letters and the General Epistles; and Revelation brings to a close the New Testament canon. Box 2 contains a listing of New Testament books in a suggested chronological order. Some scholars would order the books differently, pushing 2 Peter and Jude to a later date, while others might put 1 and 2 Timothy and Titus at earlier or later dates. Still others would put the Gospels and Acts much earlier. Generally, we can say that all the books were written between A.D. 45–100. In many cases we have so little information on which to base a decision that a great variety of suggestions emerge as to chronology. The *writer* and *reader* sections of the discussion of each New Testament book contain some of the considerations about dates of writings and their places of origin.

Literary Helps for Interpreting the New Testament

Fortunately, helps for interpreting the New Testament abound, beginning with English translations. The New Testament was written in Greek; and if a student has a choice, it is best to study the New Testament in Greek. However, excellent translations are available which render accurately the Greek text into English.

The *King James Version* remains a favorite of many people because of its familiarity as well as its majestic language and pleasing cadence. Translated in 1611, it has gone through several revisions, the latest of which is the *New King James Version* of the Bible. The *New Revised Standard Version*, the *New American Standard Bible*, and the *New International Version* are recent translations that have gained wide approval. These translations take into account the latest information about Greek manuscripts as well as advancements in historical and archaeological information. Also, they are results of the work of committees of scholars from diverse Christian backgrounds.

A translation by a committee is usually stronger than one by a single translator because the theological biases of the translator creep into the translation if no one is present to challenge or present an alternate possibility. Also, one person does not have expertise in as many areas of Old or New Testament studies as does a diverse committee of scholars with expertise in a number of areas. The translations mentioned here are the results of years of painstaking work by a number of different scholars. Their intention was to represent the text accurately in translation. As a case in point, translation of the *New American Standard Bible* began in 1959 and was completed in 1971; revisions and refinements have occurred with the publication of new editions since then.

Bible dictionaries, commentaries, and books on special topics also aid in interpretation. A Bible dictionary contains articles on important words, concepts, and people of the Bible. Commentaries give background information on a book or books of the Bible, and extended comments on the meaning of the biblical text follow the background information. Dictionaries and commentaries come in one-volume or

multi-volume sets. In choosing a dictionary, a commentary, or book, the user should ask certain questions. Who researched and wrote the work? Did that person or persons have the educational background to research and write the book or books? For instance, some people have attempted to present a detailed interpretation of the Book of Revelation and have no knowledge or even awareness of the existence and nature of apocalyptic literature. While valuable insights can be gained without such specialized knowledge, serious study of the Book of Revelation must take apocalyptic literature into consideration. The same kind of expertise applies to studies in other books of the Bible as well. The reading suggestions and endnotes at the ends of the chapters list dictionaries, commentaries, and books widely accepted for their expertise and integrity.

Other questions need consideration. Does the approach and content of a work stand in the stream of wholesome Christian tradition? What are the theological commitments, as best as can be determined, of the author or authors? Does the work present different possibilities or opinions so that readers can come to their own conclusions? Answers to these questions are important in choosing books, for prepared and careful scholarship in the service of the Lord can lead the student into greater appreciation and experience of God's truth.

The Historical-Critical Method

As regards advanced technical study of the New Testament, the student should at least be aware of some of the terminology of scholars. A scholarly study of the text of the New Testament includes what is called the historical-

A papyrus fragment of Homer's *Odyssey* found in Oxyrhynchus Egypt. *Biblical Illustrator* Photo/ David Rogers/University Museum, University of Pennsylvania.

critical method. This methodology uses textual criticism, source criticism, form criticism, redaction criticism, and canonical criticism.

Criticism is an unfortunate word, because people sometimes think that all scholars who use the methodology engage in negative and even destructive interpretation of the biblical text. *Evaluation* may have been a better word. The purpose of the scholar is to evaluate the text, use analytical abilities in study, and draw conclusions resulting from the study. Nevertheless, some have used the historical-critical method in destructive ways. If the interpreter has a respectful attitude toward Scripture, as Scripture deserves, then many aspects of the methodology can serve the interpreter well.

Textual criticism deals with the Hebrew or Greek text of the Bible. Before the New Testament became a collection, it existed as individual manuscripts. No original manuscripts (called autographs) for the Old or New Testament are in existence—only copies several times removed from the original. Suppose the scholar has three copies of a book of the Bible: one dating from the fourth century, one from the fifth, and one from the sixth. As these are placed side by side, variations in readings appear here and there.

Determining which of the texts most accurately represents the oldest and perhaps the original reading, when a conflict of reading occurs between the three copies, is the task of the textual critic. The process the critic uses is technical and scientific. The student should understand that the variations in the texts do not affect the theological truth of the Bible. Indeed, the variations are evidences of the history of the text and accent the power of God to use weak, imperfect human beings to get His truth into written form.

Source criticism, sometimes called literary criticism, attempts to determine the sources behind New Testament writings, especially the Gospels. The Gospel of Luke opens with reference to sources in compiling accounts of the events of Christianity (Luke 1:1–4). What sources did Luke or Matthew use? Through careful analysis of the texts, certain source relationships can be proposed. One discussion that arose out of this kind of study is related to the literary relationship between the Gospels of Matthew, Mark, and Luke. In narrative portions they have the same phrasing and word usage at points. This agreement is a question for source criticism. Later in this book, Matthew, Mark, and Luke will be discussed with reference to some of the results of source criticism.

Form criticism arose out of source criticism. This discipline concerns itself with the history of sayings, stories, and narratives in the Gospels. At first the gospel circulated orally, and sayings and stories were repeated over and over. What was the historical situation in which sayings and stories first were spoken? Analyzing smaller units of materials led to the attempt to classify these units by certain forms. Some of the forms are obvious; others are not so obvious. A parable is a form; in what context would a certain parable in the New Testament most likely be taught, and to whom? Form criticism attempts to answer this question. While a complex and an inexact science, form criticism can aid the student in understanding the history and development of some texts.

Redaction criticism relates especially to the study of the Gospels. The authors of the Gospels wrote with a message in mind for a particular audience or audiences. Why did they choose the materials they used to write their books and not include other materials? Why did they arrange some of the materials in certain ways? Critics answer such questions in relationship to the purpose and audience of the authors by means of redaction criticism. The Gospels of Matthew, Mark, and Luke resemble each other, but they have distinct differences in arrangement, choice of materials, and emphases. Each presents a slightly different portrait of Jesus. Redaction criticism helps the interpreter to place the reason for the differences in perspective.

Canonical criticism is a more recent variation in historical-critical methodology. For canonical critics, the most important benchmark in the development of the text occurred when the church accepted the New Testament canon as authoritative and inspired. The end result is the significant aspect of the text, not the historical process by which it came to be. Canonical critics emphasize that the text as it is should be the focus of biblical interpretation; as canonical Scripture, it is normative for the life of the church. Canonical criticism helps us to understand the importance of the church in the formation of the New Testament and the value of the text as we have it now in the canonical New Testament.

The Holy Spirit

Historical-critical methodology provides tools for interpretation. The tools are of value, but not ultimate value. They cannot explain the inspiration of Scripture. They are valuable when used with a healthy reverence for the Bible.

The ultimate help in interpreting the revelation of God is the Holy Spirit. Jesus told His disciples that the Spirit was the "Spirit of truth" (John 14:17) and that the Spirit would be the disciples' teacher so that they could understand and remember the teachings and meaning of Jesus (John 14:26). The Christian faith believes in this continuing ministry of the Spirit. God meets with us, and this is the basic moment of teaching.

Yet disciples are not to be passive receptacles. God meets with us as we engage our minds and abilities. The information and applications we have considered to this point can be vehicles of God's illumination to us. Part of Christian growth is searching and reaching for understanding, using the stream of God's revelation in both tradition and the written revelation, the Bible. *Tradition* refers the interpretations and experiences of the church, where God has given His illumination to people in times past. Even these must be judged in the light of the Bible, rightly interpreted and rightly applied, because sometimes traditions are wrong. At the same time, Christians must be wary of someone who claims to have a totally new insight that goes against the stream of God's revelation of Himself to the church and past interpretations of the biblical revelation. The burden of proof is upon the variant interpretation.

The Goals of Interpretation

Having set a broad background for understanding the history and nature of the New Testament text, we are ready to focus upon the text itself. Our purpose is to read and interpret the New Testament in order to apply it to our present life situation.

How should we approach the New Testament in interpretation? Dana and Glaze suggest that interpreters should seek three results in interpretation: the historical, the universal, and the practical.[2] These form excellent general guidelines for interpreting the New Testament.

The interpreter achieves the *historical result* by asking a question: What did this text (verse, paragraph, or book) mean to the original readers? The authors of the texts of the New Testament wrote to particular readers with particular needs at a particular point in history. Without understanding these elements, interpreters may be tempted to read into the text their own particular situation, needs, and historical context. In doing so they obscure, even ignore, the original meaning to the original readers. To read one's own views back into the text and then to receive them back in interpretation is to engage in *eisegesis*. We want to engage in *exegesis*, which is the attempt to get out of the text what the writer originally meant. While all of us do become involved with the text from our own culture and viewpoint, we do want to understand as much as possible what the original readers understood in their context.

Seeking the historical result also requires us to keep the verse, paragraph, or book in its original context. Putting verses together from different contexts usually results in incorrect interpretation. With such usage, some people make a new Bible by putting verses together from different contexts to create a new statement, which may, at worst, totally differ or, at best, show some similarity to the original meanings of the verses. Similar meanings arising out of different contexts may be used to support or explain one another, but may not be used to make new meanings.

For example, one reason so many interpretations of the Book of Revelation exist is the failure to put the book in its original context. As evidenced by the content of the book, the people who received and read Revelation were undergoing terrible persecution. Revelation must be understood first in terms of its meaning to them.

In order to treat Holy Scripture with dignity and respect, interpreters must seek the historical result. Much of the historical context of the texts of the New Testament is evident to the reader. Much meaning, however, awaits those who diligently study the historical situation of the writer and the original readers of the texts being interpreted.

In addition, the interpreter should seek the *universal result*. Although texts have historical contexts, they also have meanings that transcend history and are true for all times. The interpreter achieves the universal result by asking what is true in this text for all time. Truth then is truth now. For example, Nicodemus' encounter with Jesus occurred in a particular historical context, and the meeting with Jesus resulted in Nicodemus being told that he needed a rebirth. That was true for

Nicodemus. But if true for Nicodemus it is true for everyone, as John 3:16 makes evident by including such terms as "world" and "whoever." God loves the whole "world," gave his only Son, that "whoever" believes in Him has eternal life. *World* and *whoever* are inclusive terms. Everyone needs the rebirth offered freely by God through Jesus Christ, not only Nicodemus in a certain place in the first century. The text has truth for all time for everyone.

Finally, the interpreter should seek the *practical result.* The practical result is found by answering these questions: What does this text mean to me? What am I going to do about it? Since Nicodemus needed a new birth, and since everyone needs a new birth from God through Jesus, what am I going to do about my own new birth? Until the practical result is achieved, the interpreter has not finished the process of interpretation. Interpreting the Bible is a life-changing and life-enriching process, not simply an intellectual exercise. Proper interpretation leads one to understand the New Testament faith as something one lives, not only something one reads about.

FOR STUDY AND REVIEW

IDENTIFY:

Criticism
Textual Criticism
Source Criticism
Form Criticism
Redaction Criticism
Canonical Criticism
Historical result
Universal result
Practical result
Eisegesis

Exegesis

QUESTIONS FOR CONSIDERATION

1. What are some helpful translations, dictionaries, and commentaries of the Bible?
2. What are the factors to consider in choosing a translation, dictionary, or commentary?
3. What is the ultimate goal of interpretation?
4. Why is achieving the historical result so important?
5. What are the types and characteristics of the literature of the New Testament?
6. What is the structural arrangement of the New Testament?

FOR FURTHER READING

Bruce, F. F. *The English Bible: A History of Translations.* New York: Oxford University Press, 1961.

Fee, Gordon D. *New Testament Exegesis.* Philadelphia: Westminster, 1983.

_____ and Douglas Stewart. *How to Read the Bible for All Its Worth: A Guide to Understanding the Bible.* Grand Rapids: Zondervan, 1982.

Keegan, Terence J. *Interpreting the Bible: A Popular Introduction to Biblical Hermeneutics.* New York: Paulist Press, 1985.

Kubo, Sakae, and Specht, Walter. *So Many Translations? Twentieth Century English Versions of the Bible.* Grand Rapids: Zondervan, 1975.

Linton, C. D. "Literature, The Bible as." *The International Standard Bible Encyclopedia.* Vol 3. Edited by Geoffrey W. Bromiley. Grand Rapids: Eerdmans, 1986: 143–46.

ENDNOTES

1. See Frank Stagg, *The Book of Acts: The Early Struggle for an Unhindered Gospel* (Nashville: Broadman Press, 1955).

2. H. E. Dana and R. E. Glaze, *Interpreting the New Testament* (Nashville: Broadman Press, 1961), 123–25.

Influences Arising During Early Jewish History

Jesus did not live in a vacuum of time. A number of formative influences shaped the times and powers in which He lived, died, and lived again. While these influences are as old as history itself, we begin with the Old Testament for our purposes. *Testament* is another word for *covenant*. On several occasions God made covenants—agreements, contracts—with His people; they are recorded in several places in the Bible.

A basic idea of these biblical covenants is *how God creates for Himself a people*. In the Old Covenant (Old Testament), God created for Himself a people in and through Israel. In the New Covenant (New Testament), God creates for Himself a people in and through Jesus Christ. Consequently, we have the names of the two sections of our Bible. The Old tells how God previously made for Himself a people, and the New tells how God now creates or saves for Himself a people.

One of the most important covenants God made was with Abraham (see Gen. 12:1–3). This is a good place for us to begin in reviewing formative influences, because Abraham was the father of the Jewish nation. Our purpose here is to trace some obvious influences arising from Abraham and several other people and events, which will be pivotal in having a basic understanding of the background of the New Testament.

Abraham

The Hebrews were the focus of that Old Testament world, beginning with Abram, who, between 2000 and 1700 B.C., left his home in Mesopotamia at the call of God to go where God wanted him to go and be what God wanted him to be. In those days, the blessing, land, and people were everything to the eldest son in the family. God called Abram to leave his blessing, his land, and his people, but promised him blessing, land, and people in return (Gen. 12:1–3). This was God's covenant with Abram, and this is the basic covenant out of which the Old Testament arises.

God blessed Abram, gave him safe journey, sustained him by supplying the needs of life, and protected him from the threats of others and from his own failures. Abram's name, meaning *exalted father*, became Abraham, meaning *father of a multitude* (Gen. 17:5), which indicated God's promise to give him a large family or nation. Abraham did have descendants who became the nation of Israel. The land given to Abraham became known as the promised land. Originally called Canaan, the promised land was Israel's, the land in which Jesus walked, taught, preached, healed, died, and was raised.

Jacob

Abraham's son was Isaac, who had two sons, Esau and Jacob. Jacob became the one through whom God's covenant with Abraham continued. At one point, Jacob's name became Israel (Gen. 32:28). The new name indicated a significant change for Jacob, which better prepared him to be God's instrument as God continued to make for Himself a people and fulfill the covenant made with Abraham and his descendants.

The name *Israel* has three uses in the Old Testament. First, as just indicated, it was the new name of Jacob. Second, it became the name designating the people of God, Israel, sometimes as a national, political identity and sometimes as the people who belonged to God. Third, Israel became the name of the Northern Kingdom when Israel divided into two nations. The northern part of the nation retained the name Israel and the southern part chose the name Judah.

Israel, or Jacob, had twelve sons. These twelve sons had families, and these sons and their families became the twelve tribes of Israel. The number twelve is significant in the New Testament for referring to God's people. Jesus' choosing of twelve disciples indicated that Jesus intended to reconstitute Israel on a new basis. He did this in the church, the new Israel of God. For example, James (1:1, NRSV) addressed Christians scattered everywhere as the "twelve tribes in the Dispersion," obviously writing to the church dispersed throughout the land. Likewise, 1 Peter referred to the church with terms normally reserved for the nation of Israel (2:9–10). Applying terminology for Israel to the church affirms that the church is now the Israel of God.

At a certain time in history, Jacob, or Israel, and his family escaped famine in Palestine by going to Egypt, where there was sufficient food. The families prospered in Egypt for many years. They multiplied in numbers and succeeded in providing a relatively good life for themselves. But a different Pharaoh, who was not ruling when Jacob and his family came, considered them to be a threat to the security of Egypt, so he enslaved them (Ex. 1:8–14).

Moses and the Exodus

Under slavery, the people cried out to God for deliverance. God heard their cry, sent Moses to lead them out of bondage into freedom, and delivered the people out of the slavery of Egypt. The deliverance and journey toward the promised land is the exodus (see the Book of Exodus), which may have begun around 1290 B.C.

The exodus shaped the Hebrews' understanding of God and their relationship to Him more than any other event in Jewish history. God was their Deliverer, their Savior, and He sustained them throughout the exodus. God gave them the law and made a new covenant with them(see Ex. 20). Israelites today still celebrate their deliverance from Egypt in the Feast of the Passover. Through the Passover celebration the Israelites remind themselves of God's great act of delivering His people from bondage and of His sustaining care throughout the exodus and the journey back to the promised land, the land of Israel.

During the Feast of the Passover in Jesus' time, participants observed the passover meal by eating a lamb, and unleavened bread. The lamb reminded them of the first passover lamb in Egypt whose blood was smeared on the doorposts of the people's houses for their

Chronological Overview
(All Dates Are Approximate)

Abraham Heard Call of God	2000–1700 B.C.
Moses and the Exodus	1290 B.C.
David United the Kingdom of Israel	1000 –960 B.C.
Divided Kingdom (Northern Kingdom, Israel;	922 B.C.
Southern Kingdom, Judah)	
Fall of the Northern Kingdom, Israel	721 B.C.
Fall of the Southern Kingdom, Judah	587 B.C.
Domination of Israel by Various Powers	
The Babylonian Period (Exilic)	605–537 B.C.
The Persian Period (Post-exilic)	537–331 B.C.
The Greek Period	331–167 B.C.
The Maccabean Period	167– 63 B.C.
The Roman Period	63 B.C.–A.D. 135
The Interbiblical Period	400 B.C.–A.D. 135

The following lists contain ranges of dates, from an early date to the latest date, with possibilities in between. For example, the latest Jesus could have been born is 4 B.C. Probably the earliest he could have been born is 7 B.C. to agree with other information. He was born in the rule of Herod the Great, who died in 4 B.C.

Life of Jesus	
Birth	7–4 B.C.
Public Ministry	A.D. 26–33
Death	A.D. 29–33
Pentecost (Acts 2)	A.D. 29–33
Paul's Life	
Birth	A.D. 10–15
Conversion	A.D. 33–35
Death	A.D. 62–65
Writing of the New Testament	A.D. 48–100

deliverance from death. The passover meal is the meal of the Old Covenant. The meal of the New Covenant is the Lord's Supper, which Jesus instituted at the last supper He ate with His apostles (Mark 14:12–25). In the Lord's Supper Jesus Himself is the passover, or *paschal* lamb, remembered in the eating of the bread and drinking of the cup. Jesus sacrificed Himself to deliver humanity from sin and death (John 1:29).

David and the United Kingdom

Long after the people settled the Promised Land, they had kings ruling over them. Their most famous king was David, who ruled from about 1000 B.C. to about 960 B.C. David united the twelve tribes of Israel into one nation, establishing Jerusalem as the capital of the united kingdom. King David was a failure in many ways, but his successes and abilities were so remarkable that the people considered him to be their greatest king. Later generations perceived that God's specially anointed king, the Messiah, whom God would send to them, would be like King David but even greater.

The kingdom of God and the nation of Israel became identified in the minds of many Israelites as the same. Jesus' major emphasis in His ministry was upon the kingdom of God, a kingdom of quite different nature and power than the Jews expected the Messiah to establish when He came. The Israelites had difficulty perceiving the kingdom of God on this earth apart from identification with national and political Israel, so they did not accept Jesus as the king of Israel when He did not meet their expectations.

Solomon succeeded his father David to the throne, and he ruled the one nation of Israel from 960–922 B.C. Solomon built the temple at Jerusalem that David had wanted to build. Jerusalem, the city of David, and the temple, God's special meeting place with the nation of Israel, became focal points for the hopes and aspirations of the people in their relationship to God.

Although Solomon began well in his rule over the people of Israel, he did not end well. His alliances with other nations encouraged the introduction of pagan worship into the life of Israel. He conscripted people into his work force to labor on his building projects, causing many to feel hostile toward Solomon and his descendants.

The Divided Kingdom

When Solomon died, the people, especially those of the ten tribes living north of Palestine, demanded change. Rehoboam, Solomon's son and heir to the throne, did not change, and the people rebelled. The kingdom divided in about 922 B.C.

The kingdom in the southern part of Palestine was known as Judah; the kingdom in the northern part was known as Israel. Judah had Jerusalem as its capital city, and Israel had Shechem and later Samaria as its capital. The Northern Kingdom, or Israel, had ten of the twelve tribes. The Southern Kingdom, or Judah, had two tribes, of which the tribe of Judah predominated—hence the name Judah for the Southern Kingdom.

The Northern Kingdom continued in existence until 721 B.C., when the Assyrians destroyed the capital of Samaria and deported leaders and other powerful people. The cultures of their conquerors permeated the people of the Northern Kingdom, and the ten tribes of Israel ceased to exist as an identifiable entity. People still refer to the "ten lost tribes" and have tried to identify their descendants with various groups, including certain people of America and the English monarchy. No historical basis exists for such conclusions.

Under King Nebuchadnezzar, the Babylonians destroyed Jerusalem, the temple, and the Kingdom of Judah in 587 B.C. Nebuchadnezzar deported into Babylonia many Hebrews from Jerusalem and the surrounding area. The years during which the Hebrews were in Babylonia became known as the period of exile.

The nation of Israel had much promise and lived up to expectations at times, but it was declining. The prophets warned Israel about the drift away from God. The prophet Amos spoke to the Northern Kingdom about their disregard for God. He warned them of their oppression of the poor and their immorality (Amos 2:6–8, for example). Their worship and devotion to God were empty because they lacked obedience to righteousness. God found unacceptable even their sacrifices and other expressions of worship (Amos 5:21–23). Rather, God desired righteousness: "Let justice roll on like a river, righteousness like a never-failing stream!" (Amos 5:24).

Despite such warnings to Israel and Judah and attempts to redirect them, they both fell. However, the nations' fall was not the end of the story. God's purposes did not ultimately hinge upon the fate of a nation. He did continue to work His purposes through people who were faithful to Him.

FOR STUDY AND REVIEW

IDENTIFY:

The two meals
Covenant
Moses

Abram (Abraham)
Names of the two kingdoms
Capital, United Kingdom
Jacob

DATES TO REMEMBER

Abraham
David
Exodus
Division of the Kingdom
Destruction of the Northern and Southern Kingdoms

QUESTIONS FOR CONSIDERATION

1. The name *Israel* was used in what three ways?

2. What is the significance of the number twelve?

3. Why was the Exodus so influential upon Israel?

4. Who destroyed each of the two kingdoms?

FOR FURTHER READING

Bright, John. *A History of Israel.* 3rd ed. Philadelphia: Westminster, 1981.

Cate, Robert L. *These Sought a Country: A History of Israel in Old Testament Times.* Nashville: Broadman Press, 1985.

Eakin, Frank E., Jr. "Israel, History of." *Holman Bible Dictionary.* Edited by Trent C. Butler. Nashville: Holman Bible Publishers, 1991. 722–31.

Rowley, H. H. "Israel, History of." *Interpreter's Dictionary of the Bible.* Vol. 2. Edited by George A. Buttrick. New York: Abingdon, 1962. 750–65.

❧ 5 ❧

Influences Arising During Later Jewish History

With the Babylonian domination of the Hebrews, the first of five significant historical periods for the Hebrews and their homeland began. Out of these periods arose influences that directly impacted Jesus, His disciples, and His church during and beyond New Testament times.

Under the Babylonians

The *Babylonian period* (605–538 B.C.) is also known as the *Exilic period*. Since the Hebrews had no temple in exile, what was it that helped them retain their identity and coherence as a group? They could not sacrifice, for the sacrificial system had its locus in the temple at Jerusalem. Actually, two things helped them remain together and remain faithful to God: the Law and the Sabbath. These two were inseparable, for the Hebrews considered the Sabbath as a sign of God's covenant with them, and they considered the observance of the Law as the means for keeping their obligations under the covenant.

By the time of Jesus, the prominence of the Sabbath and the Law had intensified until, for some people, they practically were ends in themselves rather than the means to the end of responding to and being faithful to God. Jesus was frequently in conflict with certain religious authorities in His day, primarily

Portion of a clay tablet inscribed with the annals of the reign of Nabonidus, king of Babylon (556-539 B.C.). The annals record the defeat of Astyaces by Cyrus, the capture and spoiling of Ecbatana, the taking of Babylon, and the downfall and death of Nabonidus. *Biblical Illustrator* Photo/David Rogers/British Museum.

over their understanding of the Sabbath and their interpretations of the Law.

Also, the synagogue likely had its genesis in the Babylonian period. In exile, Hebrew men began to meet to discuss the Law and its applications to God's people. Eventually these meetings took on a formal shape and developed into the institution known as a

31

synagogue. The New Testament refers to numerous synagogues, the dominant religious institution among the Jews during New Testament times.

Under the Persians

Second came the *Persian period* (538–331 B.C.). Under King Cyrus, Persia defeated Babylonia and became the major power of the Old Testament world during this time. Cyrus' policy was to allow captured peoples to return home and rebuild their cities and societies; he even provided money grants to help them. These reestablished national groups became greater sources of tax revenue, or tribute, for Cyrus than would have been true had they remained displaced peoples. Cyrus gave the Hebrews in captivity the option of returning to Israel. Several groups of Hebrews returned. The Persian period became known as the beginning of the *post-exilic period* since the people who returned were no longer away from the homeland.

A shift in terminology occurred at this point. The designation of the people of Israel as "Hebrews" changed when they returned from captivity. While the designation of "Hebrews" was still applied, the dominant designation became Jews, primarily because most of those returning were of the tribe of Judah. The "Jews" figure prominently in the New Testament, and most prominently of all in the Gospels, for Jesus was a Jew.

The Jews eventually rebuilt the temple, the city of Jerusalem, and the walls after they returned from captivity. During the rebuilding process, the Samaritans wanted to help. Originally, the Samaritans were simply those Hebrews of the ten tribes of Israel, so called because their capital was Samaria. After the destruction of the Northern Kingdom, some

of those left behind by the Assyrians intermarried with non-Jews. *Samaritan* became a term applied in disgust by some Jews in reference to the offspring of mixed marriages. The Northern and Southern Kingdoms were often in conflict with each other, so a long history of hostility existed between the Samaritans and the Jews before the rebuilding process began. The enmity only deepened when the Samaritans were not allowed to participate in the rebuilding of Jerusalem and the temple.

In the latter part of the Persian period, Ezra, a Jewish leader, became a strict enforcer of the Law and even trained selected men to interpret the Law. These interpreters, including Ezra, were the scribes. They were the forerunners of the class of scribes referred to in the New Testament. Some interpretations eventually became strict and exclusive, such as required renunciation by Samaritan Jews of non-Jewish wives and children if they wanted to be numbered among the people of God. Excluded for a number of reasons, the Samaritans eventually established their place of worship on Mount Gerizim, referred to by the woman at the well in her discussion with Jesus (John 4:20).

Whether the term *Samaritan* was applied in a general sense and a particular sense is difficult to determine. In a general sense, Samaritans were those who married non-Jews and were assimilated into other cultures around them. In a particular sense, Samaritans may have been a group of loyal Hebrews who maintained their identity with the Law of Moses. In any case, religious Samaritans believed in the first five books of the Bible. Moses, therefore, was their only prophet. Jesus took direct actions to reach out to the Samaritans and to include them in the Kingdom just as they were, for although Jesus was a Jew, He did not share the prejudice which

Marble bust of Alexander the Great. Probably found in Italy. Castellani Collection. Roman copy of a portrait by Lysippos. *Biblical Illustrator* Photo/David Rogers/British Museum.

some held against the Samaritans (see Luke 9:52–56; 10:30–37; 17:11–19; John 4:4–42).

Under the Greeks

Third was the *Greek period* (331–167 B.C.). Alexander the Great dominated this period. Taught by Aristotle, he committed himself to Greek ways of thinking and Greek culture. Even as a youth he demonstrated great capability as a military leader, becoming a successful general in his father's army at seventeen. When he became ruler in his father's place, he set out to conquer the world, with the purpose of spreading Greek culture and Greek thought as well as acquiring power for himself. He was very successful. Greek thought and Greek culture became dominant in the world of Alexander the Great.

Alexander brought Western and Eastern cultures together through his conquests, introducing Greek culture into the whole process. Opening the East to the West resulted in the interchange of language, customs, ideas, and other aspects of culture. The East was Palestine, Syria, Asia Minor, and other countries. The West began with areas of Macedonia, Achaia, and other nations of Europe. Greek, primarily *koine* Greek, became the common language of both West and East. Koine Greek is the language of the New Testament Greek text from which our English translations come.

After the death of Alexander the Great, four generals finally prevailed in the struggle for Alexander's place of power. They divided the conquered lands among themselves. In Palestine, the homeland of Jesus, two generals and their dynasties dominated the Israelites for years. One general was Ptolemy I (304–283 B.C.), who ruled Egypt and the surrounding area, and the other was Seleucus I (312–281 B.C.), who ruled Syria and surrounding areas. The Ptolemies controlled Palestine for about one hundred years.

During the reign of Ptolemy II or Philadelphus (285–247 B.C.), the translation of the Old Testament into Greek began with the first five books of the Old Testament. Translations of the other books followed over a long period of time. Known as the *Septuagint* (or

LXX) the Greek translation of the Old Testament was the Bible for many New Testament Christians as the New Testament itself took shape. LXX and Septuagint mean *seventy*, and the translation is so named because of the legend that seventy translators worked on the production of the text. New Testament writers often quoted from the Septuagint as they used Old Testament Scriptures in their witness about Christ.

The Seleucids finally wrested Palestine from the control of the Ptolemies. Seleucid kings ruled Palestine for about thirty years. During the Ptolemaic and the Seleucid reigns, the Jews were subject to the process of Hellenization. *Hellenes* was another name for Greeks, after Hellas, the ancient name for Greece. To become Hellenized was to adopt Greek thought and Greek culture. Some Jews saw nothing wrong with this adaptation and determined to retain their relationship to the Law and Jewish worship in the context of Hellenization. Others among those who were amenable to Greek ways went further and embraced some of the Greek religious commitments as well. Tension existed between those Jews sympathetic to Greek ways and those who rejected not only Greek thoughts and customs but the Greek language as well.[1] Still, those Jews who maintained their traditional culture existed rather peaceably in relationship to the Ptolemies and the Seleucids because the rulers made no overt effort to force Greek ways upon them.

The situation changed with Antiochus Epiphanes IV, a Seleucid king. He tried to force those Jews who rejected Greek ways into worshiping Greek gods. His efforts became increasingly aggressive. He finally entered the temple at Jerusalem in 167 B.C. and offered a sacrifice of swine to Zeus. The Jews called this the "abomination of desolation" (see Dan. 11:31; 12:11; Mark 13:14).[2]

The Jews blamed themselves for this incident. Because of their sins, they believed, God left the temple desolate of His presence, allowing Antiochus to desecrate the temple.

Inspired by an elderly Jew named Mattathias, loyal Jews finally rebelled against Antiochus Epiphanes.[3] When an emissary of Antiochus came to the village of Modein to offer a sacrifice to a Greek god and attempt to force the Jews there to participate, Mattathias in anger killed the emissary and a young Jewish assistant. Mattathias' act of anger sparked a rebellion that rapidly gained momentum.

Under the Maccabeans

The rebellion marked the beginning of the *Maccabean period* (167–63 B.C.). Mattathias and his five sons escaped into the hill country to prepare for resistance to Antiochus' forces. A group of pious Jews, dedicated to obedience to the Law and the preservation of the Jewish way of life, joined Mattathias and his sons in the rebellion. These pious Jews were known as the *Hasidim*, who may have been the forerunners of the Pharisees. The Essenes also may have been of the lineage of the Hasidim (see the discussion under "Jewish Groups" in Chapter 6).

The five sons of Mattathias were Judas, Jonathan, Simon, Eleazer, and John. Judas succeeded his father as leader, for Mattathias died not long after the rebellion began. Judas became known as Judas the Maccabee, which means the "Hammer," and from him the period takes its name. Judas achieved some spectacular victories, using the tactics of guerilla warfare in much of his fighting. The armies of Antiochus Epiphanes assisted the success of Judas by fighting among themselves, preventing them from using their combined strength

Tetradrachm of Antiochus IV Epiphanes. Obverse: Head of Antiochus IV. Obverse: Zeus sitting on a throne. Inscription: "Of the King Antiochus, the god made manifested and the victorious." Antiochus IV was the Seleucid ruler responsible for religious persecutions that led to the revolt of the Maccabees. *Biblical Illustrator* Photo/David Rogers/Jewish Museum, New York

to put down the Jewish rebellion. Judas' army fought and won against impressive forces. Finally, Judas and his forces regained control of Jerusalem and the temple. The Jews cleansed and rededicated the temple in December of 165 B.C., an event still celebrated as *Hanukkah*, the Festival of Lights.[4] Under Judas, the Jews regained religious freedom.

Jonathan became leader after Judas died in battle, and he extended the territory under Jewish control. Simon followed Jonathan in leadership, and he secured political independence for the nation by 143 B.C. He minted his own coins by that date, something only an independent nation could do. Consequently, for the first time in almost four hundred years, the Jews controlled their political destiny as a free nation once again.

Under the Romans

Independence lasted until the beginning of the next historical period of our survey, the *Roman period* (63 B.C.–A.D. 135). After Pompey captured Palestine in 63 B.C., certain vassals of Rome (Hyrcanus II, Antipater, and Herod the Great) ruled over Palestine. Taxes levied by the Romans weighed heavily on the Jews. Coupled with a number of actions that insulted the Jewish faith, excessive taxation engendered Jewish hostility toward the Romans.

Herod the Great ruled from around 37–4 B.C. Jesus was born toward the end of his reign. Other rulers and procurators followed Herod, but none were acceptable to most of the Jews. As any people would, the Jews wanted freedom from all foreign dominance. The Romans were the political power to which Jesus and his followers of the first and second centuries had to relate. Christianity did not advocate violence, and Christians resisted the Roman government only when the government attempted to undermine their faith. In a way, Roman rule made a contribution to Christianity. Routes of travel, made relatively safe by the presence of Roman soldiers who enforced Roman law, aided apostles, teachers, and missionaries as they traveled with the gospel throughout the known world. In general, however, the Jews did not have peaceful times with the Romans. Many Jews awaited eagerly the time when a Messiah would come and deliver them from all Roman and every other disagreeable influence.

A Jewish rebellion began in A.D. 66 and lasted until A.D. 70. Vespasian and his forces, and later the same forces under his son, Titus, put down the rebellion. The Romans severely punished the Jews and destroyed the temple. The Jews continued as something of a political entity for some time after that defeat. Finally a Jewish rebellion in about A.D. 135 resulted in the loss of Jewish political identity. They would not be a true nation again until A.D. 1948, when the Allies established a homeland for the Jews after World War II.

Many significant events of Christian history happened during the Roman period. The birth, death, and resurrection of Christ; the beginning and explosive progress of the church; the travels and experiences of the apostle Paul; and the work of many other disciples instrumental in the spread of Christianity across the Mediterranean landscape occurred during the Roman rule. But as strong as the Romans were, Jesus Christ was stronger still.

FOR STUDY AND REVIEW

IDENTIFY:

Exilic Period
Mattathias
Synagogue
Modein
Cyrus
Hasidim
Post-exilic period
"Hammer"
Jews
Hanukkah
Samaritans
Antiochus Epiphanes IV
Alexander the Great
Hellenization
Aristotle
Septuagint
Koine
Ptolemy II
Ptolemies
Seleucids

DATES TO REMEMBER

The names and dates of the five historical periods
Rededication of the temple
The restoration of political freedom
The Jewish rebellions in the Roman period

QUESTIONS FOR CONSIDERATION

1. What was the significance of the Law and the Sabbath in the Exilic Period?

2. Why were the Jews and Samaritans antagonistic toward each other?

3. What did Antiochus Epiphanes attempt to do to the Jews?

4. Who were the sons of Mattathias?

5. Which of the sons led in the restoration of freedom of worship and which in political freedom?

6. What were the influences arising out of each period?

FOR FURTHER READING

Bruce, F. F. *Israel and the Nations: From the Exodus to the Fall of the Second Temple.* Grand Rapids:Eerdmans, 1969.

Cate, Robert L. *A History of the New Testament and Its Times.* Nashville: Broadman, 1991: 63–93.

Ferguson, Everett. *Backgrounds of Early Christianity.* Grand Rapids: Eerdmans, 1987: 1–36.

Russell, D. S. *Between the Testaments.* Rev. ed. Philadelphia: Fortress, 1965: 13–40.

ENDNOTES

1. See 1 Maccabees 1:11–15; 2 Maccabees 4:9–17. These writings may be found in *The Oxford Annotated Apocrypha,* rev. ed., ed. Bruce M. Metzger (New York: Oxford University Press, 1977).

2. See 1 Maccabees 1:16–62; 2 Maccabees 6:1–11.

3. See 1 Maccabees 2:1–48.

4. See 1 Maccabees 4:36–59.

Influences Arising During the Interbiblical Period

The interbiblical (or intertestamental) period overlaps the Persian, Greek, and Roman periods. As the name indicates, the interbiblical period ocurred between and overlapping the end of the Old Testament and the writing of the New Testament, from about 400 B.C. to A.D. 135. By looking at this period of history more pointedly, we can see previous influences taking identifiable shape in dominant philosophies, Jewish sects, and religions and cults.

Major Philosophies

Major philosophies during the time of Christ were Platonism, Epicurianism, and Stoicism. Gnosticism also began taking shape in the first Christian century but did not reach full development until the second century. The New Testament world did not experience these philosophies in delineated or pure form. Often philosophical ideas from different points of view overlapped. The people of the first century usually encountered these philosophies in popular forms or mixed with each other.

Platonism

Plato (427–347 B.C.) proposed two worlds, or dimensions, of reality. First is the world of change or becoming. This world, our world, is in constant flux; entities are born and then die. It is a world of the senses, and the senses cannot be trusted for the perception of reality. The second dimension is the world of forms or ideas, a world of perfect and changeless prototypes or patterns. This world is true and real. All realities in the world of change are imperfect, material copies of the changeless types or forms. Even expressions of concepts in this life have behind them perfect forms. Court cases, for instance which express justice, share in the perfect form of justice. Such court cases are copies in this material world of the perfect form in the immaterial world.

For Plato, the soul of a person was a spiritual, eternal, and immaterial entity that resided in a physical body. The soul existed before the body and also survived the body at death. As it resides in the body, the soul has the capacity to remember, although imperfectly, the world of forms. Generally, the Platonic tradition has depreciated the body and exalted the soul, holding that the soul is central to identity, intellect, and character.

The Platonic concept of soul permeated much of the philosophical thought of New Testament times and even modern-day thinking. In the Jewish-Christian view, however, a person does not *have* a soul; a person *is* a soul. The whole person is involved in a unity of personhood. Sometimes the New Testament speakers or writers view a person from different perspectives, but the whole person is still meant. At the beginning of her song of praise, Mary knew that she was to bear the Christ-child; she said, "My soul glorifies, the Lord / and my spirit rejoices in God my Savior" (Luke 1:46–47). Mary referred to herself as "soul" and "spirit." As is true with some Hebrew poetry, the second line of her song, which contains the word "spirit," means the same as the first line, which has the word "soul." In both cases Mary referred to her whole self, not a compartment or an element of her body.

At times Christians adapted certain concepts and ideas of Platonism to convey the truth of the Christian message to their contemporaries. The writer of Hebrews, in order to give a more pointed witness to his readers, may have employed Platonic expression in the statement, "They serve at a sanctuary that is a copy and shadow of what is in heaven" (Heb. 8:5). Of course, in the heavenly sanctuary there is one high priest forever, the exalted Lord, as the context of Hebrews 7—8 makes clear. Such terminology and concepts were a point of contact between Christians and the world around them through which they gave convincing witness to Jesus Christ.

Epicureanism

Epicureanism, named after its founder, Epicurus (342–270 B.C.), contrasts with Platonism. Epicurus rejected Plato's ideas about the senses. He believed that the senses should be trusted in determining reality. Epicurus taught that pleasure was the purpose and goal of a person. Reason should lead an individual to simple, natural, and necessary pleasures. Later Christians would find wisdom in the Epicurean Effort to seek wise virtues.

Epicurus held an interesting belief about the gods. Gods did exist and were national and temporal, but had minimal participation in human life. They concerned themselves primarily with their own pleasurable fulfillment. In other words, Epicurus allowed the existence of gods in his thought system, but they made no difference to human life. A human being, even the soul, consisted of atoms. Body and soul disintegrated at death, leaving no possibility for an afterlife. Many sophisticated people found Epicurus' philosophy attractive amid the fantastic religious claims of that day, especially since the gods of many religious systems appeared implausible.

Stoicism

The name for Stoicism came from the place where the adherents met: a *stoa*, or porch, in Athens. Zeno of Cyprus (336–263 B.C.) was their founder. Stoics believed that divine reason pervaded the whole material world and that humanity's goal should be to live in cooperation with that divine reason. The soul was the divine spark in a person's body. The Stoics believed that when the divine spark, or soul, was in right relationship to the divine reason, a person could live above the circumstances of life in a steady, stable existence. Even today, a person who seems to be relatively unaffected by emotions, keeping equilibrium amid positive and negative circumstances, may be said to be "stoic."

Stoics believed that living in harmony with their own natures and the nature around them determined their destiny. According to their thought, divine reason (*logos*) pervaded all things. To be in harmony with the divine reason, humans needed to accept their destinies in order to be set free from the destructive excesses of life. Also, embracing virtue, they believed, freed them from the passions that led to life's destructive excesses. The divine reason which pervaded all things, made a unity of all things. People who were in harmony with divine reason were also one with each other, which meant that they were brothers and sisters.

With a strong moral emphasis and its attempt at unity of thought, Stoicism became a widely accepted philosophical approach to life. However, Christianity provided the superior and realistic unity with God in Jesus Christ. Also, Christianity challenged the unhealthy repression of emotion and the Stoics' unhealthy belief that people's lives were determined by natural law. Some first-century Christians admired the Stoic call for courage in the face of difficulty and suffering. Paul preached to those holding this philosophy as well, as is indicated in Acts 17:18.

Gnosticism

Gnosticism is a modern term given to philosophic ideas present in the first century. These ideas became somewhat more systematized in the second century. The term arises from the Greek word *gnosis*, which means "knowledge." Adherents of this diverse philosophical approach put great emphasis upon knowledge and reason. Also, they had a dualistic world view which posited the spiritual and the material (or matter) in opposition to each other. The spiritual was good and the material was evil. On the other side stood evil, darkness, and manifestations of unrighteousness. To some adherents, an evil god, who belonged to a hierarchy of intermediary beings between the good god and creation, created the world. Since creation had an evil source, all matter inherently was evil.

Gnostic groups, therefore, rejected the belief that the creation of the world was a good act by a good and sovereign God. Furthermore, they rejected the humanity of Jesus since they believed that the word of God could not become flesh in Jesus of Nazareth. After all, flesh was matter, and matter was evil.

Human beings also were of a dual nature in the Gnostic view. They were composed of matter; therefore, they were evil. Within the evil body was a divine spark, which was good, deposited in some who had been especially elected by the deity. The human body, evil as it was, imprisoned the divine spark. Since human beings could think and reason, however, the elect had a route of escape. Special knowledge and secret rituals could awaken the divine and enable the elect to overcome the evil deity who had created them. They then could live in relationship to the good god and be reunited with him at death. Not just any knowledge would do, however.

To some gnostic groups Jesus was the source of a revealed knowledge that came from outside the created order. They could then lay claim to a body of revelation that included but went beyond the witness and teachings of the apostles and traditional teachings of the church. "Christian" Gnostics convinced some Christians to follow their heretical teachings.

The Gospel of John, Colossians, 1 and 2 John, and 1 and 2 Timothy countered heretical teachings and beliefs influenced and sometimes dominated by proto-Gnostic ideas. Gnostic ideas became attractive to many who labeled themselves as Christians in the latter part of the first century and in the second century. The ideas were attractive in part because they enabled people to fit certain Christian beliefs into a complex of Greek philosophical ideas which dominated the scene at that time. Christian converts were in danger of being enticed away to such "hollow and deceptive philosophy" (Col. 2:8), so leaders such as Paul met the challenge head-on with sound teaching and preaching of the gospel.

Sometimes we think Christians had an easier time proclaiming the gospel of Christ in the first century than we do in our scientific, skeptical age. But on every hand were those, such as the Epicureans, who scoffed at the claims of Christianity. When Paul proclaimed the resurrection at Athens, for example, the Epicureans and others ridiculed him (Acts 17:18, 32).

Jewish Groups

Certain Jewish groups became prominent during the interbiblical and New Testament periods. These groups are important for a study of the New Testament. Most Jews were not members of any of the Jewish parties or sects. Even so, the impact of some of the groups was great.

Sadducees

The Sadducees were the priestly aristocratic group, primarily connected with the temple. Their origin is not certain, although one persistent suggestion is that they were descendants of Zadok, Solomon's priest. Whatever their origin, they continued the priestly line of Aaron. They had the responsibility for the temple and its activities. To their party belonged the most important political post in the Jewish nation, the office of the high priest. This meant that they had the most to offer the Romans in terms of the Roman government's relationship to the Jewish state. The Sadducees often used their political

strength to work political relationships to benefit themselves and, they believed, the Jewish nation.

The Sadducees accepted only the first five books, called the Pentateuch (five books or scrolls), of the Old Testament as Scripture. Since no direct mention of an afterlife or angels occurred in the first five books, they believed in neither angels nor the resurrection.

In addition to their strong influence arising out of their relationship to the temple, the Sadducees held the majority influence in the Sanhedrin. The Sanhedrin (Council of the Seventy) was the ruling body or council among the Jews, having ultimate authority in religious matters, as well as some authority in civil matters among their own people. At the urging of the high priest, the Sanhedrin condemned Jesus for blasphemy and proposed the death sentence (see Matt. 26:57–68; 27:1–2).

Pharisees

The Pharisees, another well-known Jewish party, probably developed from the Hasidim, the "pious ones" who joined with Mattathias and his sons when they rebelled against Antiochus Epiphanes. The Pharisees devoted themselves to interpretation and application of the Law. They believed in the resurrection, an afterlife, angels, and demons. Their Scripture included the first five books of the Old Testament (the Law) and ultimately the other Old Testament books now found in the Hebrew Bible.

The synagogues were under their control and leadership. Since the synagogues were in the villages and towns where most of the Jewish people lived, the Pharisees influenced more Israelites than other groups. The Pharisees were not official or professional religious leaders, which added to their popular standing. In addition, many Jews living outside Palestine had local synagogues in which they studied and worshiped, a fact that extended the Pharisees' influence beyond the borders of Israel.

In some ways, unfortunately, the Pharisees created a gulf between themselves and many Jews. The Jews in the villages and on the farms worked hard, so they did not have time to keep the minute legal requirements placed upon them by the Pharisees. Such demands made many feel as if they stood outside the blessings of God. In Jesus, sinners and tax collectors (Luke 15:1) found acceptance and inclusion as He invited people to come to God just as they were.

The Pharisees had traditional interpretations and pronouncements upon the Law which assumed equal authority with the Scriptures. Over a period of time, rabbis interpreted and made application of the Law which they and their followers handed on orally to succeeding generations. Eventually, the pronouncements and applications were recorded as written collections known as the *Mishna* and *Talmud*. The Talmud actually includes the Mishna and the *Gemara*, which is a commentary on the Mishna. To keep the Law a person had to keep the interpretations of the Law as determined in this body of material.

For example, what constituted work on the Sabbath (Ex. 20:8–11)? Was it work to tie or untie a knot in a rope? Was walking a certain distance work? Such matters as these became the focal point of many discussions. The faithful Jew was to abide by the Pharisees' decisions on these points. Jesus' disagreements with their interpretations, as evidenced in His actions, brought Him into much conflict with the Pharisees. When Jesus healed a man on the Sabbath and told him to pick up

his bed and walk, He gave the man permission to break the "law" of the Sabbath by carrying his bed, considered to be unlawful work by the strict Pharisee (John 5:10). Not all Pharisees were "legalistic" and insensitive, for among them were many good people, and many did respond to the message and ministry of Jesus.

Recent studies indicate that the Pharisees of Jesus' time worked for renewal in the totality of Israel's life.[1] Their emphasis upon maintaining ritual purity in the home, much as temple priests did in the temple, was the way to turn Israel into the holy nation that God wanted them to be. Many Pharisees found affinity with Jesus in His renewal emphasis; some of them even invited Jesus to dine with them (Luke 7:36; 14:1). Some (Joseph of Animetea and Nicodemus) apparently even became his disciples (Mat. 27:57–60; Mal. 15:43–46; Luke 23:50–53; John 3:1–2; 7:48–51; 19:38–41). Yet other Pharisees contended with Jesus over what they perceived to be His disregard for the Law.

Essenes

The Essenes are not mentioned in the New Testament, but are discussed in various sources current in the first century.[2] Evidently they separated themselves from mainstream Israel, who, in the Essenes' view, failed to keep the Law. They considered themselves to be the true Israel, and they intended to keep themselves pure and obey the Law according to their interpretation. Other Jewish groups had contaminated themselves in some way, and they could not be considered the true Israel.

The Essenes perhaps lived as several smaller groups at different locales in Israel, but that is uncertain. One such group may have been the Qumran community. The dis-

Qumran. *Biblical Illustrator* Photo/David Rogers/Oriental Institute

covery of the remains of the community came after a series of events beginning in 1947, when three shepherd boys were tending their goats. One boy, seeing a cave in the rocks, threw a stone through the opening, and he heard the sound of the rock hitting a container. Later, one of the three came back to investigate and discovered some clay pots with old scrolls in them. Searchers later found other caves and containers, discovering ancient manuscripts and manuscript frag-ments. The manuscripts and fragments discovered in those caves became known as the Dead Sea Scrolls.

The scrolls and other archaeological evidence revealed that a community had lived near the caves, at times intermittently, between approximately 150 B.C. and A.D. 68. Scholars gave the community the name Qumran, after its location, which was near a *wadi*, or stream, named Qumran. Some scholars believe that the Qumran community hid the scrolls in the caves to keep them from being destroyed by their enemies. Some recent scholarly opinion, however, has questioned whether the Qumran community is to be identified with the community that preserved the scrolls. At first considered to be an Essene group, that identity for the Qumran community has also been questioned. Nonetheless, that the Dead Sea Scrolls were written, treasured, and deposited by Essenes who lived of Qumran remains the scholarly concensus.

Regardless of the identity of the community, the discovery of the scrolls and fragments was explosive. Many of them were scrolls and fragments of Old Testament Scripture, while others were writings about the community's life and teaching. These extra-biblical writings of the community seem to reflect characteristics that might identify it as Essene, whether the community is to be identified with the Qumran remains or not. The biblical scrolls and fragments were about a thousand years older than Old Testament manuscripts and fragments scholars possessed before the discovery.

The discovery not only provided ancient manuscripts and fragments of the Old Testament, but yielded important information about the thought, culture, and religious practices of a group that existed before and in the time of Jesus. The community represented much of the religious thought and practice among some Jews outside their community as well, all of which is vitally important to biblical studies.

Possibly John the Baptist had some connection with a group much like that described in the extra-biblical writings of the Dead Sea Scrolls, but this cannot be proven. However, John's manner of dress, his diet, his appearance out of the desert or wilderness, his message of repentance, and his practice of baptism may reflect Essene influences (Matt. 3:1–6). That Jesus lived or studied with an Essene community is highly unlikely. Jesus reflects no parallel thought or practice that may be connected exclusively with the Essenes.

Zealots

While there is some question whether the *Zealots* were a distinct party, they at least represented a movement by a radical element in Judaism. Revolutionary zeal characterized them, and they may have taken on distinctiveness as a party by A.D. 66, when they inspired the Jewish rebellion against Rome. Advocates of armed rebellion, they even considered it unlawful to pay taxes to Rome. A more radical group among the Zealots was the sicarii, meaning "dagger-men," a name apparently inspired by the knives carried under their cloaks which they used to assassinate their enemies. They were terrorists who kept tensions heightened between Jews and Romans.

Although Jesus was tempted by the "Zealot option," he refused to embrace the violence of the revolutionaries or to grasp for political power. He never shared the view that national power would make possible the accomplishment of His mission. Jesus' revolutionary way was the way of self-giving love, and his crucificton was the ultimate rejection of violence as a means to restore the kingdom of God to Israel.

Other Jewish Groups

Besides these major Jewish groups which occur frequently in New Testament discussions, a number of other groups existed but were not as prominent. The Herodians, Jews who were loyal to the family of Herod, made up one such group. While they are difficult to identify, they were opponents of Jesus, even joining the Pharisees against Him (Matt. 22:16; Mark 3:6; 12:13). They especially supported Herod Antipas, perhaps indicating that in their belief a descendant of Herod was the best answer and best hope for Israel. Other groups appeared on the scene briefly and with little impact. Apparently, a group loyal to John the Baptist believed that he could lead the way to the renewal of Israel.

The Jewish groups reflected certain philosophies or approaches to life within Judaism. The Sadducees, centered in the Temple and the sacrificial cultus, saw the Pentateuch, the sacrificial ritual, and acceptable political alliance with Rome as the way the Jews were to survive and obey God in the process. Until the Messiah came to deliver Israel, the Pharisees believed that the purifying of Israel by means of the Law was the people's hope and salvation as a nation. The Essenes endeavored to make themselves into a people acceptable to God. They believed they lived in the last days, and some expected a Messiah of Aaron and/or a Messiah of Israel to deliver them from oppression soon.[3] The Zealots thought that the proper way of deliverance was through taking up the sword. God, they believed, would help Israel defeat its enemy of superior forces if Israel rebelled violently against Rome. These various approaches placed the Jewish population as a whole in a state of tension. Into this state of tension Jesus came with His message of redeeming love.

The Dominance of Law, the Absence of Prophecy

During the interbiblical period, the Law, in the mind of many Jews, completed what God wanted His people to know and to do. The Law was the revealed will of God included in the first five book of Moses and other religious writings and traditions accepted as the authoritative revelation of God. Law often translates into the Hebrew word *Torah*, meaning "teaching" or "instruction." *Torah* designated the first five books of the Old Testament, sometimes for the "Law of Moses", and sometimes it referred generally to God's revelation and work with His people. Religious leaders among the Jews, believing that God spoke His ultimate revelation in the Law, felt that the function of prophets and prophecy had been fulfilled. Prophets were no longer considered necessary. Then John the Baptist burst on the scene, calling the Israelites to repent and announcing the impending arrival of the Messiah and His kingdom (see Mark 1:1–8).

The Apocrypha

Although written prophecy ceased to function during the period between the testaments, messages of an interpretative and prophetic quality continued through Jewish religious literature. One such body of literature is referred to as the Apocrypha. The books of the Apocrypha may be dated from approximately 200 B.C. to A.D. 100.

The collection of books now considered as the Apocrypha include First and Second Esdras, Tobit, Judith, Additions to the Book of Esther, The Wisdom of Solomon, Ecclesiaticus (or the Wisdom of Jesus the Son of Sirach), Baruch, The Letter of Jeremiah, The Prayer of Azariah, First and Second Maccabees, The Prayer of Manasseh, Song of the Three Young Men, Susanna, and Bel and the Dragon. These are included in the Old Testament for the Catholic, Orthodox, and Anglican churches. Other Protestants may consider them a source for information about the thought and times in which they appeared, but do not include them in the Old Testament. The Catholic Church does not call the Apocrypha by that name, referring to the collection instead as Deutero-canonical, giving the books a status of authority but not the same degree of authority as other books of the Old Testament.

Two collections or canons of Old Testament books developed during the interbiblical period. One was the Hebrew collection of Old Testament Scriptures, or Hebrew canon, that originated in Israel, sometimes referred to as the Jewish canon. Like most Protestant Bibles, the Jewish canon does not include the apocryphal books.

On the other hand, the Alexandrian canon found expression in the Septuagint, the Greek translation of the Old Testament (see discussion under the Greek period). Some copies of the Septuagint eventually included the Apocrypha. The Septuagint with the Apocrypha influenced the Latin Vulgate (Jerome's version, fourth century A.D.), which in turn influenced the books included in the English translation of the Old Testament for the Catholic, Orthodox, and Anglican churches. Many in the early Christian church used the Septuagint as their Old Testament, including the books of the Apocrypha.

FOR STUDY AND REVIEW

IDENTIFY:

Platonism
Gemara
Epicurianism
Zealots
Stoicism

Essenes
Gnosticism
Qumran Community
Sadducees
Dead Sea Scrolls
Sanhedrin
Zealots
Pharisees
Sicarii
Mishna
Apocrypha

DATES TO REMEMBER

Interbiblical Period
Apocrypha

QUESTIONS FOR CONSIDERATION

1. Why did the law take the place of prophecy?

2. Which canon included the Apocrypha, and how did that inclusion occur?

3. How did the Pharisees plan for the renewal of the nation?

4. What are the indications that John the Baptist may have been influenced by an Essene group?

5. What was the Stoic concept of divine reason *(logos)*?

FOR FURTHER READING

Cate, Robert L. *A History of Bible Lands in the Interbiblical Period.* Nashville: Broadman Press, 1989.

Ferguson, Everett. *Backgrounds of Early Christianity.* Grand Rapids: Eerdmans, 1987: 402–23.

Harrop, Clayton. "Apocrypha." *Holman Bible Dictionary.* Edited by Trent C. Butler.

Nashville: Holman Bible Publishers, 1991: 69–74.

Jeremias, Joachim. *Jerusalem in the Time of Jesus: An Investigation into Economic and Social Conditions During the New Testament Period.* 3rd ed. Philadelphia:Fortress, 1967.

ENDNOTES

1. Graham N. Stanton, *The Gospels and Jesus* (Oxford: Oxford University Press, 1989), 241.

2. John Bright, *A History of Israel*, 3rd ed. (Philadelphia: Westminster Press, 1981), 462–463.

3. The Community Rule, IX. See G. Vermes, *The Dead Sea Scrolls in English* (Baltimore: Penguin, 1968), 87.

❧ 7 ❧

The Gospels

The Gospels, the first four books in the New Testament canon, are sometimes referred to by number according to their sequential order. Hence, Matthew is the *First* Gospel, Mark the *Second* Gospel, Luke the *Third* Gospel, and John the *Fourth* Gospel. This discussion includes both names and number designations so students may become familiar with both usages.

The discussion focuses on the Gospel of John and the Synoptic Gospels, Matthew, Mark, and Luke. The word *synoptic* is from the Greek word *synopsis*, which means "seeing together" or "viewing together." Matthew, Mark, and Luke are the Synoptic Gospels because they give the life and teachings of Jesus in a similar presentation. John gives witness to Christ from another viewpoint, although some of the material in the Fourth Gospel is like that of the Synoptics. Treating the Fourth Gospel separately gives opportunity to emphasize its uniqueness.

The Synoptics share so much in common that somehow they are dependent upon a common source or sources of oral tradition or written materials. While we expect the words and phrases to be similar when quoting Jesus, even the narrative portions in many places share the same words and phrasing. Is one of the Gospels an abbreviation of another? Did two of the Gospel writers use the other Gospel as a source? Were all three Gospels dependent upon an earlier source? These questions indicate that the matter of sources is a problem to be solved, usually referred to as the *synoptic problem.*

Possible solutions offered for the Synoptic problem are several, some of them from early Christian history. Augustine (A.D. 354–430) believed that Matthew wrote first and Mark later abbreviated Matthew, a position held for a long time. In the eighteenth century, Johann Griesbach claimed that the composition of Matthew and Luke preceded Mark, and Mark used both of them for sources as he wrote. Other suggested solutions to the synoptic problem include:[1]

1. *A shared oral tradition:* The Synoptics show commonality because they drew not from shared written sources but from the same oral tradition, very familiar to the authors.

2. *A common written source:* The three gospels shared the same written source, perhaps a written first Gospel upon which they depended.

3. *Dependence upon one another:* The authors each used the others' materials.

4. *Multi-document hypotheses:* These include the two-document hypothesis, the four-document hypothesis, and the multiple-document hypothesis (as many as seven sources).

5. *Independent hypothesis:* The Gospel

writers were not directly dependent upon one another or upon the same sources. Each used his own direct knowledge, including oral teachings and brief written sources in his possession.

The prevailing position today among biblical scholars is that the Gospel of Mark came first and the other two Synoptics depended partially upon Mark. A complex course of reasoning supports this conclusion, but a few statements serve to point the direction of the position. Matthew and Luke reproduce some 95 percent of Mark, sometimes word for word, and Matthew contains all but about forty verses of Mark. Luke contains less of the material in common with Mark, but significant identity occurs between the two. Interestingly, while Matthew and Luke have materials of their own different from one another, Mark has very little not found also in Matthew and Luke.

Did Mark take materials from both Matthew and Luke? Probably not, for why would Mark shorten the account? Why would he leave out so much important material, such as the Sermon on he Mount? It is more likely that Matthew and Luke expanded upon the account of Mark, and an analysis of their materials suggests such expansion.

Matthew and Luke contain about two hundred verses in common with each other which Mark does not have, indicating that they may have used another common source. Scholars call this other source *Q*, the first letter of the German word *Quell*, which means *source*. Mark and Q are the basis for what is called the *two-document hypothesis*, found in the preceding list, which means that the gospel as presented in the Synoptics has at its base two source documents, Mark and *Q*. In addition, Matthew and Luke each have special materials, designated by the letters *M* and *L* respectively, not contained in the other two

Synoptic Gospels. Combining Mark, *Q*, *M*, and *L* means that four sources stand behind the Gospels, the basis for the *four-document hypothesis* mentioned in the preceding list. A general consensus of opinion, disregarding the particulars of which documents and how many, is that the authors did depend upon other sources besides themselves as is indicated in Luke 1:1–4. Certainly behind all three of the Gospels stands the earlier oral transmission of the text and some earlier written documents.

What is the significance of, or indeed why even consider, the sources for the gospel? First, the discussion does illuminate to a significant degree how God guided human beings to write Scripture. Second, these sources should encourage us about the strength of the Gospels' witness, because they mean that the good news we have about Christ comes from a variety of witnesses supported by a number of other witnesses. Third, the authors of the Gospels did not write in a vacuum, nor even in total dependence upon their own memories and experiences, but upon the basis of other providentially prepared witnesses. What we have in the Gospels, therefore, is a rich telling of the most important life in all of history, that of Jesus Christ!

Dates suggested for the writing of the Synoptics vary from before A.D. 50 to as late as A.D. 100. Usually the dating occurs in relationship to A.D. 70, which is the year Titus and the Roman forces put down the Jewish rebellion against Rome. The rebellion began in A.D. 66, experienced success at first, and then ended in A.D. 70 in terrible defeat. The Romans destroyed Jerusalem and the temple, marking a dramatic change in history for Israel.

Conditions of life before and after A.D. 70 had distinct differences, which may be reflected in the people and their circumstances addressed by each Gospel. A question may be asked of each of the Synoptics, "Does this Gospel reflect conditions of life prevailing before or after A.D. 70?" In particular, "Does each Gospel reflect a situation in which the temple and Jerusalem still stand?" Nonetheless, the answers are not obvious as the various dates assigned to the Gospels indicate.

Assigning dates for the Synoptics falls into three categories. First, all may be dated before A.D. 70, sometime between A.D. 50 and 70. Second, all may be dated after A.D. 70, between A.D. 70 and 100. Third, one or the other may be dated before or after A.D. 70.

In the final analysis, we are limited by the evidence available in determining a date for the writing of the Synoptics. Strong reasons exist for dating on each side of A.D. 70. A range within which several specific dates have found rather wide acceptance include dating Mark between A. D. 63–68 and Luke and Matthew between A. D. 70–85. However, strong arguments can be made for dating all the Gospels between A. D. 50–70, and the dating schemes now seem to be moving toward earlier dates.

FOR STUDY AND REVIEW

IDENTIFY:

Q
Two-document hypothesis
Four-document hypothesis

QUESTIONS FOR CONSIDERATION

1. What is another method of referring to the Gospels?
2. What is the meaning of the word *Synoptic?*
3. What is the Synoptic problem?
4. What are some solutions to the synoptic problem?
5. What is the significance of studying sources for the Gospels?
6. What are the possible dates for the Synoptic Gospels?

FOR FURTHER READING

Carson, Moo, D.A., Morris, Douglas J. and Leo. *An Introduction to the New Testament.* Grand Rapids: Zondervan, 1992, 19–60.

Drane, John. *Introducing the New Testament.* San Francisco: Harper and Row, 1986: 160–80.

Kümmel, W. G. *Introduction to the New Testament,* translated by H. C. Kee. Revised and enlarged ed. Nashville: Abingdon Press, 1975, 38–80.

ENDNOTE

1. For a full survey of these and other proposed solutions to thesynoptic problem, see D. A. Carson, D. J. Moo, and Leon Morris, *An Introduction to the New Testament* (Grand Rapids: Zondervan, 1992), 19–45.

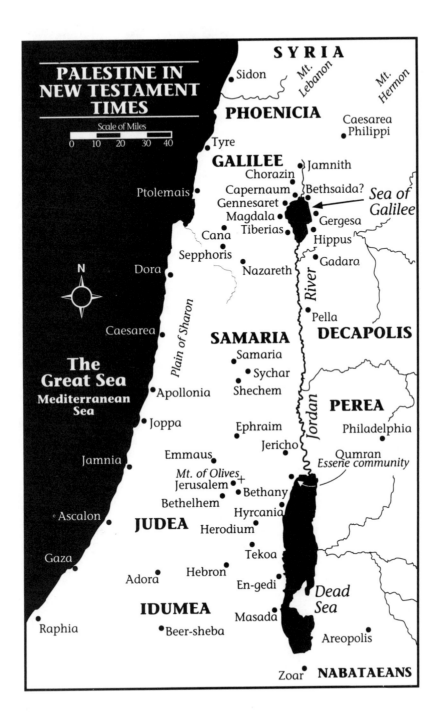

PALESTINE IN NEW TESTAMENT TIMES

Scale of Miles
0 10 20 30 40

SYRIA

Sidon

Mt. Lebanon

Mt. Hermon

PHOENICIA

Caesarea Philippi

Tyre

GALILEE

Jamnith

Chorazin

Capernaum

Bethsaida?

Sea of Galilee

Ptolemais

Gennesaret

Magdala

Gergesa

Tiberias

Hippus

Cana

Gadara

Sepphoris

Nazareth

River

Dora

Pella

N

DECAPOLIS

Caesarea

SAMARIA

Plain of Sharon

Samaria

Sychar

Shechem

Jordan

PEREA

The Great Sea
Mediterranean Sea

Apollonia

Philadelphia

Joppa

Ephraim

Jericho

Qumran
Essene community

Emmaus

Mt. of Olives

Jamnia

Jerusalem

Bethany

Bethelhem

Hyrcania

Ascalon

JUDEA

Herodium

Gaza

Tekoa

Dead Sea

Adora

Hebron

En-gedi

IDUMEA

Masada

Raphia

Beer-sheba

Areopolis

Zoar **NABATAEANS**

✤ 8 ✤

The Gospel of Matthew: Jesus the King

Writer

We have specific if not abundant information about the man named Matthew. We know that he was a tax collector, a Jew who worked for the Roman government, which made him a traitor in the eyes of many Jews. The Gospels know him by two names, Matthew in the Gospel of Matthew and Levi in the Gospels of Mark and Luke. We also know that Christ sought Matthew out, called him to follow Him, and Matthew did. The name Matthew means "gift of God." Consequently, Levi may have been his tax-collector name, but when he became a Christian he became known by Matthew. Finally, Mark 2:14 tells us that he was the son of Alphaeus.

The title of the First Gospel indicates that a person named Matthew was its author. Generally, the position prevails that the church added the titles in the last half of second century. Martin Hengel challenged this position with a study of book distribution in the ancient world. According to his position, affixing titles was the practice in book writing and distribution, so the Gospels likely had titles from the beginning. If so, little doubt would exist about the authorship of Matthew.[1] His point is not absolutely conclusive, so the best we can say for the titles is that they give especially strong witness to the person who wrote

or influenced the writing of the book. The truth remains that the text of the Gospel does not identify its author as Matthew. The same can be said of all four Gospels.

Evidence for Matthew the apostle as author is significant but limited outside the title of the First Gospel itself. Some early writers[2] such as Papias (c. 60–130), as quoted by Eusebius (c. 260–340), Irenaeus (c. 130–200), and Origen (c. 185–254) seem to refer to the Gospel as having been written by Matthew the apostle. Each of these references, however, could point to a writing other than the First Gospel.

Some indicators in the text of the First Gospel itself give limited support. Matthew and Levi are the same person, but Luke (5:27) and Mark (2:14) refer to him as Levi, while the Gospel of Matthew never refers to him as Levi. Perhaps Matthew, in writing his Gospel, preferred the name he used after his conversion from tax collector to disciple of Jesus. So the exclusive use of the name Matthew may support Matthean authorship.

In addition, Matthew is a structured, orderly Gospel. A tax collector, accustomed to keeping records, could be the kind of person to write an orderly and structured account about Jesus. Hence, orderliness may support Matthew the apostle as author.

Challenges to Matthean authorship occur for several reasons. Matthew was an eyewitness to Jesus Christ. An eyewitness would not have had to depend upon the Gospel of Mark as a source, as the author of Matthew seems to have done. The Gospel of Matthew does not seem to carry the passion of one involved in the events reported, which would again speak against an eyewitness writing the Gospel. In addition, some interpreters believe that Matthew seems to reflect a developed church situation in the latter part of the first century, which would make less likely the possibility that Matthew wrote the First Gospel.

Such objections may be answered in the first case by the fact that Matthew thought it wise to use sources other than himself in writing his account. In the second case, some of the passion of the reporting may be removed simply by the lapse of time from the actual events observed. In the third case, the rapidity of church development in some areas cannot be determined. Other objections exist against Matthean authorship. While the interpreter cannot be dogmatic about Matthew as author and be honest to the evidence presented in the Bible itself, Matthew may have written the Gospel or in some way have influenced significantly its shape and content.[3]

Matthew is the first book in the New Testament. If Mark wrote first, why is Matthew the first in the canon? The book's orderliness, its adaptability as a teaching tool to new converts in the church, and its presentation of themes must have appealed to early readers, making it the book of dominant use and earning the Gospel its priority position in the New Testament.

Readers

The Gospel seems to have three groups of readers in view. Primarily, the message is directed to a *Jewish audience*. Matthew cited much Old Testament material to support the claim that Jesus is the Messiah, the king, and thus the fulfillment of Jewish expectation about a Messiah. He came "not . . . to abolish the Law or the Prophets . . . but to fulfill them" (5:17). Too, He even has the authority to interpret the law of Moses (see 5:21, 27, 31, 33, 43), a fact of much significance for a Jewish audience.

A second audience addressed by the Gospel was the *Christian community*. Because of the orderly presentation of its witness, the Book of Matthew was particularly suited to instruct Christians, especially new converts, in the teaching and way of Jesus. Jesus Himself, as presented in Matthew, is the master teacher. So Matthew wrote with the community in mind. The record and teachings of Jesus prepared Christians to meet the questions and challenges posed by those both skeptical of to and interested in Christianity.

A third audience must have been the *world beyond* Judaism and the Christian community. Although Matthew addressed primarily a Jewish audience, careful emphases exist to show that Christ is for everybody, as a few examples will demonstrate. The genealogy in Matthew includes three Gentiles, two of whom are women (see 1:1–16). The "Magi" ("wise men," NRSV) come from another place and another culture to worship the one "born king of the Jews" (2:1–2). In addition, the Gospel ends with the charge to go and "make disciples of all nations" (28:19). Although the First Gospel demonstrates that Jesus is the fulfillment of Old Testament and Jewish expectations, He is the Messiah, the King, for everyone who will become a disciple, a fact even supported by Old Testament evidence. Such evidence would deflect Jewish criticism aimed at the Gospel's inclusiveness of everybody.

The book reflects a tension between Jews and the Christian community. Tension would develop in a locale where a Jewish synagogue-connected majority and a Jewish-Gentile Christian minority lived. Antioch of Syria had such elements, although it was not the only place of that composition. A location in Palestine, such as Jerusalem, or Phoenicia in Syria has been suggested for the origin of the book, We cannot be certain of the homeland of the readers, but they probably lived in a place where a Jewish synagogue majority was critical of a Jewish-Gentile Christian minority.

Message

The First Gospel affirms that Jesus is the King, the Messiah, who has come and whose reign has begun. A number of Old Testament texts included in Matthew support the claim that Jesus is the fulfillment of messianic expectations. Also, the Gospel ends with the affirmation that all authority in heaven and on earth has been given to Christ (28:18), which means that His reign continues. Significant to Matthew's organization of the message of and about Jesus are the five great discourse sections. A discourse is a collection of the sayings of Jesus about a certain subject or subjects. Preceding each discourse section is a narrative section which tells of other facts and actions in relationship to Jesus. Consequently, the material in chapters 3—25 may divide quite naturally into five divisions, each containing a narrative section and a discourse section. In each case the narrative prepares the way for the discourse or follows the discourse. The five discourses are the heart of the five divisions. The five discourse sections are the Sermon on the Mount (Chaps. 5—7), the instruction to the twelve for their mission (Chap. 10), the parables of the kingdom (Chap. 13), the teaching about the church (Chap. 18), and the teaching concerning things to come (Chaps. 24—25).

Box 3: Five Sections of Matthew

Prologue: 1—2

Section I

Narrative: 3—4
First Discourse: 5—7

Section II

Narrative: 8—9
Second Discourse: 10

Section III

Narrative: 11—12
Third Discourse: 13

Section IV

Narrative: 14—17
Fourth Discourse: 18

Section V

Narrative: 19—23
Fifth Discourse: 24—25

Conclusion

Trial, death, burial, resurrection, 26—28

Are these five divisions intended to correspond to the first five books of the Old Testament, the Pentateuch, in order to present Jesus as the new giver of the law? Like Moses, who gave the law at Mount Sinai, the Messiah has such authority. This is one possibility for explaining the structure and content of Matthew, but the message may be viewed from other points of structure as well.

The book may be divided according to the locale of Jesus' ministry. For instance, the ministry in Galilee and in Judea and Jerusalem dominate most of the Gospel of Matthew. As Jesus moves from one locale to the other, He is the Messiah who carries out His mission, who establishes by His words and action, as well as by His suffering, death, and resurrection, that He is the Messiah.

To emphasize the stress upon Jesus as the Messiah of Jewish expectations, the following emphases may be utilized: the identification of Jesus as Messiah (1:1—4:11); the message of the Messiah (4:12—25:46); and the passion (suffering) and resurrection of the Messiah (26:1—28:20). This approach does help the reader to keep in mind that Jesus as Messiah is the major thrust of Matthew's content. Also, this approach takes into account the situation of the readers in which a mixed Christian community of Jews and Gentiles must present their beliefs in an understandable way in the context of a Jewish majority.

The Identification of Jesus as Messiah (1:1-4:11)

The genealogy, birth, and childhood references help us to mark Jesus' identity (1:1—2:23). Matthew's genealogy traces the lineage of Jesus to David and Abraham, from whom the Messiah was to descend according to Jewish expectation. Jesus' birth was of divine motivation and announcement.

While the Gospel of John speaks of the birth of Jesus as the Word becoming flesh, the Gospels of Matthew and Luke give other details about this unique event. They tell us

of the virgin named Mary to whom the announcement came that she would bear the Christ-child, the child who was to be the Messiah of Jewish expectation. Joseph was her promised husband (Matt. 1:18). In effect Mary already belonged to Joseph, which was a much stronger commitment than an engagement in our society. When Joseph heard that Mary was pregnant, he decided to break his obligation to her privately, so as not to cause her embarrassment. But an angel of the Lord appeared to him in a dream, and said, "Joseph son of David, do not be afraid to take Mary home as your wife, because what is conceived in her is from the Holy Spirit" (1:20).

Matthew recorded two significant names in relationship to the child to be born. The first is "Immanuel," meaning "God with us" (1:23), which echoes Isaiah 7:14 where a child was named Immanuel as a sign of God's deliverance. Jesus is the ultimate fulfillment of that deliverance of all people who call on God for salvation. Matthew's Gospel tells us that the name of the baby was to be "Jesus" (1:21). The Hebrew form of Jesus is "Joshua," a name meaning "God is salvation" or "God saves." As the message to Joseph indicates, the name Jesus expresses what He will be and do, "for he will save his people from their sins" (1:21).

Mary could have been as young as fifteen years when she received the announcement that she would be the mother of the Messiah, although we do not know her age. Joseph probably was somewhat older than Mary, a conjecture supported by the likelihood that he died well before Jesus left home, his death in effect placing Jesus at the head of the family and responsible for their well-being.

Having heard and accepted their responsibilities in relation to the Christ-child, after their marriage Joseph and Mary traveled to

Bethlehem. Mary gave birth to Jesus there, in Bethlehem, as had been foretold for the place of the Messiah's birth (2:5–6). Remarkable things happened at the birth of Jesus such as the special star and the visit of the Magi (2:1–2). Of course, the most striking thing was Jesus. He was God's Son, the Savior, Lord of all, God Himself coming into the middle of humanity. Immediately, in this context, Herod the Great struck at the vulnerability of the Christ-child and tried to find and destroy Jesus, causing Joseph and Mary to flee into Egypt to escape his designs (2:13–21).

After these initial events, Matthew's Gospel tells us little of the life of Jesus. They did return from Egypt, and they settled in Nazareth, Jesus' home for most of His life. We assume that he learned a trade from Joseph. The people of Jesus' home area identified Him as the "carpenter's son" (Matt. 13:55). Did Jesus support His family as a carpenter? Interestingly, the word translated "carpenter" (*tekton*) may be translated "farmer." The word *tekton* basically means "to cut," and the regular usage referred to cutting wood as a carpenter does. But another usage, although rare, refers to cutting ground as a farmer does.[4] Could Joseph and Jesus have been farmers? Most of Jesus' illustrations were from agricultural life rather than the carpenter's shop, so the view that He was a farmer may have some support. Or He may have been a carpenter who chose agricultural stories simply because of their familiarity to His audiences.

Since Joseph disappears from the story during and after this time, we assume that he died and that Jesus, as the eldest child, took responsibility for providing for the family. Evidently the family included at least two sisters and four brothers: James, Joseph, Simon, and Judas (13:55–56). The sisters are not named, but we know that there was more than one because of the plural form, "sisters."

The baptism and temptation of Jesus also mark His identity and signal the beginning of His ministry (3:1–4:25). He was "about thirty years" of age (Luke 3:23). If He had been responsible for Mary and His brothers and sisters up to this point, He could at this time give the responsibility of the care of His mother over to His brothers. Other family responsibilities could be discharged in the same way. He was prepared, God had prepared the times, and the public ministry began.

John the Baptist (3:1–17) burst from the wilderness, clothed in camel skins bound up by a leather girdle. He had an interesting diet of wild honey and locusts, an insect high in protein eaten either raw, boiled, or roasted. With his dramatic appearance and dramatic message, John looked and sounded like a prophet.

"Prepare the way for the Lord, make straight paths for him" (Matt. 3:3) was the message of the Baptist. In those days, when a ruler was to travel in his territory, a messenger went out along the way of the king's planned route to announce to the people that their king would soon travel this way. The people were to straighten roads, build bridges, and do other work to make the roads passable and smooth for the king's journey. John told people to prepare their lives, not roads, for the coming of their king, the Messiah. After all, the Lord would baptize them with the Holy Spirit, while John could only baptize with water. In other words, John could immerse them in water, but the Messiah who was about to come would immerse them into the very presence of God (see 3:3).

John refused to baptize Jesus at first when Jesus came to him for that purpose, but Jesus insisted that he do so (3:13–17). Why was Jesus baptized when John was calling for sinners to repent and be baptized as a sign of that repentance? The biblical witness is that

Jesus was sinless, so no need existed for Him to engage in a baptism of repentance. Jesus said the baptism was necessary to "fulfill all righteousness" (3:15). Jesus' baptism really epitomized His character and the nature of the commitment by which He would fulfill in faithful obedience His mission.

Jesus' baptism expressed His self-giving to His Father and to others, which characterized His whole life. He never was Messiah for Himself, but for His Father and for others. Consequently, as there was a baptism at the beginning of His ministry, there also was a baptism at the end of His ministry: His crucifixion and resurrection. Ultimately He would take on Himself the self-centered evil of humankind and bury it, by conquering death and sin through God's power working in His self-giving life (see 1 Cor. 15:54–57). Then He would be raised to new life in exultation to all "authority in heaven and on earth" (28:18). In reality, then, His baptism was a sign of the character and action of His whole life. Followers of His are now baptized, following the pattern of Jesus as He calls us to a self-giving life.

The temptations of Jesus (4:1–11) were three: to turn the stones into bread, to throw Himself from the pinnacle of the Temple, and to worship the devil so as to secure the kingdoms of this world. These may be viewed, in order, as a temptation to selfish interest, a temptation to popularity, and a temptation to power.

Another way to consider the temptations is in relationship to Jesus' identity, for each of the temptations was an effort to make Him deny who He was. The first temptation struck

Traditional site of the Mount of Temptation. *Biblical Illustrator* Photo/David Rogers.

at His *human identity*. As *Son of Man*, He was representative of all human beings. Human beings needed to be shown who we are and what it means to be human as God made us to be. If the tempter could get Him to deny His humanness by turning the stones into bread, Jesus would no longer be the human being for others but for Himself. The tempter would have defeated Jesus at this point had he been successful.

The second temptation was at the point of His *divine identity*. He was tempted to live as if He were not the *Son of God*. In essence, throwing Himself from the pinnacle of the temple was a temptation to get God to prove that Jesus was His Son. If Jesus did jump, and the angels did "lift" Him up (4:6), then He could prove to Himself and others that He was God's Son. "After all," the tempter seems to be saying, "You may not be the Son of God. Prove it. Test ("tempt," 4:7, KJV) God to see if it is so." Jesus had settled the matter about His sonship, and to test to see if it were so would have been a denial of what had been revealed to Him already by His Father—an act of "no faith" in His Father.

Jesus also came to be *Messiah*, the specially designated king-deliverer of God, which was the focal point of the third temptation. He was tempted at the point of His *mission identity*. "Here is the power to be king," the tempter offered, "just fall down and worship me." But Jesus did not come to be a king to subject people by power and self-interest, but with self-giving love, which is a special power in itself. Besides, the tempter lied; the kingdoms were not his to give. Had the devil succeeded at this point, he would have set Jesus on an impossible quest.

Notice that in each temptation Jesus' relationship with the Father turned the temptation away. He responded to the first temptation with, "Man does not live on bread

The pinnacle of the Temple. *Biblical Illustrator* Photo/David Rogers.

alone, but on every word that comes from the mouth of God" (4:4). As important as bread is to a person's existence, what God says or wills is more important than that, and Jesus was committed to do and be what His Father willed. To the second temptation Jesus said, "Do not put the Lord your God to the test" (4:7). Testing God to see if He is true is to live by doubt rather than faith. Jesus lived by faith in His Father; He had perfect confidence in His Father. In response to the third temptation, Jesus replied, "Worship the Lord your God, and serve him only" (4:10). We will be like what we worship; we will give ourselves to that, whatever it is. Jesus gave Himself to the Father, not to Satan.

The Message of the Messiah (4:12—25:46)

As we survey the message of Jesus in Matthew, we will give special attention to the five major discourse sections. They all have to do with the reign of God and the meaning of that reign to humanity. Jesus' preaching primarily involved the proclamation of the kingdom (4:17). Matthew used the expression "kingdom of heaven" rather than "kingdom of God" because it was more palatable to the Jews. They preferred to use the name of God as little as possible out of respect for the name, so they substituted "heaven" for the name of God. Actually, kingdom of heaven and kingdom of God are the same reality, which basically means "rule of God."

The Sermon on the Mount (Matt. 5:1—7:29), the first discourse section, contains some of the most moving and challenging teachings of Jesus. By means of this sermon, Jesus told His hearers what a citizen of God's kingdom is to be and do. The ethical demands of this sermon are lofty. Jesus demanded a standard of righteousness that exceeded that righteousness defined by the laws and conduct of the Pharisees (5:20). Jesus defined righteousness primarily in terms of relationship, not in simply keeping the rules.

In the sermon, relationship to God, to human emotions, to our own selves, to possessions, to fellow believers, to family, to enemies, and ultimately to Jesus came under the demands of Jesus' righteousness. Why does Jesus want us to live as defined by the Sermon on the Mount? Because He wants us to build a life that is worth living. In other words, He wants us to aspire to His righ-

teousness for our benefit. As He closed the sermon and spoke of building a house on a rock or on sand, He was talking about building life (7:24–27). If we want to build a life that will stand, then we need to hear and do the words of Jesus (7:24).

In chapters 8—9, Matthew recorded a number of miracles of Jesus. Jesus' healing activity marked Him as one who had power over evil and over that which threatened Christ's followers. Also, the miracles should have helped Matthew's readers to see that the Messiah had arrived and that His reign had begun.

In a second major teaching or discourse section (10:1–42), Jesus instructed the twelve apostles as He sent them out to minister as He had done (10:1). The twelve are named to be His close associates (10:2–4). These He sent to the "lost sheep of Israel" (10:6). By this means Matthew emphasized that Jesus gave priority to the house of Israel. While a matter of strategy was a reason for doing so, God, in His relationship in Jesus Christ to the house of Israel, gave them opportunity to respond. Probably Matthew wrote out of a consciousness of Jewish criticism about the inclusion of Gentiles in the reign of the Messiah. After all, if Jesus were the Messiah, would He not have come to Israel? He did.

Jesus' warnings about how the apostles might be received by some people (10:16–25) indicated the difficulty of proclaiming to a people the reign of Jesus as Messiah when they had another kind of reign in mind. Jesus encouraged them not to be afraid (10:26–31), for God would care for them. Nonetheless, He called for supreme commitment from His followers to His kingdom (10:32). The commitment is costly, disrupting some relationships as the relationship to Christ is put first (10:34–39). Jesus did not advocate that His disciples should reject father, daughter, mother, or others; but these might reject the disciples as they placed Christ as the priority relationship among all relationships.

Chapters 11—12 depict the growing rejection of Jesus by the religious establishment. The rejection began to affect those closest to Him. What He said might be true of His disciples' families was true of Him. His mother and brothers (12:46–50) evidently thought Jesus needed rescuing from His mission as resistance built against Him, so they came for Him. Jesus gave priority to His mission, and His mother and brothers could not influence Him away from that, for He was doing the will of the Father.

The parables of chapter 13 constitute the third major message or discourse section of Matthew. Parables of the sower (13:3–23), weeds (13:24–30), mustard seed (13:31–32), yeast (13:33), hidden treasure and pearl (13:44–46), and net (13:47–50) are presented. They comprise a dazzling array of stories in which the nature of the kingdom, or rule of God, is explained. The kingdom eventuates in a superabundant harvest, as when the seed falls in the good soil, despite evidences to the contrary, as when the seed falls in the bad soil (sower). Judgment and separation eventually result in the reign of God in Christ (weeds). The kingdom produces unimaginable results, although it has seemingly insignificant beginnings (mustard seeds). All of life is affected by the kingdom (yeast). A crisis of decision comes to life as the kingdom comes, but if hearers understand the value of the kingdom, they will give everything they have in order to possess and be possessed by the kingdom (hidden treasure and pearl).

Matthew related various activities of Jesus in chapters 14–17, such as His response to the beheading of John the Baptist (14:1–13), feeding of five thousand (14:14–21), walking on water (14:22–36), conflicts with the Pharisees

and teachers of the Law (15:1–19), encounter with a Canaanite woman (15:21–28), feeding of four thousand (15:29–39), conflicts with Pharisees and Sadducees (16:1–12), and Peter's confession (16:13–20). In 16:21–28 Jesus predicted His death, and 17:1–13 records His transfiguration. The healing of the epileptic boy (17:14–23) and discussion of the temple tax (17:24–27) completes chapter 17. These events and activities occur in a brief period of time. Witnessing even one such mighty event would be remarkable, but here one event follows another as the dramatic reign of God in Jesus Christ, literally the kingdom of heaven, was brought to bear on human existence.

The fourth major message or discourse of Jesus is in chapter 18. Interpreters usually consider this to be teaching about the church. During the activities recorded in chapters 14—17, Jesus attempted to be alone with His apostles to prepare them for the events ahead. He did succeed in being alone with them at Caesarea Philippi (16:13–20), which eventuated in the great confession of Simon Peter. After asking His disciples how people identified Him, Jesus wanted to know how the disciples answered. As spokesman for the group, Simon Peter answered: "You are the Christ, the Son of the living God" (Matt. 16:16). Jesus' reply to Simon was, "And I tell you that you are Peter, and on this rock I will build my church, and the gates of Hades will not overcome it" (16:18). In other words, Jesus would take people like Simon Peter, with all his faults and limitations, who confessed a faith like Peter's and build His church.

We sometimes picture the church, the people of God in Christ, as being in a fortress position, protecting itself from evil. But the picture that Jesus gave is quite different (Matt. 16:17–19). The gates of Hades are the powers of death, and they shall not stand against the church. Gates were for keeping something out in order to protect something within. The church, Jesus said, would storm the gates of the powers of death to rescue people from death to life.

The church, as chapter 18 teaches, is the manifestation of the reign of God, or kingdom of heaven in people's lives. Kingdom citizens have childlike characteristics (to be distinguished from childishness), relating to God in trusting and faithful dependence and obedience. The church is composed of little ones, epitomized in children themselves for whom the church is to care. God is not willing for any of these little ones, all of those under His kingdom, to be neglected or hurt, as the parable of the lost sheep vividly depicts (18:10–14). In the church, gracious forgiveness is to dominate and is to be both given and received (18:15–20). Those who do not forgive are not a part of the kingdom of heaven, as emphasized in the parable of the unmerciful servant (18:21–35).

The last major narrative and discourse section (chapters 19—25), which presents the message of Jesus through His activities and teachings, takes us up to the dramatic final events of Jesus' life. We should remember that this life is the inbreaking of the reign of God, the kingdom of heaven, in a person, Jesus Christ the Messiah (King). The narrative section features, among other important events, Jesus' triumphal entry into Jerusalem (21:1-17). He enters as a king of peace, as depicted by His riding the donkey, and the people proclaim Him as king. He is the "son of David," and He "comes in the name of the Lord!" (21:9). These were kingly (messianic) acclamations by the people.

After Jesus made this dramatic entrance, He aggressively pressed His call to real kingdom rule. He confronted the chief priests and elders in the temple courts (21:23–27).

Through parables (two sons, 21:28–32; tenants, 21:33–46; wedding banquet, 22:1–14) He confronted the religious leaders and showed them that they were in a crisis situation. Then Jesus pronounced upon them "woes" (23:1–36) by which He showed their failure to follow the righteousness of the law. They needed the grace of the righteousness of the kingdom, and perhaps Jesus' confrontation was to shock them into realizing their needs. In 23:37–39 Jesus mourned Jerusalem's fate.

The last discourse or teaching section, chapters 24—25, is in an "end of the age" context (24:3). However, much of what Jesus said pointed to the fall of Jerusalem, for the disciples' first question addressed the destruction of the temple, while the second addressed "your coming and . . . the end of the age" (24:3). Therefore, in chapter 24, at times Jesus spoke to the first question, and other parts of the discourse apply to the second question. As regards the second question, no one knows the "day or hour" (24:36). Three parables (ten virgins, 25:1–13; talents, 25:14–30; sheep and goats, 25:31–46) stress the need to be prepared and the judgment upon unpreparedness which comes at the "end of the age" (24:3).

Final Events of the Messiah (26:1—28:20)

Religious leaders plotted against Jesus (26:1–5), even enlisting Judas, one of the twelve, who agreed to betray Jesus (26:14–16) into their hands. Jesus shared a last meal with his disciples, at which He instituted the Lord's Supper (26:17–29). Jesus predicted Peter's betrayal (26:31–35) and retired to Gethsemane, where he struggled with the suffering He knew was before Him (26:36–46). Matthew recorded that a "large crowd" (26:47) came to arrest Jesus. Jesus was tried before the Sanhedrin (26:57–68), while outside Peter denied Him (26:69–75). Judas hanged himself in remorse over his betrayal (27:1–10), and Jesus was tried before Pilate.

After being handed over to the soldiers, who treated Him badly (Matt. 27:27–31), Jesus was crucified. A number of events occurred at the crucifixion, and Jesus uttered His last words from the cross. Seven statements of Jesus from the cross, usually referred to as the "seven last words," are found in the four Gospels. For convenience's sake, and so the reader may see the words and their sources at once, a listing and discussion of the words is included at this point. Note the word found in Matthew.

Box 4: Jesus' Seven Last Words as Found in the Gospels

1. "Father, forgive them, for they do not know what they are doing" (Luke 23:34); said of all, including His enemies.
2. "I tell you the truth, today you will be with me in paradise" (Luke 23:43); said to one of the robbers crucified with Him.
3. "Dear woman, here is your son . . . Here is your mother" (John 19:26–27); spoken to His mother and the disciple whom He loved most, respectively.
4. "My God, my God, why have you forsaken me?" (Matt. 27:46).
5. "I am thirsty" (John 19:28).
6. "It is finished" (John 19:30).
7. "Father, into your hands I commit my spirit" (Luke 23:46).

Although Jesus suffered terribly, His concern was for others, as His words from the

cross confirm. The first word affirms Jesus' reason for being on the cross. He expressed the suffering and forgiving love of God for all people, including those who crucified Him. Even a thief received immediate forgiveness and inclusion into eternal relationship with Jesus, as the second word shows. The third word provided for the care of His mother.

The fourth word from the cross, found in Matthew's Gospel, has proved to be the most perplexing for interpreters. Did God forsake Jesus? One answer is that He did, proposing that as Jesus took the sins of the world upon Himself God turned His back on Jesus. As the reasoning goes, God did so because, being holy, He could not be involved with sin. Therefore, He could not be involved with Jesus at this point. The fourth word is sometimes referred to as the "cry of dereliction," because Jesus was left alone like a derelict ship which all have deserted.

But this interpretation poses some problems. First, God has always been involved in delivering His people from their sin. God is not afraid to look upon sin or to deal with it, as numerous cases in the Old Testament confirm. Second, the biblical witness stresses that God and Jesus were one. Second Corinthians 5:19 states that "God was reconciling the world to himself in Christ." Was the Father not with Christ on the cross? The best answer is that He was.

A second answer to the question, "Did the Father forsake Jesus?" is in the negative. Jesus, in His intense suffering in the absence of human contact and terrible pain, felt alone and forsaken, but was not in reality. This explanation has much to commend it because it takes seriously Jesus' humanness.

A third answer to the question involves Psalm 22, which begins with the words, "My God, my God, why have you forsaken me?" In this explanation, Jesus did not feel forsaken at all, but began to recite Psalm 22 for himself and others for the purposes of strength and comfort. A reading of Psalm 22 reveals a description of suffering that parallels the suffering of Jesus (22:6,14–18). Although the suffering described is intense, the psalm ends in victory (22:27–31).

The victory, of course, did come. On the first day of the week, Jesus was raised from the dead. His resurrection appearances included a number of individuals and groups (Matt. 28:1–20; Mark 16:2–20; Luke 24:1–53; John 20:1—21:25; Acts 1:3–11). The number of people who saw Him after the resurrection eventually became more than five hundred (1 Cor. 15:6). The power of sin and death had been defeated. Jesus had been true to Himself and His Father and had accomplished His mission. "All authority in heaven and earth" belong to him, as befits the Messiah of all humankind. By that authority He has sent, and continues to send, His followers into all the world (Matt. 28:18–20).

FOR STUDY AND REVIEW

IDENTIFY:

Papias (endnote 2)
Irenaeus (endnote 2)
Polycarp (endnote 2)
Eusebius (endnote 2)
Gethsemane

QUESTIONS FOR CONSIDERATION

1. What are some of the considerations for the authorship of Matthew?
2. Who were the audiences addressed by Matthew?

3. What was the possible location for the Christian community of Matthew? What was their situation?
4. What is the message of Matthew?
5. What is the structure of Matthew according to the five section approach?
6. What is the reasoning behind the proposal that Jesus may have been a farmer?
7. What was the major thrust of Jesus' preaching? What did "kingdom of heaven" mean?
8. How are the "gates of Hades" in Matthew 16:17–19 to be explained?

FOR FURTHER READING

Aland, Kurt, ed. *Synopsis of the Four Gospels.* Rev. Eng. ed. United Bible Societies, 1985.

Barclay, William. *Jesus as They Saw Him.* New York: Harper and Row, 1963.

Carson, D. A., Douglas J. Moo, and Leon Morris. *An Introduction to the New Testament.* Grand Rapids: Zondervan, 1992: 61–87.

Cate, Robert L. *A History of the New Testament and Its Times.* Nashville: Broadman Press, 1991.

Kümmel, W. G. *Introduction to the New Testament.* trans. H. C. Kee. Rev., enlarged ed. Nashville: Abingdon Press, 1975: 72–86.

Michaels, J. R. "Gospel of Matthew." *Mercer Dictionary of the Bible.* Edited by Watson E. Mills. Macon, Ga.: Mercer University Press, 1990, 558–60.

ENDNOTES

1. Martin Hengel, *Studies in the Gospel of Mark* (Philadelphia: Fortress, 1985), 54–84.

2. Some support for Matthew as author can be gleaned from the quotes of later Christian writers. In fact, these early writers are important in discussing all of the New

Testament writers. They give us our earliest information about some of the authors of the books of the New Testament and sometimes information about the books themselves. While there are many early writers, some of the earliest from whom we have direct or indirect information about the New Testament are given here.

Papias lived from approximately A.D. 60 to 130. He was a companion of Polycarp and gives us some information about what Polycarp said. He was bishop of Hierapolis, in southern Asia Minor. Hierapolis was the place where Epaphras, a colaborer with Paul, had worked (Col. 4:13).

Polycarp an early Christian martyr, was given an opportunity to deny Christ and live. But Polycarp replied, "Eighty and six years have I served him, and he hath done me no wrong; how then can I blaspheme my king who saved me?" He lived from about A.D. 69 to 185. He was bishop of Smyrna.

Irenaeus gives us some interesting information about the Gospel writers in his *Against Heresies*. He lived from around A.D. 130 to 200. He was bishop of Lyons, in what was known as Gaul but much later became France.

Eusebius is a pivotal historian who recorded in his *Ecclesiastical History* so much of what early Christian leaders wrote or were reported to have said. He was from Caesarea, not to be confused with Eusebius of Nicomedia. He lived from around A.D. 260 to 340.

3. In writing about the documents, I often refer to the titled authors. The reader should keep in mind the various questions of authorship raised.

4. Robert L. Cate, *A History of the New Testament and Its Times* (Nashville: Broadman Press, 1991), 150–51.

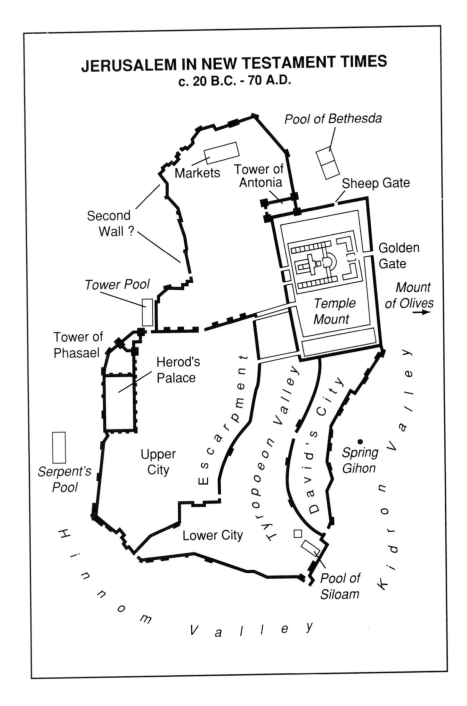

JERUSALEM IN NEW TESTAMENT TIMES
c. 20 B.C. - 70 A.D.

Pool of Bethesda

Markets Tower of Antonia

Sheep Gate

Second Wall ?

Golden Gate

Tower Pool

Mount of Olives

Tower of Phasael

Herod's Palace

Temple Mount

Escarpment

Tyropoeon Valley

David's City

Kidron Valley

Serpent's Pool

Upper City

Spring Gihon

Lower City

Hinnom Valley

Pool of Siloam

The Gospel of Mark: The Strong Son of God and His People

Writer

The title of the Second Gospel points to Mark as the author. What was said about the title of the First Gospel is true for the Second and Third Gospels as well. At no place in the biblical text of the Gospel are we told that John Mark was the author. However, excellent support for that position exists otherwise.

A "John Mark" is mentioned three times in Acts (12:12, 25; 15:37), and a "Mark" is found in several references (Acts 15:39, Col. 4:10, 2 Tim. 4:11, Philemon 24, 1 Pet. 5:13). Colossians 4:10 mentions that Mark was a relative of Barnabas, which identifies the name "Mark" with "John Mark" of Acts references. Therefore, Mark's name was also John. Mark, or John Mark, was not an eyewitness to Jesus as far as we know, nor was he one of the twelve apostles. We do know that he was a kinsman to Barnabas and that he turned back from a missionary journey with Paul and Barnabas (Acts 13:13), after which Paul rejected Mark as a worthy missionary associate. But because Paul refers to Mark in positive ways in later references (Col. 4:10, 2 Tim. 4:11; Philemon 24), we know that they became friends and fellow missionaries. In addition, John Mark was a Jewish Christian originally from Jerusalem. The Christian church, or a portion of it, met in his mother's home at Jerusalem (see Acts 12:12).

Outside biblical texts, early Christian leaders make interesting references to Mark. The Elder, perhaps John the Elder (latter part of first century), was quoted by Papias (c. A.D. 60–130), who in turn was quoted by Eusebius. The quote of the quote occurs in Eusebius' *Ecclesiastical History.*[1] According to Eusebius, Papias related that the Elder said, "Mark became Peter's interpreter and wrote accurately all that he remembered, not, indeed, in order, of the things said or done by the Lord." Irenaeus, about the end of the second century, wrote that Mark was the disciple and interpreter of Peter and that he handed down in writing what he heard Peter preach. These are two strong early witnesses to John Mark as the author of the book of Mark, although we cannot be certain that the writings referred to by the Elder and Irenaeus were the Gospel of Mark.

One textual record gives support to John Mark as the author in relationship to writing down the preaching of Peter. First Peter 5:13 suggests that Mark was a close associate of Peter and that they were at Babylon (Rome), where Peter did much of his work and where Mark could have heard and written down the preaching of Simon Peter. Other interpreters reject this evidence as too inconclusive for deciding who wrote the Second Gospel.[2]

Readers

A long tradition points to the readers of the Gospel as being Christians in Rome and Italy.[3] The same tradition connects the place of writing also as Rome. Other interpreters do suggest a location in Syria or Palestine for the origin of the book. The Second Gospel has indicators that Mark addressed a Roman audience. Mark spoke of the Roman division of four watches of the night rather than the Jewish division of three; he explained Jewish customs and practices as would need to be done for Gentile readers. A climactic confession near the end of the Second Gospel is that of a Roman centurion, a Gentile, who says, "Surely this man was the Son of God!" (Mark 15:39).

A generally accepted position is that the origin, author, connection with Simon Peter, and content of the Gospel place it just prior to or within the persecution of Christians under the Roman emperor Nero. Christians had a bad reputation among many Roman citizens. Those outside the Christian faith considered them antisocial and abnormal human beings, since they refused to participate in the pagan rituals important to many Romans.

In the summer of A.D. 64 much of Rome burned. Angered by the burning, leading citizens of Rome sought out the cause, and they suspected Nero ordered the fire so that places in poor repair could be destroyed and rebuilt. If that were the purpose, those setting the fire lost control and much more burned than they planned.

Tacitus (A.D. 55–120), a Roman historian, told the story of the events, including suspicions about Nero. Nero shifted blame from himself by accusing Christians of burning Rome. After convictions for crimes to which the authorities forced them to admit, not, as Tacitus said, "so much for arson as for hatred of the human race," many Christians received the death penalty. Some were torn to death by dogs as a means of execution; some were covered with pitch, attached to crosses, and set afire to provide light at night. The cruelty to these unpopular Christians was so great that a backlash of sympathy for them occurred among some of the citizens of Rome.[4]

The writing of Mark may have preceded the fire in Rome, but the church who read Mark's writing probably had to live under Nero's rule. Apparently, Christ's people were unpopular with the general populace. Christians suffered, and the author of the Second Gospel had them in view as he wrote.

Message

The Second Gospel opens with, "The beginning of the Gospel about Jesus Christ, the Son of God" (1:1). Near the end of Mark's account, at the death of Jesus, a Roman centurion says of Jesus, "Surely this man was the Son of God!" (15:39). From beginning to end, Mark presented Jesus the Messiah as the strong Son of God. The Second Gospel simply tells the story so that people will give attention to Jesus Christ. In the telling of the story, important realities about Christ emerge. He is the strong Son of God who also suffers and dies. He is victorious in His living, His dying, and, most importantly, in His resurrection. Mark's readers knew struggle and suffering; and in learning from and following their Master, they could be victorious, too.

Mark told this story in his own way. In contrast to parts of Matthew's Gospel, Mark did not have Jesus giving lengthy discourses. The Second Gospel presents Jesus in action, and the frequently occurring word *euthus*, translated "at once" or "without delay" (see 1:12,18,20; 2:12, for example; the NRSVB translates "immediately"), signals the rapid movement of the narrative. Jesus actively took on the powers of evil as well as the powers of the religious establishment. He initiated events that took Him steadily down the road to suffering, the cross, and the resurrection.

Mark had evangelistic motivations for writing as well. The Romans who read the Second Gospel would have seen that Jesus was not a revolutionary who deserved to die at the hands of the Roman government. Also, outsiders must have wondered why, if Jesus was the Messiah by divine initiative, He was not more widely known. Mark seemed to understand and answer such questions by a messianic secret emphasis he related in his Gospel (1:24,34,44; 3:11–12; 5:43; 7:36; 8:26,30; 9:9 are examples). The preconceived ideas that people of Jesus' time had of the Messiah were contrary to His true identity and mission. Therefore, Jesus disassociated Himself from those ideas and defined Himself ultimately on His basis by urging that His messiahship be kept a secret.

In addition, Romans and other Gentiles had difficulty understanding how a Messiah, or king, could be a strong king if he suffered and died by execution. Mark's Gospel dispels such concerns since the suffering and death of the Messiah, the Son of God, are shown to be divine initiatives to accomplish the salvation of humankind.

The Gospel of Mark has a fast-paced narrative, as befits an action-packed account of Jesus' ministry, which we will consider along the following lines. The story begins with the public ministry of John and the baptism of Jesus (1:1–13). Again, as in Matthew, the ministry in Galilee (1:14—9:50) occupies a great portion of the Second Gospel. In chapter 10 Jesus' journey to Jerusalem began, and as Jesus made His way He ministered to people. Finally, there is the Passion Week (11—15) and the resurrection (16). Since Matthew and Luke reflect the basic order of events in Jesus' life as also presented in Mark, we will list these events in a blocked section under each of the major divisions. This will enable the student to have a sense of the basic event structure of the Synoptic Gospels.

The Beginning (1:1–13)

Mark briefly presented several pivotal events at the beginning of Jesus' ministry. He started with a rush, almost as if to say, "This is the Christ, the Son of God, and here goes." John the Baptist first appears as the one preparing the way "for the Lord" (1:1–6). Jesus appeared then, to be baptized by John, followed by a period of temptation in the wilderness (1:9–12).

Box 5: Mark 1:1–13

The Beginning (1:1)
John the Baptist (1:2–8)
Jesus' Baptism (1:9–11)
Jesus' Temptation (1:12–13)

The Galilean Ministry (1:14–9:50)

After John the Baptist's arrest, Jesus "went into Galilee proclaiming the good news of God" (1:14) and called His first disciples (1:16–20). The ministry in Galilee occupied the major portion of Jesus' public ministry—the reason this period is sometimes referred to as *the Great Galilean Ministry.*

Box 6: The Galilean Ministry

The Beginning in Galilee (1:14–15)

Calling of the First Disciples (1:16–20)

Disciples (1:16–20)

Jesus Delivers from Illness and Evil (1:21—3:12)

Jesus Appoints Twelve Apostles; Teaches in Parables (3:13–34)

Healing and Teaching Around the Sea of Galilee (4:35—5:43)

Rejection at Nazareth (6:1–6)

The Mission of the Twelve (6:7–13)

The Death of John the Baptist (6:14–29)

Feeding of the Crowd of Five Thousand (6:30–44)

Jesus Walks on the Water and Heals (6:45–56)

The Growing Opposition from the Pharisees (7:1–23)

Ministry in Tyre and Decapolis (7:24–37)

Feeding of the Crowd of Four Thousand (8:1–21)

Healing of a Blind Man at Bethsaida (8:22–26)

Peter's Great Confession and Jesus' Prediction of His Death (8:27—9:1)

The Transfiguration of Jesus (9:2–13)

Healing of a Boy (9:14–32)

Instructions to the Disciples (9:33–50)

As Jesus ministered, He revealed Himself as one in authority and power over evil, illness, nature, and ultimately death itself. The reality of Jesus as the strong Son of God comes through to us in the recognitions and events recorded during His ministry.

Shortly after arriving at Capernaum (1:21), Jesus exorcised an evil spirit from a man who interrupted Him when He spoke in the synagogue. The people responded in amazement and recognized the power of Jesus (1:27). "A few days later" (2:1), again at Capernaum, Jesus healed a paralytic. This healing was evidence that He had the "authority on earth to forgive sins" (2:10).

Jesus found Levi (Matthew) at the tax table and invited him to be a disciple (2:13–14). Levi left all and followed Him. Many tax collectors and sinners came to Him; Jesus even ate with them (2:15–17). The Pharisees objected to Jesus' association with these people, for no truly righteous person would associate with those standing outside the law. The tax collectors and sinners would not be ritually pure for table-fellowship with fellow Israelites, and table-fellowship in their view should not be contaminated.

The Pharisees were most serious in doing what they thought was right for Israel. Graham Stanton says, "At the time of Jesus the Pharisees were attempting to replicate the Temple cult in everyday life in the home. The purity laws kept by priests in the Temple were to be observed at the table of the ordinary Jew; thus, quite literally, Israel would be turned into a 'kingdom of priests and a holy nation.'"[5]

In the view of many of the Pharisees, therefore, Jesus could not be the Messiah. If He were, they reasoned, He would not contaminate the table-fellowship of Israel by sharing the table with tax collectors and sinners. On His own authority, Jesus engaged in the process of Israel's renewal or salvation, beginning with those who were the outsiders or the disenfranchised.

Jesus established His authority in regard to the Sabbath as well. As the disciples went through the grain fields, they picked some grain for their own use (2:23). The Pharisees accused them of breaking the law of the Sab-

Sea of Galilee, view from Tiberias. *Biblical Illustrator* Photo/David Rogers.

bath (2:24). But, as Jesus pointed out to them, "The Sabbath was made for man, not man for the Sabbath" (2:27). Then He said that the Son of Man, a title that Jesus preferred for Himself, "is Lord even of the Sabbath" (2:28).

The forces of evil recognized who Jesus was. Crowds followed Him (3:7–8). He healed many people, and "whenever evil spirits saw him, they fell down before him and cried out, 'You are the Son of God'"(3:11). Although the evil spirits recognized Jesus, the strange reality is that others did not. The teachers of the law who came from Jerusalem said that He was "possessed by Beelzebub! By the prince of demons he is driving out demons" (3:22).

One of the characteristics of Mark's Gospel is stress upon the failure of people to recognize who He was. Even the disciples struggle to discern his true identity. Mark 4:35–41 tells the story of Jesus calming the storm that caught the disciples in their boat at sea. What was their response? "They were terrified and asked each other, 'Who is this? Even the wind and the waves obey him!'" (4:41).

Jesus reached a turning point in His ministry. The crowds grew, but opposition to Him increased as well. Time was short; much work needed to be done. Therefore he finalized His selection of twelve associates to be His apostles in His ministry (3:13–19). Mark's list contains the following names: Simon Peter and Andrew his brother; brothers James and John, sons of Zebedee; Philip; Bartholomew (Nathanael?); Matthew; Thomas; James the son of Alphaeus; Thaddaeus; Simon the Zealot; and Judas Iscariot. These twelve symbolized the twelve tribes of Israel, and they were to serve under Christ as those who reconstituted Israel, over which Christ reigns.

Followed by the crowds to the Sea of Galilee, Jesus taught them and the disciples (Mark 4:1–34). He told several parables, such as the Sower, Seed Growing Secretly, Tares, Mustard Seed, and Leaven. Each of these parables, properly understood, illuminates the nature of the kingdom of God. Throughout Jesus' ministry people, including Jesus' disciples, wanted the kingdom to be a national and political reality in nature. Because of their preconceived ideas, they had trouble accepting the spiritual reality of the kingdom of God, the rule of God, which Jesus brought to their lives.

Crossing the sea to the land of the Gerasenes, Jesus encountered the Gerasene demoniac (5:1–20). Described as a wild, fierce, demon-possessed individual, the demoniac lived among the tombs, and at times cried out and cut himself with stones. The fact that he lived among tombs pointed to his isolation from everyone and perhaps indicated the deadness inside the man himself. That he abused himself physically probably indicated the self-loathing and pain within the man. This pitiable man had given himself over to evil so much that his name was Legion, a name signifying that he had a whole collection of demons in his life.

Jesus changed his life. A telling statement in this account is that in describing the demoniac after the ministry of Jesus, the people found him "sitting there, dressed and in his right mind" (5:15). The contrast before and after the demoniac met Jesus was apparent. Christ returned the demoniac to the status of a human being, forgiven and cleansed, with a whole new life ahead of him. The healed demoniac epitomizes what Jesus was about in Galilee and in all of His ministry: to restore people to wholeness in right relationship to God and right relationship to one another.

Still, the failure to recognize Jesus continued. In brief form, Mark told about Jesus' rejection at His hometown in Nazareth (6:1–6, see a more detailed discussion of this event in Luke 4:16–30) although "many who heard him were amazed" (6:1). Yet Jesus manifested His authority not only at Nazareth but in other places and ways as well. He gave the twelve His authority and sent them out (6:6–13), and they too exercised power over evil and illness (6:13).

Herod Antipas executed John the Baptist during the Galilean ministry of Jesus (Mark 6:14–29). Herod married his brother Philip's wife, Herodias, a marriage which John the Baptist denounced. Not long after John's denunciation, the daughter of Herodias danced before Herod, so pleasing Herod that he promised the daughter anything she wanted. Her mother instructed her to ask for the head of John the Baptist, which Herod gave to her on a platter (Mark 6:28). Later when Herod heard of Jesus' work, he believed that Jesus was John the Baptist risen from the dead. The case of John the Baptist and Herod points to the reality of the violent world in which Jesus and His followers labored and to the difficulty Jesus had in communicating to people who He was.

Note in Box 6 the authoritative and powerful actions in the remander of Jesus ministry in Galilee. People continued to be amazed at Jesus' power and authority, yet they still did not understand who He was. Opposition from the Pharisees grew, and Jesus continued to respond to them with authority, pointing out their failures and needs (7:1–23).

Chapters 8—9 constitute a pivotal section in the Second Gospel as Jesus gave direct instruction to the disciples from the events of His ministry. Here, too, is the confession of Simon Peter that Jesus is "the Christ," the Messiah of Israel (8:29). Jesus then predicted His death and resurrection (8:31). Peter "rebuked" Jesus for predicting His death (8:32), probably because Peter and his fellow disciples expected Jesus to be a victorious political Messiah. But Jesus rebuked Peter: "'Get behind me, Satan!' he said. 'You do not have in mind the things of God, but the things of men'" (8:33). The disciples understood that

Jesus was the Christ, but did not understand everything that identity should mean to them.

The Journey Toward Jerusalem (10:1–52)

When asked about divorce, a test question from the Pharisees, Jesus emphasized that permanency in marriage was God's will (10:2–9). That the two be "one" was the purpose of marriage (10:8). Jesus gave marriage, and consequently women, a dignity that was not the general attitude in that world.

Box 7: Journey Toward Jerusalem

Teaching about Divorce (10:1–12)
Jesus and the Children (10:13–16)
The Rich Young Man (10:17–31)
Again Jesus Predicts His Death (10:32–34)
The Importance of Service (10:35–45)
Bartimaeus Healed (10:46–52)

Children sought out Jesus, and Jesus said that "the kingdom of God belongs to such as these" (10:14). The children came to Jesus more openly and willingly, responding to Him as He was, than did others who wanted to make Him into their kind of Messiah or reject Him altogether. That childlike, willing, trusting response was necessary for people to come under the rule of God (the kingdom), as God was inaugurating the kingdom and establishing it in and through Jesus Christ.

A rich man, who was quite moral in his attitudes, could not come with such open trusting (10:17–31). He looked upon what Jesus had to offer, eternal life, as something to be added to what he already had. The rich man did not perceive that God's rule in Christ, the kingdom of God, came first and encompassed everything else. Jesus pointed out his idolatry by

challenging him to sell all that he had (10:21). The young man went away, and Jesus taught His disciples regarding the dangers of wealth and the rewards of discipleship.

Again, Jesus predicted His death and His resurrection, the third such prediction (see 8:31–32; 9:30–32; 10:32–34). This was another of those pivotal moments. Jesus stated to His disciples, "We are going up to Jerusalem" (10:33). He aggressively embraced the route that He knew would lead to confrontation, suffering, and death. Still the disciples did not understand, for James and John wanted the right- and left-hand positions to Him "in [His] glory" (10:37). In other words, they anticipated a kingdom of political proportions and they wanted positions of power. The nature of Jesus' kingdom, rule, however, is self-giving service, not to "lord it over" others (10:42).

The blind man, Bartimaeus, did see more than some others. He addressed Jesus as Israel's deliverer, "Son of David" (10:47–48). Jesus went to him, and he came to Jesus. His response and trust were those elements necessary for people to share in what Jesus planned to do as He made His way to Jerusalem. But others did not see, as evidenced by the events in Jerusalem.

The Week of Suffering (11:1—15:47)

Prior to His arrest and trial, Jesus received both affirmation and resistance (note box 8). As Jesus entered Jerusalem, people proclaimed Him as the expected Messiah with their shouts of "Hosanna!" (praise by means of a phrase meaning "save") and their expressions about "Blessed is he who comes in the name of the Lord!" and "Blessed is the coming kingdom of our father David!" (11:9–10).

Jesus, previously intent upon keeping His identity a secret, now entered Jerusalem in a way certain to draw attention to His identity and allowed the people to proclaim Him openly as Messiah. They did not understand the kind of Messiah He was, however, because He did not immediately start a revolution to overthrow the rule of Rome and inaugurate a political kingdom. This may explain what seems to have been a cooling of fervor for Jesus in subsequent hours. He did was not to assemble an army and trounce the Romans. Instead, He entered the temple

---

Box 8: The Week of Suffering

The Entry into Jerusalem (11:1–11)

The Case of the Fig Tree (11:12–14,20–26)

The Cleansing of the Temple (11:15–19)

Religious Leaders Question Jesus' Authority (11:27–33)

The Parable of the Wicked Tenants (12:1–12)

Taxes and Caesar (12:13–17)

Question About Marriage at the Resurrection (12:18–27)

The Great Commandment (12:28–34)

Warning About the Teachers of the Law (12:35–40)

Widow's Offering (12:41–44)

The End of the Age (13:1–37)

Jesus Anointed at Bethany (14:1–11)

The Lord's Supper (14:12–26)

Peter's Denial Predicted (14:27–31)

Struggle in Gethsemane (14:32–42)

The Arrest and Trial of Jesus (14:43—15:20)

The Crucifixion and Burial of Jesus (15:21–47)

The Resurrection and Resurrection Appearances (16:1–20)

---

and cleared it out (11:15–19), hardly a place to begin a political revolution at the important Passover season.

He was intent on confronting the religious leadership; consequently, resistance from them intensified. If He had wanted to save the ultimate confrontation and prevent the crucifixion, He should have left Jerusalem shortly after His entrance. But confrontation was the only way. The religious leaders plotted to kill Him (11:18), questioned His authority (11:27–33), and tried to trap Him with questions in order to build a better case against Him (taxes to Caesar, 12:13–17; marriage and the resurrection, 12:18–27; the greatest commandment, 12:28–34). In each instance Jesus turned the questions back, and the questioners became the questioned. Mark recorded a parable of Jesus about some wicked tenants, an obvious reference to the religious leaders and their failure to care for the vineyard of Israel (12:1–12; see Isa. 5:1–10).

Chapter 13 has been called the "little apocalypse" (apocalypse means an "unveiling" or "revealing") because Jesus discussed the end of the age. Containing picture language, Chapter 13 should be read with the sense that events greater than mere human history are and will be at work. Yet there are two issues, as previously discussed in the parallel passage in Matthew (Matt. 24:3–51). The first matter relates to the temple and its destruction (13:5–23). Jesus warned them by telling them signs of that event. He could discern Israel's political leanings, foreseeing that revolution would come against the Romans, and the Romans would crush them mercilessly. When Jews did begin to rebel in A.D. 66, at first they were successful in some areas, and many thought the age of victory had come for Israel. Some would then have claimed to be the Messiah. But Rome crushed the rebellion, and the temple was destroyed (in A.D. 70).

Jesus moved to a different focus in the latter part of chapter 13. He spoke of the end of time, yet He emphasized that no one knew the day or the hour (13:32). Some readers have given a peculiar twist on this statement. They admit that no one can know the day or the hour, but interpreters who put all the signs together can know the year, the week, and the time within a day. However, Jesus meant that no one—not even Himself—knew when the end time would be. Disciples are to live life in the light of the end of time (13:33–37), which is not a negative matter, because that means that they are moving toward their destiny. History has a purpose and a goal, which is connected to the sovereignty of Christ over life.

Among other events of these last days was the Lord's Supper. Here Jesus instituted the new meal of the new covenant. The new covenant relationship with God is in and through the self-giving life of Jesus Christ. As was emphasized earlier, God created for Himself a people in and through Israel in the Old Testament and in and through Jesus in the New Testament (covenant). As the Passover was the meal of the Old Covenant, the Lord's Supper is the meal of the New Covenant. When Jesus instructed His disciples to take the bread and the cup in remembrance of Him, He pointed to the giving of Himself in an act of self-sacrifice for humanity. Now, when Christians use those elements in remembrance, they point to and celebrate the reality that our relationship to God, our forgiveness and gift of life, is mediated through Jesus Christ, our Lord and Savior.

Jesus struggled in Gethsemane. He did not have a death wish or a martyr's complex. He wanted to avoid the "cup" of suffering (14:36). But the path ahead of Him, including the cross, was the only way to meet humanity's needs. Soon religious authorities arrested, tried, and sentenced Jesus to death (14:43—15:15), all at the cost of terrible suffering and a great miscarriage of justice. On the day before the Sabbath, Joseph of Arimathea obtained permission to take the body of Jesus from the cross, and he gave Jesus a proper burial. Jesus was placed in a tomb, and a stone was rolled in front of the opening (15:42–47). So the life was over—the whole exhilarating, successful mission, as well as the disappointments and sufferings. Had all of that come only to this, a tomb?

The Resurrected Jesus (16:1–20)

Some disciples, the women, came early that Sunday morning, the first day of the week, to properly anoint Jesus' body. The message awaiting them was surprising and bewildering: "You are looking for Jesus the Nazarene, who was crucified. He has risen! He is not here. See the place where they laid him" (16:6). With this message a whole new kind of existence was confirmed for humanity, an existence in which all could participate if they chose to do so by faith.

By putting the Messiah's suffering in perspective, Mark helped his readers to put their own suffering and anticipated suffering into perspective. Jesus stayed true to His mission, although He was alone after all His friends and disciples deserted Him at the crucifixion. But Mark's account stops with the resurrection, not the crucifixion. So the Messiah was victorious after all, although He chose the path of suffering. By Christ's example and presence in their lives, Mark's readers could know that remaining faithful under the stress of rejection and persecution would lead to victory.

FOR STUDY AND REVIEW

IDENTIFY:

Tacitus
Great Galilean Ministry
Messianic secret
euthus

QUESTIONS FOR CONSIDERATION

1. What are the arguments for Mark as author?

2. In what situation was the Second Gospel written?

3. What is the message of Mark?

4. Why was the suffering of Jesus a problem to many who did not believe that he was the Messiah?

5. According to Mark's Gospel, who were the twelve apostles?

FOR FURTHER READING

Harrison, Everett F. *Introduction to the New Testament*. Rev. ed. Grand Rapids: Eerdmans, 1982: 59–86.

Rhoads, David, and Donald Michie. *Mark as Story: An Introduction to the Narrative of a Gospel*. Philadelphia: Fortress Press, 1982.

Gundry, Robert H. *A Survey of the New Testament*. Rev. ed. Grand Rapids: Zondervan, 1981: 76–81.

Martin, R. P. "Gospel According to Mark." *The International Standard Bible Encyclopedia*, vol. 3: 248–59.

ENDNOTES

1. Eusebius, *Ecclesiastical History*, III, 39, 12–16.

2. See W. G. Kümmel, *Introduction to the New Testament*, translated by H. C. Kee, revised and enlarged edition (Nashville, Abingdon Press, 1975), 95–97.

3. *The Anti-Marcionite Prologue* (around A.D. 160–180). For the Latin rendition and a translation, see Vincent Taylor, *The Gospel According to St. Mark* (London: The MacMillan Company, 1952); Irenaeus, *Against Heresies*, III, i. 2; Eusebius, *Ecclesiastical History*, III, xxxix, 14–15.

4. Tacitus, *Annals*, XV, xliv, as translated by John Jackson in *Tacitus in Five Volumes, The Loeb Classical Library*. Edited by G. P. Goold (Cambridge: Harvard University Press, 1981), 283–84.

5. Graham N. Stanton, *The Gospels and Jesus. The Oxford Bible Series*. Edited by P. R. Ackroyd and G. N. Stanton (Oxford: University Press, 1989), 241.

❖ 10 ❖

The Gospel of Luke: Jesus, the Savior for All People

Writer

Few interpreters will contest that the same person who wrote the Third Gospel also wrote Acts. The introductory material in each connects the two books, since both are addressed to a person named Theophilus. Consequently, Luke is volume 1 and Acts is volume 2 by the same author.

Early Christian leaders seem to point to Luke as the author. Irenaeus (c. 185) wrote that "Luke, the follower of Paul, put in a book the Gospel that was preached by him."[1] Tertullian (c. 200) referred to a writing of Luke, an obvious reference to Acts, about certain events in the lives of the apostles. The Muratorian Canon (c. 175–180), a canon of the church at Rome, relates that the Third Gospel was written by Luke, the physician. Within the first half of the fourth century A.D., Eusebius indicated that Luke was the author of the Third Gospel and The Acts of the Apostles.

At one time a strong argument was made that Luke and Acts contain medical language, which would have been the natural vocabulary of a physician. This argument was countered, however, by showing that obviously nonmedical writers used similar terminology to that found in Luke. Nonetheless, some medical terminology is present, which sup-

ports to a slight degree the argument for a physician as author of the Gospel.

One of the strong evidences for Luke as author is that He is the most likely candidate to fit the "we" sections of Acts. Here the author shifts to the first personal pronoun (we) from the third personal pronoun (they) in writing his account. This suggests that he was present when the events recorded in the "we" sections happened. The "we" sections in Acts are 16:10–17; 20:5–15; 21:1–18; 27:1–29; 28:11–16. In Philemon (24), Paul, writing from prison, sends greetings from Luke as well. Luke's presence with Paul in prison agrees with the "we" section of Acts 28:11–16. A companion in prison, one of whom was Luke, was likely the writer who included himself in the "we" and "us" used in Acts 28:11–16. Again, Luke seems to be the most likely person to fit the situation for the authorship of the Third Gospel.

What else do we know of Luke? He was probably a Gentile, in all likelihood Greek. We do not know anything of his conversion experience. He appeared with Paul at Troas as one who was already a follower of Jesus. We know that he was a companion of Paul and a fellow-laborer in the Gospel. Luke also was a physician, perhaps using his medical abilities to minister to Paul while the apostle was in prison.

The Third Gospel is the longest of the four, and together with Acts comprises the largest segment of the New Testament by any one writer. Therefore, if Luke indeed was the author, he wrote more of the New Testament than did Paul.

Readers

The author addresses the primary reader, Theophilus, in 1:3. One of three views may be taken of Theophilus. First, it has been suggested that he was a Greek or Roman official because Luke addresses him as "most excellent" (1:3), an address used specifically for high-ranking political officials. Second, Theophilus may have been a name meant to represent many people. Since Theophilus means "lover of God," Luke may have been addressing any reader who was, even potentially, a lover of God. Third, Luke may have been addressing a convert and friend who had basic knowledge and experience of Christ but needed additional instruction in an orderly way.

Luke seemed to have a real person in view, but he wrote his books for readers other than Theophilus. His introduction about his purpose and use of sources indicates that he intended for his account of Jesus to take its place among the other accounts consulted by believers and seekers. Perhaps Theophilus was addressed because through him Luke could make his account available to a wider audience. Theophilus may have been a friend who had the means to reproduce Luke's account so that it could have wider readership. The content of the Gospel indicates the expectation of a wide readership, especially a non-Jewish readership. The place of writing is uncertain, but suggestions include a place in Achaia, Rome, or Caesarea.

Message

A brief overview of the structure of the Third Gospel demonstrates the similarity to Matthew and Mark, as the outline in box 9 demonstrates. Readers needed an orderly account of Christ and His ministry. Luke is the only author who explains even briefly his methodology in compiling his account of Christ (see 1:1–4). Many others had attempted to compile a narrative (1:1) about what had happened. Evidently, Luke felt that these were either inaccurate at worst or inadequate at best. Therefore, he purposed to "draw up an account of the things that have been fulfilled" (1:1), with the aid of "eyewitnesses and servants of the word" (1:2) to fulfill the need for an "orderly account" (1:3).

Box 9: An Overview of Luke

Preface or Introduction (1:1–4)
Birth and Early Events of John the Baptist and Jesus (1:5—2:52)
Jesus' Baptism and Temptation (3:1—4:13)
Ministry in Galilee (4:14—9:50)
Ministry on the Journey to Jerusalem (9:51—18:30)
Ministry in Jerusalem (18:31—21:38)
The Passion of Christ (22:1—23:56)
The Resurrection (24:1–53)

Some interpreters see Luke-Acts as giving a sweeping view of God at work in history through Jesus Christ. The history, however, is theological history, or history interpreted from a theological point of view. While scholars' views of Luke as theologian-historian have gone through stages of development,[2] the ideas of Hans Conzelmann have dominated the discussion.[3]

According to Conzelmann, Luke had a three-stage view of *salvation history*—a term used to discuss history from the viewpoint of God's saving work in history. Conzelmann's three stages were Israel, Jesus, and the church. The Israel period ended with John the Baptist, who was a transition figure. Jesus dominated the middle stage, and the church formed the final stage, which is of indefinite duration. While Conzelmann's views have not received universal acceptance, he did impress upon interpreters the need to see Luke as a theologian-historian who wrote with a particular purpose in mind.

For our purposes, we consider Luke as a theologian-historian along the lines of the author's own statement. In Acts (1:1) the author referred to his first volume (Luke) as telling what Jesus "began to do and teach." The implication of this statement is that the Third Gospel tells what Jesus began to do and teach in His earthly ministry, while Acts tells what Jesus continues to do and teach through the church.

Each of the Gospels has a distinctive message, and Luke is no exception. How Luke is distinctive evokes considerable discussion among interpreters.[4] Luke presents Jesus as the universal Savior. That is, He is the Savior for anyone, regardless of the racial, cultural, national, or economic distinctions that people give to each other. The poor and isolated come into view in Luke's Gospel.

God's Special Identity with Humanity

Jesus' birth and genealogy point to both His reality and His identity with all of humanity. Luke was the writer who told us that Jesus was born in a manger, or stable (2:7), probably a cave in the side of a hill normally used for holding animals. The local innkeeper may have secured the stable for Mary and Joseph, and he often receives bad reviews for not providing a place for them in his crowded inn. Yet Robert Cate points out that the normal inn of that time was a large space enclosed by walls. People kept the animals in the center of the enclosure and slept around the walls, sometimes building fires to keep warm or to cook. A smoke-filled, large room with people around the walls and animals in the center would have afforded no privacy for Mary, so the innkeeper may have done them a special favor by directing them to a stable.[5] God's Son was born in a stable, not in a palace or to a wealthy family. Jesus began His life at the bottom of the socio-economic scale.

That God would enter human existence as a tiny, vulnerable baby is remarkable. Why did He not come as a mighty warrior, fully mature and fully armed for battle? Why did He not come as a mighty whirling wind, with identifiable shape to "lord it over" human beings and force them into compliance? Or, why did he not come as a burst of pure energy, recognizable, but of such illuminating and irresistible power that everyone would be forced to conform? Rather, He came as a tiny, vulnerable baby. That vulnerability seemed to indicate that God intended by Jesus' birth (and life) to identify with and to deliver all the vulnerable, weak, and hurting humans who would allow Him to do so.

Luke's genealogy (Luke 3:23–38) signifies the universality of Jesus. Luke traces the family tree all the way back to Adam, not stopping with Abraham as Matthew did. While Abraham is the father of the Jewish nation, Adam was the father of the whole human race. The genealogy demonstrates the humanity of Jesus and suggests that Jesus was the Savior for all of humanity.

That Jesus is Savior for everyone is certainly present as an emphasis in the other Gospels, but Luke especially brought it to the attention of his readers. In order to write his account from the perspective of Jesus' universality, the author had to be sensitive to various groups of people and individuals.[6]

Jews and Gentiles

Luke demonstrated the universality of Christ by stressing the inclusion of Israelites and Gentiles in Jesus' ministry. Both were included in God's saving work in Jesus from the beginning. By reading Luke's Gospel, Israelites certainly would see the strong connection with orthodox Judaism, even in the opening accounts. Zechariah, Elizabeth, and Mary move in orthodox Judaism. The dedication and circumcision of Jesus in the temple (2:21–24) were according to orthodox Jewish procedure. Yet Simeon, a "righteous and devout" Jew (2:25), proclaims Jesus as the means of salvation for all people. Simeon sings,

> For my eyes have seen your salvation,
> which you have prepared in the sight of
> all people, a light for revelation to the
> Gentiles and for glory to your people
> Israel. (2:30-32)

Jesus was the Messiah for everyone, both Israelites and Gentiles, in direct fulfillment of Isaiah's prophecy.

While Jesus was accepting and inclusive, rejection was often His experience. His return home to Nazareth brought Him rejection by His neighbors (4:16–30). As was his custom, He attended the synagogue services on the Sabbath after arriving in Nazareth. The synagogue leader invited Him to read, and He selected a portion of Isaiah. He stood to read, but according to custom He sat down to comment on the Scripture He had read.

The Isaiah passage spoke of the deliverance of the poor, the prisoners, the blind, and the oppressed. The first impression the people had of Jesus' comments was very favorable (4:22). Their attitude changed, however, when Jesus refused to do for them what they wanted—to perform a sign of some kind as he had done in Capernaum (4:23).

The demand for some mighty work was evidence that they did not accept Jesus on the basis of His own testimony. The axiom was true that "no prophet is accepted in his hometown" (4:24). The two examples He used in His comments on the Isaiah passage, a woman of Sidon to whom God sent Elijah and a Syrian leper named Naaman to whom God sent Elisha (4:26–27), made non-Israelites a focus of God's deliverance. For Jesus to assume the position of deliverer and to emphasize strongly the deliverance of non-Israelites raised their anger toward Him.

Through these two examples, Jesus showed the people of Nazareth that they expected the wrong kind of deliverance. They were told, in effect, that the blessing that they felt should be theirs would be shared with outsiders such as the woman of Sidon and Naaman. Jesus' neighbors would have preferred favor to the Israelites above all others and a deliverer primarily for themselves. But Jesus was the deliverer for everybody, and He refused even the demands of His hometown neighbors to be an exclusive Savior.

The Romans and Government Officials

Luke had to be sensitive to the political climate of his day. Roman citizens may have perceived Jesus as a political revolutionary intent on disrupting or overthrowing the Roman government. They must have won-

Modern Nazareth, Christ's boyhood hometown. *Biblical Illustrator* Photo/David Rogers.

dered if Christ's disciples harbored and nurtured revolutionary motives. After all, claims that Jesus was the Messiah, the king, must have sounded like a political, revolutionary movement.

Luke's account brings out to Theophilus and other readers the non-political intentions of Jesus. Tax collectors and soldiers responded to the Baptist's preaching. To the tax collector John said, "Don't collect any more than you are required to" (3:13); and the soldiers were told not to "extort money" and not to "accuse people falsely" (3:14). In either case, John the Baptist did not demand that they leave their professions. Jesus also said to "give to Caesar what is Caesar's, and to God what is God's" (20:25). Too, the account of Jesus' trial shows that Pilate, the

Roman governor, believed Jesus to be innocent of the political crimes charged to him by the Jewish religious leaders (23:2). Pilate affirmed the innocence of Jesus three different times (23:4,14,22). While Jesus revolutionized life, Luke pointedly demonstratesd that He had no political ambitions. And, as is evident in the Book of Acts, neither did the early Christian church.

Women and Children

Elizabeth and Mary occupy central roles in the very beginning of Luke's account. That women receive special commendation in Luke is impressive, since women occupied mostly a subservient or limited role in society.

When Mary visited Elizabeth she expressed her song of praise to God (1:46–55), a song often titled "The Magnificat" by theologians, musicians, and others. Notice how the proud and the mighty are brought down and the humble and the hungry are elevated in Mary's song (1:52–53). The compassionate, inclusive Christ would reach out to those who were the social underclass or on the fringes of society. In Luke's account, Mary was a pivotal means of revelation of the nature and mission of Christ.

When Jesus was twelve years of age, he went with Mary and Joseph on their yearly visit to Jerusalem for the Feast of the Passover. When they left to return home, Joseph and Mary thought Jesus was with their traveling group, but He had remained behind. When they returned to search for Him, they found Him in the temple, sitting among the teachers, listening and asking questions. Jesus amazed those who heard him ask questions and give insights. When Mary confronted Jesus about His having remained behind and causing them anxiety, Jesus' reply was, "Why were you searching for me? . . . Didn't you know I had to be in my Father's house?" (Luke 2:49), a statement that pointed to His unique relationship to the Father.

The account of this incident ends with Luke writing that Mary "treasured all these things in her heart. And Jesus grew in wisdom and stature, and in favor with God and men" (2:51–52). He grew intellectually, or in wisdom, informing the knowledge He gained with His Father's perspective, making for growth in wisdom. Increasing in stature is another way of saying that he grew up or increased in years. Significantly, He grew to adulthood in "favor with God and men," which means that His life was a healthy experience to those around Him and pleasing to His Father. By inference in this context, Mary,

who treasured these things, played a key role in the development and growth of Jesus. In effect, Luke gave to Mary a respect and dignity which was surely hers.

Women come into view in other places in the Third Gospel. Luke recorded the extended account of the sinful woman who anointed Jesus' feet (7:36–50). The attitude of Simon the Pharisee, the host of the meal where the anointing occurred, was that of rejection toward the woman. Jesus' attitude was one of acceptance and forgiveness. The contrast between the woman's recognition of her need for forgiveness with the failure of Simon to recognize his need is apparent. Jesus pointed out to Simon that the woman's act grew out of love resulting from her forgiveness (7:47). Simon had shown little response to Jesus, again a sharp contrast to the woman. Jesus praised her for her faith and forgave her sins (7:48–50).

Luke told of the women who aided Jesus in His work (8:1–3) by helping to provide materially for Him and His disciples. The presence of women around the cross of Jesus (23:49) and at the tomb (23:55—24:12) are other examples. That such status was given to women in a world where women often were second-class citizens is remarkable. The same was true for children, who also received special attention from Jesus (8:41–42,49–55; 9:38–43).

The Disenfranchised of Society

The underclass, the isolated, marginalized people of society, received the attention of Jesus. The tax collectors and sinners, considered unacceptable by much of the religious leadership, at times stood outside looking in on the blessings of God as taught by Judaism.

Luke 15:1 tells us that these people came to Jesus and found acceptance. Some of the religious leaders criticized Jesus for associating with these people (15:2). Jesus responded to their criticism with three parables, the lost sheep (15:3–7), the lost coin (15:8–10), and the lost sons (15:11–32). The first two end with the same conclusion. As the shepherd calls together his friends and neighbors to celebrate the finding of the lost sheep (15:6), and as the woman calls her neighbors to celebrate with her over the finding of the coin (15:9), so God and heaven rejoice over "one sinner who repents" (15:7,10).

The parable about the two sons, often called the parable of the prodigal, is best understood from the standpoint of the father because he is the central figure. The younger son (15:12–24) takes his inheritance, wastes all that he has, and ends up isolated, desperate, and separated from his father. He decides to return home. Although he has done terrible wrong and dishonored his father, his father receives him back with joy and even honors him. The elder son (15:25–32) who has remained at home is also alienated from the father because of his anger at his brother. He refuses to welcome his brother and join in the celebration over his return. The tax collectors and sinners (15:1), who were like the younger son, were returning home to the Heavenly Father as Jesus received them. Certain Pharisees and teachers of the law (15:2) acted like the elder son, who refused to rejoice over the return of God's children through Jesus' ministry.

Ten lepers "stood at a distance" from Jesus and pled for His help (17:12). By virtue of their disease, lepers were isolated from society as the law commanded (Lev. 13:46), although they did associate with others who had the disease. Jesus heard them and healed them (Luke 17:14). Only one returned to thank Him and to praise Him, and that was a Samaritan (17:16). Being both a leper and a Samaritan marked this man as an outsider in two ways in some social circumstances. Jesus included this man and his group into His ministry.

Other destitute outcasts received praise and inclusion from Jesus. In the parable of the tax collector and the Pharisee (18:9–14), the tax collector offered acceptable prayer toward God, while the Pharisee did not. Jesus sought out and included Zacchaeus the tax collector although some hated this traitor who worked for the Roman government (19:1–10). Finally, the thief on the cross, in his utter state of rejection, received the ministry of Jesus and the promise that he would be in paradise with Jesus (23:39–43).

A Person-Centered Ministry

Since Jesus included individuals often excluded by others, to say that His ministry was person-centered is almost redundant. Yet without the Gospel of Luke we would not have some of the most moving and person-centered parables of Jesus. Often the parables deal with the kingdom of God, but Luke's Gospel gives special place to parables of fascinating personalities, such as the good Samaritan (10:30–37), the prodigal son (15:11–32), the rich man and Lazarus (16:19–31), and the importunate widow (18:1–8).

The parable of the good Samaritan is found only in Luke (10:25–37). In it Jesus answered the question, "Who is our neighbor?" (10:29). We understand the answer to be, from the parable, that our neighbor is anyone who needs us. The right question is not, "Who is my neighbor?" but "Who needs me and the resources I have?" The Samaritan of the parable approached it that way. So did

Stairs of Caiaphas up which Roman guards led Jesus to trial. *Biblical Illustrator* Photo/David Rogers.

Jesus. Jesus was a neighbor to those who needed Him, including the excluded and destitute of society.

In the parable of the rich man and Lazarus (16:19–31), the rich man and poor man have their fortunes reversed after death. This parable should not be taken as a description of the afterlife. A parable has one primary message, and this parable was a message to certain religious leaders. Probably the story was a popular one, but Jesus told it in His unique way. The poor man receives blessing, in contrast to the rich man, who was in torment. Some people of Jesus' day thought that wealth was a sign of God's blessing bestowed because of righteousness. The parable constitutes a warning to the religious leaders. They

were like the rich man. They were like the five brothers to whom the rich man wanted Lazarus sent from the dead in order to warn them of their plight (16:27–28). They were like those who did not listen to Moses and the prophets (16:31). Jesus said that if they did not listen to Moses and the prophets, they would not listen even if someone, such as Lazarus, came back from the dead. The implication is that the poor man did listen to Moses and the prophets. The poor man becomes the hero of this story. The good Samaritan was also a hero, although both were members of the underclass of that society.

The same is true for the parable of the unjust judge (18:1–8). Although the judge is the central figure, the poor widow who desires justice is the hero of the parable. The point of the parable is made by contrast. Persistence in prayer as a means for convincing God to do something is not the point of the parable. Rather, if the judge who cares nothing about the woman will grant her request simply because she persists, think how different the matter is with God. God loves and is ready to act in behalf of His people. He will hear them readily and respond quickly. Jesus certainly epitomized this reality in His ministry. These person-centered parables point to the ministry of Jesus to people in need.

The Suffering, Death, and Resurrection of Christ

The elements of the suffering, crucifixion, and resurrection of Jesus are essentially the same as in the other Gospels. However, Luke shared some additional material. In the account of the Last Supper, statements about the Passover, the meal, and the cup (22:15–18), service and sitting at the table in Christ's kingdom (22:27–30a), and Jesus' discussion about Peter's betrayal and the crises about to come to the apostles (22:31–32,35–38) are unique to Luke. Luke's Gospel tells us of the first word of Jesus from the cross, "Father, forgive them, for they do not know what they are doing" (23:34). We learn from Luke about Jesus' forgiveness of the penitent thief on the cross (23:40–43), the appearance of Jesus to the two disciples on their way to Emmaus (24:13-35), the appearance of Jesus to the eleven in Jerusalem (24:36–49), and the ascension of Jesus (24:50–53; see also Acts 1:9). Luke is a rich Gospel, telling us of the compassionate, inclusive Savior for all people.

FOR STUDY AND REVIEW

IDENTIFY:

Theophilus
"Began to do and teach"

QUESTIONS FOR CONSIDERATION

1. What support does Lukan authorship have from early Christian leaders?
2. What are the "we" sections? What is their significance?
3. Who was Luke? What do we know about him?
4. What is the message of Luke?
5. What are some of the distinctive emphases in Luke?

FOR FURTHER READING

Harrison, Everett F. *Introduction to the New Testament,* rev. ed. Grand Rapids: Eerdmans, 1982: 194–210.

Davies, W. D. *Invitation to the New Testament.* Garden City: Doubleday, 1966: 219–30.

Tolbert, Malcolm O. *Luke.* Volume 9, *The Broadman Bible Commentary.* Edited by Clifton J. Allen. Nashville: Broadman, 1970: 1–16.

ENDNOTES

1. Irenaeus, *Against Heresies, III, i, 1.* See quote in Eusebius, *Ecclesiastical History,* V, vi-ii.

2. See Charles H. Talbert, "Luke-Acts," *The New Testament and Its Modern Interpreters,*

ed. Eldon Jay Epp and George W. MacRae (Atlanta: Scholars Press, 1989), 298–99, 301–02.

3. Hans Conzelmann, *The Theology of St. Luke*, trans. Geoffrey Buswell (New York: Harper, 1961).

4. For a scholarly discussion see Talbert, 297–320.

5. Robert L. Cate, *A History of the New Testament and Its Times* (Nashville: Broadman Press, 1991), 147–148.

6. See Malcolm Tolbert's excellent summary of the purposes of Luke in *Luke*, vol. 9, *The Broadman Bible Commentary*, ed. Clifton J. Allen (Nashville: Broadman Press, 1970), 9–12.

❖ 11 ❖

The Gospel of John: Christ, the Source of Life

Writer

Questions of authorship about the Fourth Gospel extend to other writings attributed to John: 1, 2, 3 John and Revelation. Who is this John, with whom this sizable body of material has been connected? Possible answers to this question are John the apostle, John the Elder, John Mark, an unknown John, and a "school" of John.

John the apostle as the author became the established tradition, and often he has been identified as the "beloved disciple" referred to in the Fourth Gospel (13:23; 19:26; 20:2; 21:7,20). The earliest reference to that tradition may be that of Irenaeus (c. 181–189), who said that "John the disciple of the lord, who also reclined on His [Christ's] bosom, published the Gospel while he was residing at Ephesus in Asia." Eusebius indicates that Irenaeus' source of information for this statement was Polycarp (c. 69–155).[1]

Of course, at no place in the text does the Fourth Gospel say that John the apostle was the author. The name *John* does not occur in the Fourth Gospel or in 1, 2, and 3 John except in the titles. Revelation 1:4 identifies the writer as John; but again, which John?

Following the traditional position of John the apostle as the author, what do we know about him? He was the son of Zebedee and the brother of James. As he was making his living as a fisherman at the Sea of Galilee (Mark 1:19–20), Jesus called him to follow, and he became one of the three (Peter, James, and John) upon whom Jesus relied as His first line of assistants. Evidently, John was a close associate of Simon Peter; the Book of Acts mentions him in relationship to Peter. John and James also were known as the "sons of thunder," which may mean that they were boisterous and aggressive.

Some reasons for not accepting John the apostle as the author include a tradition about his early martyrdom, which means that he died before the Gospel could have been written. However, the attestation of this tradition is limited, coming from fifth- and ninth-century writings. The tradition of early martyrdom is traceable to Mark 10:39, where Jesus indicated that James and John would drink the same cup as He, possibly suggesting that they would suffer and die at the hands of persecutors. James did suffer martyrdom (Acts 12:1–2), and some interpreters suggest that John must have died at the same time. In addition, John the apostle could not have written all the writings attributed to him, other interpreters claim, for the timespan for his life would be excessive. But nothing establishes that John did not live long enough to do so.

John the Elder is suggested as the author of some of the Johannine literature for two reasons. First, in 2 and 3 John, the writer identifies himself as the "elder." Second, a quote of a quote of Eusebius, found in his *Ecclesiastical History*, seems to separate a John the Elder from the other apostles.[2] However, some interpreters point out that the quote is not clear in this matter. Indeed, from the quote a case can be made that the Elder and the apostle John were really the same person.

John Mark is a possibility for authorship, because of his association with the disciples and community in Jerusalem. Also, he was a close associate of Simon Peter (Acts 12:12, 1 Pet. 5:13). However, John Mark does not meet the "beloved disciple" characteristic, a title in John which may refer to the author, requiring that the author be one of the twelve apostles if the beloved disciple is the author (see John 13:21-24; 21:20-24).

A school of John—that is, disciples of John taught by him in a school-like setting—has been suggested as the source of authorship. Others take the position that John the apostle wrote some of the Johannine material and the Elder John some; or perhaps some of John's disciples or an unknown John, or a school of John produced some of the materials. These approaches to authorship would explain the variety and similarity of the Johannine material. However, the apostle John as author or as giving direct influence to the writing of the Gospel and the Johannine materials best fits all the variant information for authorship.

The date assigned to the Fourth Gospel ranges from around A.D. 60 to 100 or even later, although most interpreters set the date after A.D. 70, at some time between A.D. 80 and 100. Ephesus persists as the place of composition in the traditional and somewhat standard view. A Palestinian or Syrian locale also are possibilities for the place of writing.

Readers

The recipients or original readers of the Fourth Gospel were probably a diverse people in diverse places. Perhaps those in and around Ephesus were its first recipients, but the author meant the Gospel for an even wider audience. By his presentation, the author invites the readers to go behind the events in Jesus' life to deeper meanings. Even common things, things like bread, water, shepherd and door, take on new maening in Jesus.

Message

Obviously, the Fourth Gospel has many differences in comparison with the Synoptics. These differences include material in the Synoptics omitted from John, material not found in the Synoptics (see box 10), differences in chronology, differences in style, and differences in certain themes.[3] The Gospel of John is one of the most popular books of the New Testament, at once possessing a simplicity that even a child can appreciate yet having such depth of meaning that scholars keep working to make it all understood.

John stated his purpose clearly in 20:31. He wrote so that people may "believe" in Jesus Christ and receive, consequently, "life in his name." *Life* is a particular theme of John's Gospel—the kind of life that is in and through Jesus. Consideration of the conversation with Nicodemus (3:1–21) and the woman at the well (4:4–26), and Jesus' statements to them about "life," certainly establishes life as a major emphasis of the Fourth Gospel.

Box 10: Selected Materials Found Only in the Gospel of John

The Pre-existence of Jesus (1:1–5)

The Presentation as the Divine *Logos* or Word (1:1–18)

The Turning of Water into Wine (2:1–11)

The Interview with Nicodemus (3:1–21)

The Interview with the Samaritan Woman (4:1–26)

The "I am" Sayings and their Attendant Material (See Box 13)

The Resurrection of Lazarus (11:1–44; 12:1)

The Washing of the Disciples' Feet (13:3–9)

Box 11: An Outline of John

Prologue (1:1–18)

The witness of John, Philip, and Nathanael (1:19–51)

The witness of Jesus' "signs" (2:1—11:57)

The witness of His Suffering, Death, and Resurrection (12:1—20:31)

Epilogue 21:1–25

John's presentation of Jesus as the One through whom life comes is evident in the structure of the book. He proclaims Jesus as the Messiah, the King, the "Word" become flesh, the only-one-of-a-kind Son of God who gives life to those who believe (1:14, 3:16). Except for the prologue and introduction (1:1–51) and the epilogue (21:1–25), the book has two major sections. The first section, the book of signs, is contained in 2:1—11:57; the second, the book of the passion (or suffering), is in 12:1—20:31. Nonetheless, discerning the detailed structure of the book is no small challenge. Actually, the Fourth Gospel seems to give itself to complex structures, reflecting different theological formulations. "One of the reasons why critics find so many mutually exclusive structures in John is that his repeated handling of only a few themes makes it possible to postulate all kinds of parallels"[4] The outline contained in the box does not show the complex and theological nature of John's development, but it does serve for a brief survey of the book and emphasizes the witness to the One who gives life.

Prologue (1:1–18)

The prologue establishes the pre-existence of Jesus in terms of *Logos*, or Word (1:1–2). Jesus Christ was the "Word." The Word was in the "beginning" (1:1). Basically, wherever a person wants to begin, as far back as one wants to go in saying, "This is the beginning," the Word was. The Word is eternal. Note also that the Word was "with God, and the Word was God" (1:1). In Greek the definite article *the*, is not present, so some claim that the phrase should be translated, "and the Word was *a* god." But often the article does not occur with the divine name, because one of Jewish background and thought would never think of another god existing with the God. God is the only God, so the article is not necessary. The oneness with God was the emphasis intended here; God and Jesus were/are one.

"Word" is a translation of the Greek term *logos*. Logos was a philosophical and theological concept much discussed in John's time. To the Greeks, logos, or word, meant several things, but basically it was the divine reason of God permeating the universe, including human beings. John identified, for anyone who would listen, the real *Logos*, Jesus Christ.

To the Jews, logos would call to mind the *dabar*, which is the creative power or energy of God, taking the cue for understanding from such biblical passages as the first chapter of Genesis. God spoke His word, and with his speaking were the means and the power to make the content of the word spoken a reality. God said, "Let there be lights in the expanse of the sky," and what God said happened (Gen. 1:14). Other statements, such as Psalm 33:6, "By the word of the Lord the heavens were made" (NRSV), and Isaiah 55:11, "my word . . . shall not return to me empty" (NRSV) stress the creative power of God's word. By using the concept of logos, John pointed the Israelites to Jesus as being the reality of the Creator Himself present among human beings.

The Fourth Gospel says, "And the Word became flesh and lived among us" (1:14, NRSV). That is to say, God was born into human existence in the person of Jesus Christ. Theologians refer to this as the *Incarnation*; God became incarnate in a human being, and He was fully human as well as fully God. How could such be? The reality belongs to the complexity of God's nature. But that such could be, and can be known through faith-acceptance of God in Jesus Christ, tells the reader that the birth of Jesus Christ was no ordinary event. If God were going to split history open with an act of self-revelation of world-changing proportions—and He did—the act certainly would not be ordinary, although He accomplished His act in many ordinary ways.

As one who was among humanity and also both Creator and Savior, Jesus experienced rejection: He "came to that which was his own, but his own did not receive him" (1:11). The rejection was not total, for some did receive Him. To these who received Him "he gave the right to become children of God" (1:12).

The Witness of John the Baptist, Philip, and Nathanael (1:19–51)

John the Baptist saw Jesus and announced boldly, "Look, the Lamb of God, who takes away the sin of the world!" (1:29). Andrew said, to his brother, Simon Peter, "We have found the Messiah" (1:41). Phillip found Nathanael and told him that Jesus of Nazareth was the One to Whom the Prophet and Moses had pointed. Nathanael, after he met Jesus, said, "Rabbi, you are the Son of God; you are the King of Israel" (1:49). According to the word of these three witnesses, Jesus of Nazareth was the Messiah and the Son of God.

The Witness of Jesus' "Signs" (2:1—11:57)

A particular feature of the structure of the Fourth Gospel is the section containing the signs, sometimes called the "Book of Signs." Some of the signs are identified, such as the "first of his signs" (2:11, NRSV) and "second sign" (4:54, NRSV), although others have no designated order or number. The number *seven*, evidently used because it carried the idea of completion, was very important to the author. Consequently, seven signs may be designated in the book of signs (see box 12).

In some lists by different interpreters, the fifth sign may be dropped and another sign delineated later to complete the seven. Some would place the raising of Lazarus as the sixth sign with Jesus' death and resurrection being the final sign, the greatest of all. In reality, the whole Gospel is one of signs pointing to Jesus as Messiah.[5]

The interpretation and meaning of each of these signs are enhanced by the sayings and events of Jesus which follow the signs. The sign is in actuality a miracle, but John preferred to designate them "signs." Each sign points the way to the reality of Jesus as the Messiah and Son of God who enhances and gives life.

Box 12: The Seven Signs

1. Turning the Water into Wine (2:1–11)
2. Healing of the Official's Son (4:46–54)
3. Healing of the Man by the Pool (5:1–9)
4. The Feeding of the Five thousand (6:1–14)
5. Jesus Walking on the Water (6:16–21)
6. Healing of the Man Born Blind (9:1–7 or 9:1–41)
7. The Raising of Lazarus (11:38–44 or 11:1–44)

The first sign, the turning of water into wine, was at Cana in Galilee (2:1–11). Jesus' mother urged Him to do something about the depleted wine supply. He replied that His hour had not yet come to manifest who He was. "Hour" referred to His death and resurrection, by which Jesus' accomplished mission would be finally and completely manifested. Nonetheless, Jesus did choose to point to His identity by performing a sign. Attention focused on the six stone jars. The jars were for Jewish ceremonial cleansing. The author used symbolism here. In Jewish thought, the number six was an incomplete number, so the six water jars for Jewish purification represented unfulfilled expectation of Judaism. Jesus filled them up from a seventh source, which is implied in the account. Seven represented completion. Jesus was the

seventh source, a symbolism which points out that Jesus filled up the unfulfilled expectations of Judaism.

He also turned the contents into wine, wine itself being a symbol of the joy of life and in this case a new joy. This sign points to the reality that Jesus fulfills and makes all things new. He was the new beginning for which many Israelites longed—the messianic times which God would bring about and by which God would bless Israel. Following this sign other events were revealed that pointed to the new beginning inaugurated in the person and work of Jesus Himself: the cleansing of the temple, the interview with Nicodemus, and the interview with the woman at the well.

John set the cleansing of the temple (2:13–22) at the beginning of Jesus' ministry, and the other three Gospels have a cleansing near the end (Matt. 21:12–16; Mark 11:15–18; Luke 19:45–48). Roman coins were not allowed in the Temple proper, so money needed to be changed into acceptable Jewish currency. Also, many travelers coming to worship at the temple were not able to bring their sacrificial animals with them, so animals could be purchased in the outer courts of the Temple. Jesus considered the whole process, probably even the sacrificial system itself, as having corrupted the reason for the system and in need of cleansing.

After Jesus cleansed the temple, the religious authorities asked Him for a sign to justify His act. He replied, "Destroy this temple, and I will raise it again in three days" (2:19). People thought the sacrificial system was the way to God. By His action, Jesus showed that it was both inadequate and corrupt. Clearing the temple was a sign in itself. Jesus' bold action and statement pointed to the reality that He was the new temple of God. His death and resurrection would give access to God as the sacrificial system could not. By coming to Him, people could come into the presence of God. The first sign at Cana pointed to the new beginning inaugurated by Jesus. The new beginning included the new meeting place for God with His people, namely, Jesus Christ.

Nicodemus (3:1–21) evidently was a moral man, a man serious about keeping the law and concerned with doing right. He was a religious teacher as well, with responsibility for interpreting God's will to others. Unable to explain Jesus by his own observations, Nicodemus went to Jesus in order to understand better. The account in John shows his shock when Jesus told him that he must be born "again" (3:3). Nicodemus needed a whole new orientation of His life from above, so much so that he would be made a new person, a person born again. In the new beginning with the new temple, a new birth is part of what the Messiah was doing to make all things new. He is the giver of life new and eternal (3:16).

Jesus' conversation with the woman at the well (4:5–42) was unusual for several reasons. First, He went into Samaria. Some Israelites avoided traveling through Samaria because of racial and religious prejudice. Second, He talked to a Samaritan, not a normal practice for a religious Israelite. Third, He addressed a Samaritan woman, the lowest class of Samaritan. The incident points to Jesus' acceptance and forgiveness of the woman, just as she was. In the process of conversation with her, He revealed that He is the water of life and that whoever drinks the water that He gives will never "thirst" again (4:14). In this way Jesus offered her redemption and the gift of eternal life.

Also, He led the woman to understand that He was the Messiah (4:25–26). The woman engaged Jesus in a discussion about the proper place of worship (4:19–24). Jesus stated that the "time is coming and has now come when the true worshipers will worship the Father in spirit and truth" (4:23). The woman countered that the Messiah will "explain everything" when he comes (4:25). Jesus then identified Himself as the Messiah (4:26). The meaning of this discussion is that Jesus is the new focus of worship, for in Jesus God meets human beings. Consequently, out of the first sign, which stressed the new beginning Jesus inaugurated, came the new temple, the new birth, and the new worship. Jesus the Messiah came to make all things new and to fulfill all things in Himself.

The second sign involved Jesus and an official at Capernaum who asked Jesus to heal his son (4:43–54). Jesus did not go to the son, but instructed the man to return home, for his son would live. The man believed Jesus, and returning home he found his son recovering. Distance did not keep Jesus from healing the son, a feature of this sign. Also, this sign points to the reality that Jesus is able to save life from death; that the life He gives defeats death. As in the first sign, where the disciples believed in Jesus because of the sign, in the second sign the official and his household believed in Jesus (4:53).

In the third sign Jesus healed the man by the pool of Bethesda (5:1–15). An invalid for thirty-eight years, the man took up his mat and walked according to the instruction Jesus gave him (5:8). This sign demonstrates the power of Jesus to enhance life. Yet, some people were critical of Jesus. The healing occurred on the Sabbath, and for a man to take up his bed and walk was an act that broke the Sabbath in the eyes of some religious leaders. As is often the case with religious leaders, they simply did not see the reality or believe that Jesus was the Messiah.

The fourth sign, the feeding of the five thousand (6:1–14), is found in all four of the

Gospels. A multitude of people followed Jesus out into the countryside. The Passover season was at hand, in which people were reminded of their ancestors' travels in the wilderness as the children of Israel journeyed from Egypt. God provided manna in the wilderness when the people were hungry and without resources (Ex. 16:4–16). Some people believed that when the Messiah came, he would provide manna from heaven once again. Others perceived this in terms of a great messianic banquet. Jesus provided the multitude with bread, a sign pointing to the reality that He was the Messiah and the fulfillment of their hopes. Later, He proclaimed that He was Himself the "bread of life" (John 6:35).

Jesus walking on the water (6:16–21) is considered by some interpreters to be the fifth sign. The important statement in this account transpires when Jesus approached "the boat, walking on the water" (6:19), which terrified the disciples. Jesus said to them, "It is I; don't be afraid" (6:20). In this statement Jesus marked His unique relationship to God. When Moses at the burning bush asked God His name, the answer was, "*I am who I am*" (Ex. 3:14). "It is I" is a form of "I am." Jesus and God are the same. Therefore, what Jesus demonstrated in this sign was that He can and does bear the divine name and divine majesty.[6] The "I am" sayings in the Gospel of John are a unique feature used by the author to further establish the identity of Jesus (see box 13).

The case of the man born blind (9:1–41) is the sixth sign. Jesus caused him to see, a wonderful miracle or sign. However, Jesus' action, of making clay and instructing the man to go and wash himself, violated the laws of the Sabbath (9:16). As a result of concern for breaking the law, the man's neighbors, his parents, the religious authorities, and finally Jesus questioned him. As the man was questioned by each, he revealed a progression of understanding who Jesus is. In answer to the first questioning, he identified Jesus as a "man" (9:11). Next he called Jesus a "prophet" (9:17), then the one who is "from God" (9:33). Finally, after being questioned by Jesus, he confessed Jesus as the "Son of Man" (9:35–38). The big miracle here is that the man really saw who Jesus is. His seeing was in direct contrast to that of his neighbors, his parents, and the religious leaders. Their physical sight was intact, but they did not really see who Jesus is. The healed man was blind, but then he saw; the others saw but they were blind.

Box 13: The "I am" Sayings of Jesus

"I am the bread of life" (6:35).
"I am the light of the world" (8:12).
"I am the gate" (10:7,9).
"I am the good shepherd" (10:11,14).
"I am the resurrection and the life" (11:25).
"I am the way and the truth and the life" (14:6).
"I am the true vine" (15:1,5).

The seventh sign was that of raising Lazarus from the dead (11:1–44). Lazarus, Mary, and Martha were close friends of Jesus. Lazarus died while Jesus was away from them. When Jesus returned to Bethany where they lived, Martha told Jesus that had He been there Lazarus would not have died (11:21). Jesus assured Martha that Lazarus would rise again (11:23). Martha agreed that he would "rise again in the resurrection at the last day" (11:24). Jesus persisted and made the point which the raising of Lazarus from the dead will confirm. He said to Martha, "I am the resurrection and the life" (11:25). This is another of the "I am" sayings that speak of Jesus bearing the divine name and majesty. He called forth Lazarus from the grave, raised him from the dead, and many people "put their faith in him" (11:45).

Jesus is the Messiah who delivers people ultimately from death to life. The raising of Lazarus was a sign that pointed to the eternal life that people may accept in Jesus Christ. This is why people put their faith in Him. Interestingly, chief priests and other members of the Sanhedrin did not see the sign for what it was: a manifestation that Jesus is the Messiah. They plotted to kill Jesus instead (11:47–53). Jesus, the Fourth Gospel tells us, could no longer move "about publicly among the Jews." Again, some believed, a contrast to some among the religious leaders.

The Suffering, Death, and Resurrection of Jesus (12:1—20:31)

Jesus arranged to have the Passover meal with His disciples. They gathered in a room provided by an unknown host, although one suggestion is that the meal took place at the home of John Mark's parents. Two meals took place at this last supper with His apostles, the Passover meal and the Lord's Supper. The Passover was the meal of the Old Covenant; the Lord's Supper is the meal of the New Covenant. Both involve a sacrifice. The *paschal* lamb of the Old Covenant meal involved the deliverance of people from bondage in Egypt; Jesus, the paschal lamb of the New Covenant, involves the ultimate deliverance of humanity from death to life (3:16).

During the course of the meal, Jesus confronted Judas about his betrayal. Interestingly, he dipped the bread and gave it to Judas (13:26), an act normally establishing who the honored guest was at a meal. Although John's Gospel indicated that this act identified the betrayer, was this also an act by which Jesus reached out to Judas in love? Jesus certainly loved Judas, this person who betrayed Him for thirty pieces of silver (Matt. 26:15–16).

Why Judas did betray Jesus is difficult to discern. One persistent suggestion is that he intended to force a confrontation between Jesus and the religious leaders, and ultimately the Roman government, in the expectation that Jesus would issue a call to arms and the rebellion would begin. If such were the motivation of Judas, he must have expected the kingdom of Jesus to take political shape, and he was ready to begin. Or Judas may simply have been driven by the evil, or greed, in his heart. Cates suggests that one factor motivating Judas' betrayal was Jesus' rebuke when Judas objected to Mary of Bethany's use of costly ointment to anoint Jesus (12:2–8).[7] Judas later committed suicide out of remorse for his act (Matt. 27:3–10). Judas could have had forgiveness just as Simon Peter did after Peter denied Jesus three times (Mark 14:66–72).

Another significant event at the Last Supper was that of Jesus washing the disciples' feet (13:1–17). In this scene He performed the act of a slave. When guests entered into his master's home, the slave designated to do so met the guests and washed their feet. By washing the disciples feet, Jesus taught them once again that they were to be the servants of society, aggressively assuming the servant role in order to meet the needs of humanity.

Jesus continued His dialogue with the apostles after the supper. He predicted his betrayal (13:18–27)) and Peter's denial (13:31–38). He comforted His disciples, who were anxious and unnerved about the coming events. Jesus reassured them that God's house has many rooms, and that He would prepare a place for them so they could be with Him (14:2–3). The "many rooms" (14:2) signify the truth that the eternal relationship in the presence of the Father is inclusive of the disciples and all who are the children of God in Christ. In response to Thomas' question about where He was going and how they could know the way to Him (14:5), Jesus answered, "I am the way and the truth and the life" (14:6). He is the way because He is the truth about the Father, who is the giver of life.

To His troubled disciples, Jesus promised that God would give them "another Counselor" (14:16) who is "the Spirit of truth" (14:17). The disciples would not be left without strength and direction. God was present with them in Jesus Christ, and God would be present with them in the same strength and deliverance after the death and resurrection of Jesus, although in a different way. While our purpose here is not to discuss the theological implications of these statements of Jesus about the Counselor, we should keep in mind the *oneness* of God. God incarnate in Jesus Christ, who was present with the disciples, is the same God present with them in the resurrected and transcendent God in Christ in the Holy Spirit. By the resurrection and resurrection appearances, the disciples would know that their living Lord was with them, just as Matthew recorded Jesus saying, "I am with you always, to the very end of the age" (Matt. 28:20). An important, practical application of the truth of God's presence with them was that they would not be left as "orphans" (14:18).

In chapter 15 Jesus told His disciples that He was the vine and they were the branches (15:1–17). Jesus is the life giver to those who are rightly related to Him, just as branches exist only when they are related to the vine.

Israel sometimes was referred to as a vine undergoing God's care or judgment (Isa. 5:1–7; Jer. 2:21; Ezek. 19:10–14), and in the New Covenant relationship God's people are constituted and sustained by their relationship to Christ.

In the process of facing the harsh realities of His death and its aftermath, Jesus further prepared His disciples. He warned them of hostility and rejection (15:18–25) and reminded them again that they would not be left without guidance, strength, or care, for the Holy Spirit would be with them (15:26–16:33). Jesus said, "I have told you these things, so that in me you may have peace. In this world you will have trouble. But take heart! I have overcome the world" (16:33).

Jesus prayed for them and all disciples after them (17:1–26). This prayer is the Lord's prayer, or, as it is sometimes called, the "high priestly prayer." The prayer reflects Jesus' understanding that God would work to accomplish His purposes in and through the suffering of Jesus, which was about to transpire. He prayed for Himself in the first part of the prayer (17:1–5), words marked by unselfishness and the desire to bring glory to His Father. In the second part Jesus prayed for His disciples (17:6–19), for the sustaining strength of the Father to keep them from evil as they remained in a hostile environment to continue the work of Christ. Similarly, He prayed for all believers who would come after, asking that "all of them may be one, Father, just as you are in me and I am in you" (17:21).

The death and resurrection of Jesus completed His mission and established who He was and is. He is glorified, marked in His act of self-giving by His suffering and death on the cross as the Messiah. He is both "Lord and God," as the testimony of Thomas later bears witness (20:28). Thomas' expression of insight was not his alone, but shared by many who did accept Jesus as Lord and who came later "who have not seen and yet have believed" (20:29). In this is fulfilled John's purpose in writing, that people might believe the testimony and have life (20:31).

Epilogue (21:1–25)

The final section of the Gospel presents another resurrection appearance of Jesus. Also, Jesus reinstated Peter, who denied Jesus after His arrest, as one in whom He had confidence (21:15–17). The Lord asked Peter three times if Peter loved Him. Peter's answer did not show the impulsive self-confidence he had displayed previous to the Lord's death (13:37). Rather, he relied upon what the Lord knows about him: "Yes, Lord you know that I love you" (21:15). Peter seemed to be ready, by answering the Lord essentially the same way three times, to put aside self sufficiency and to depend upon the knowledge and direction of Christ.

That Jesus asked Peter three times if he loved Him seems to be related to the number of times Peter denied Jesus; thus three denials are undone by three confessions of love. If so, this was for Peter's benefit, not Christ's, for Christ knew that Peter loved Him. Notice that Peter's love for Christ was to be shown by active ministry to Jesus' flock. The Lord instructed Peter three times with the following injunctions: "Feed my lambs" (21:15), "Take care of my sheep" (21:16), and "Feed my sheep" (21:17).

After this exchange Peter asked Jesus about the "disciple whom Jesus loved" (21:21), probably asked out of concern for the other's welfare. The disciple whom Jesus loved is the same disciple who had "leaned back against Jesus at the supper" to ask about

the identity of the traitor (21:20). Jesus told Peter that this was not his concern but that his purpose was to follow the Lord (21:22). All of this serves to establish the credibility of the disciple whom Jesus loved and "who testifies to these things and who wrote them down" (21:24).

The book ends with a statement of the impossibility of really presenting all the glory of Jesus in one book (21:25). However, we are grateful for the arresting and challenging witness to Christ which the Fourth Gospel gives.

FOR FURTHER STUDY AND REVIEW

QUESTIONS FOR CONSIDERATION:

1. Who are possible authors for John?
2. What was John's purpose in writing?
3. What is the significance of the "signs" in John?
4. What are the seven signs?
5. What is the overall structure of John in its four parts?
6. What is the development and significance of the "sign" in which the blind man is made to see?

FOR FURTHER READING

Culpepper, R. Alan. "The Gospel of John." *Holman Bible Dictionary*. Nashville: Holman Bible Publishers; 1991.

Marshall, I. Howard. "Gospel of John." *New Bible Dictionary*, 2nd ed. Ed. J. D. Douglas. Wheaton, Ill.: Tyndale, 1982: 601–12.

Hunter. A. M. *The Gospel According to John. The Cambridge Bible Commentary*. Ed. P. R. Ackroyd, A. R. C. Leaney, J. W. Packer. 1965.

ENDNOTES

1. Eusebius, *Ecclesiastical History*, III, xxiii, 3f.
2. Ibid., III, xxxix, 4.
3. See D. A. Carson, *The Gospel According to John* (Grand Rapids: William B. Eerdmans, 1991), 21–23.
4. D. A. Carson, Douglas J. Moo, Leon Morris, *An Introduction to the New Testament* (Grand Rapids: Zondervan, 1992), 136. Their whole discussion on structure should be consulted (135–38).
5. Ibid., 135.
6. Raymond Brown, *The Gospel According to John (i–xii), The Anchor Bible*, ed. W. F. Albright and David Noel Freedman (Garden City, New York: Doubleday & Company, 1966), 255.
7. Robert L. Cate, *History of the New Testament and Its Times* (Nashville: Broadman, 1991), 191.

12

Acts: The Church Breaks Through with the Good News of Christ

Good News of Christ

Although "Acts of the Apostles" is the title of the book, the author gives significant attention only to Simon Peter of the original twelve apostles. Much of the book tells of the work and life of Paul, the person who some believe completes the twelve, taking the place of Judas. The focus on others in the story of Paul is on Paul's fellow laborers, not the original apostles of Jesus. The word "apostle" also occurs in the New Testament with application to all of Christ's disciples. If that is what the author meant, then the Acts of the Apostles is about the work of the church, or all the disciples of Christ.

Another suggested title is "Acts of the Holy Spirit," which gives attention to the emphasis upon the work of the Spirit in Acts. While the theme of the Holy Spirit is very important to the book, the Holy Spirit's work is not the major subject of Acts.

What is apparent is that the Gospel began in Jerusalem and spread to Rome (1:8). As the church became the bearer of the gospel, often epitomized in individuals such as Stephen, Philip, Paul, and Paul's colaborers, barriers that separated people from God and from each other fell one after the other. Acts is a remarkable story. Christ working through His church began in the cradle of Judaism in Jerusalem, but soon burst from that boundary. Old forms of religion, or barriers of race, nationality, and culture, could not contain the explosive work of Christ through His church. The "Acts of the Apostles" is a wonderful account of God creating in Jesus Christ a people from among all nations and peoples through the work of the church.

Writer

Acts is the second volume and Luke is the first volume of a two-volume work by the same author. (See the section "Writer" under the chapter on the Gospel of Luke.) The traditional view, which has strong support, is that Luke, the physician and coworker of Paul, was the author of the two-volume work. The place of composition is uncertain, but suggestions include Caesarea, Achaia, Decapolis, Asia Minor, and Rome.

Readers

The primary reader, as with the Third Gospel, was Theophilus. Again, perhaps Luke addressed Theophilus because he could direct the message to a wider Gentile readership. The good news about Christ was for everybody. Acts shows the welcome given to people of varied backgrounds as the disciples proclaimed the gospel in an ever-widening circle. Also, Luke made apparent in his presentation that the followers of Christ, the church, were in no way a politically inspired revolutionary movement, so they posed no political or military threat to the Roman government. The Gentile readership of Luke-Acts needed to hear that message, and the followers of Christ needed that image as they proclaimed the Gospel in the world.

Message

To put the message of Acts in perspective, we should remember its connection with the Gospel of Luke.

Luke stated his purpose for both works in Luke 1:1–4. He purposed to write an orderly account to present the truth of Christ. He intended to appeal especially to Gentiles so that they might accept Christ as Lord. In Acts Luke stated that in the previous book, a reference to the Third Gospel, he had told Theophilus what Jesus "began to do and to teach" (Acts 1:1). Following the sequence, then, Acts is a continuation of the story of what Jesus continues to do and teach through His church. To state the major thrusts of the two volumes, Luke may be paraphrased this way:

Theophilus, here is my first volume about Christ, which tells and shows what Jesus began to do and teach in His ministry on earth. And here is my second volume, which tells what Jesus continues to do and teach through His church.

Some view Luke's two volumes as presenting the story of "salvation history." Hans Conzelmann brought this theological purpose of Luke-Acts to the attention of interpreters.[1] Salvation history may be divided into three periods: the period of Israel, which ends with

John the Baptist; the middle period, which tells of Jesus and His ministry; and the third period, the history of the church.[2] The pivotal historical period is the midpoint, the event of Christ and all that His salvation means. What came before, the Old Testament period, was preparation. What comes after, the church period, is result and consequence.

Christ is the central, pivotal event of all of history. He is Savior, and God works out His purposes through Him. All may come into God's salvation, as Luke demonstrated. He took pains to show that Jews, proselytes, women, Samaritans, Gentiles in general, and all manner of displaced and disenfranchised persons may receive the ministry of Jesus.

The theological theme of the Third Gospel (salvation focused in Christ) is coupled with a geographical theme in Acts. The earnest reader of the Third Gospel-Acts notices the stress of place, where people were, and movement, as the good news of salvation in Jesus Christ began in Jerusalem and headed toward the "ends of the earth" (Acts 1:8). Acts shows Jesus in His church breaking through barriers of race, religion, culture, and nationality, moving from place to place to include all people who believe under God's kingly rule in Jesus Christ.[3]

The Beginning (1:3–26)

The resurrection of Jesus is validated at the beginning of Acts. The resurrected Christ ate with the disciples (1:4) and talked with them. He instructed them to wait in Jerusalem, where they would receive the gift of the Spirit (1:4–5). The disciples wanted to know if Jesus were about "to restore the kingdom to Israel" (1:6). This question indicates that they still had difficulty understanding the nature of Christ's reign. Jesus' ascension occurred, an act that accented to the readers the authority and rule of Christ. The disciples went to Jerusalem to wait according to Jesus' instructions (1:12–26).

Into Jerusalem and Judea (2:1—8:1)

The Events at Pentecost and the Early church (2:1–13)

The disciples were together in one place when they experienced the Holy Spirit, as Jesus had promised them (1:5). Was this the first coming of the Holy Spirit upon humanity? The Holy Spirit or Spirit of God has been present with humanity previously, as recorded in the Old Testament (Ex. 19:3–6; Ps. 51:11; Isa. 51:2). Also, the disciples had experienced the Holy Spirit in the presence of Jesus, for John the Baptist had said that although he baptized with water, Jesus would baptize them in the Holy Spirit (Luke 3:16). The Holy Spirit is God present with us. When Jesus came He immersed people, as He still does, into the very presence of God. The disciples' baptism of the Spirit, as recorded in Acts 2, was a new experience in which the Spirit prepared and equipped them to do the work of God's people in the world.

As a result of this experience, the disciples spoke in tongues (2:4). The tongues-speaking here evidently was different from other cases in the New Testament, as in 1 Corinthians 12—14, for the people heard in their own languages (2:6). Several explanations exist for this event, and three are presented here. First, the speakers spoke in a tongue they did not know, which is the miraculous aspect of the event. Second, some of the disciples knew more than one language, so they spoke the gospel in tongues that they knew. God's Spirit enhanced both their knowledge and speaking, which is the miraculous aspect of the event. Third, as the disciples spoke in unknown tongues, those listening heard them in their own language, and the aspect of the miraculous in this case would be upon the hearing. Regardless of the particulars of interpretation, communication took place in a miraculous way made possible by the powerful working of God's presence in the whole event.

Simon Peter's Preaching and the Response (2:14–47)

Simon Peter stood and delivered a stirring sermon (2:14–36) in which his central point was that God had made Jesus "both Lord and Christ" (2:36). Now the miracle of communication was completed as people responded to the gospel, repented, and were baptized and added to the church (2:41). They learned the teaching of the apostles, participated in the fellowship of Christ's people, broke bread (both eating together and observing the Lord's Supper), and prayed together. These same activities are very much a part of the church today.

Those converted to Jesus as Lord were both Jews and proselytes. *Proselytes* were non-Jews who committed themselves to the Jewish faith. They went through an involved procedure, climaxed in baptism, by which they freed themselves from other national, religious, and family connections and became a part of Israel. Although proselytes were considered a part of Israel, they were not equal with the biological descendants of Abraham. Yet, as those Jews and proselytes responded to the preaching of salvation in Jesus Christ, they did so on the same basis— that of faith, not nationality or religious preparation.

Problems with Authorities and Within the Church (3:1—8:1)

The second chapter is important in demonstrating how explosively the gospel broke through to Jews and proselytes in Jerusalem. The third and fourth chapters show the boldness of the young church through the work of Peter and John. The religious authorities could not silence or intimidate them. When told to be quiet about Jesus, Peter and John replied that they must speak what they had "seen and heard" (4:20). This boldness was quite different from the timidity and terror the disciples had demonstrated immediately before and during the crucifixion. The reality of the resurrection of Christ, who now reigns, changed them radically (see Luke 24:45–53). The church, although composed of committed people had its own problems, as chapters 5—6 demonstrate. But the church never has been nor will ever be perfect.

Persecution broke out against the young church. The catalyst was Stephen. He was a Hellenistic Jew who was converted to Christ and was passionate in his witness (6:8–10). His accusers charged him with "blasphemy against Moses and against God" (6:11). Brought before the Sanhedrin, Stephen made his defense. He stressed God's inclusiveness of everyone. Especially pivotal in this message was his affirmation that God was not confined to place (7:46–50). This and other things he said implied that God was not confined to one people.

To Stephen's accusers, this meant that they were not exclusively God's chosen people and that they had failed in keeping the law, even rejecting the Messiah. Their anger exploded into mob violence as they stoned Stephen to death. Stephen, therefore, was the first Christian martyr. As he died Saul (Paul) stood by and watched, giving his consent to the stoning (8:1). Saul was probably a leader in instigating the mob-action against Stephen.

Into Samaria, Galilee, and Syria (8:1—11:30)

The persecution against the church became intense. Hellenistic Jewish converts and proselytes from places other than Jerusalem were the focus. Resident and non-Hellenistic Jews who became followers of Christ evidently did not receive the brunt of the persecution since the Jerusalem church remained strong and influential. Probably these Jewish Christians did not proclaim as strongly the inclusiveness of everyone as God's people through Christ as did Stephen and other Hellenistic Jewish converts. The apostles still had some lessons to learn in this regard (see the experience of Peter in 10:1—11:18).

Philip was one of the persecuted who led the charge of the gospel into Samaria. The Samaritans heard his witness and many believed in Christ (8:12). Response from the Samaritans to the gospel even surprised the apostles at Jerusalem, and they sent Peter and John to investigate. A special experience convinced them that the Samaritans, too, could receive the gospel and be included as God's people in Christ (8:26–39). Note the reality that the Samaritans came into the reign of Christ by faith, just as did the Jews and proselytes. Neither race nor religion entered into consideration for their becoming a part of the people of God.

An addendum to this reality is that of the conversion of an Ethiopian eunuch (8:26–39) who was a God-fearer. *God-fearers* were those who worshiped the God of Israel and kept much of the law, but would not or could not become proselytes. They were even further from being true Israelites than proselytes or Samaritans, for devout Samaritans believed many of the same things as the Jews. This meant that God-fearers could not become fully a part of the people of God from an Israelites perspective. But by faith in Christ, with baptism as a sign of his faith, the Ethiopian became a part of God's people through Jesus Christ.

Saul, later identified as Paul, appears in the account again in chapter 9, which recounts his persecuting activity. Why had he sought papers to persecute the church (9:2)? Saul, with roots in the synagogue outside of Palestine, may have been a Jewish missionary before he became a Christian missionary.[4] Evidently, some synagogues were aggressive in making proselytes and having them join the synagogue. By such missionary activity they extended the kingdom of Israel and, more importantly for a Pharisee such as Saul, the rule of God through the law beyond the confines of Palestine. Although Paul's pre-Christian missionary activity cannot be proved, F. F. Bruce pointed out that those who participated in Jewish missionary activity took seriously the prophet Isaiah's charge for Israel to declare God's praise to other nations and to be witnesses to the world.[5]

Some of those most open to the message of Jesus as Messiah would be those in synagogues outside Palestine, especially the proselytes. Saul surely recognized this. In fact, some of those delivering the message of Christ would return to their hometown synagogues from the experience at Pentecost, where they had committed themselves to the Lordship of Christ. Paul did not want the synagogues influenced in this way and changed. Most importantly, he did not want the law undermined by the proclamation of a Messiah who had been crucified. He endeavored to bring those who witnessed to Christ back to Jerusalem to face accusation.

A dramatic interruption occurred in the persecutor's activities, however. He met the living Christ in a dynamic encounter on the road to Damascus. He was changed forever. As a result, Saul the persecutor became Paul the apostle. After his conversion, Acts tells us, the church in "Judea, Galilee and Samaria enjoyed a time of peace" (9:31).

The scene now shifts to Simon Peter before Saul, or Paul, takes center stage once again. An experience of Simon Peter provides the transition between the Jewish moorings of the church and the establishing of the Gentile moorings. The experience concerned a Roman centurion, a God-fearer named Cornelius. He received instruction by means of a vision to send men to Joppa to bring Simon Peter to Caesarea (10:1–6).

In the meantime, Simon Peter had his own vision of a large sheet lowered to the earth with all kinds of animals from which he was to take, kill, and eat (10:11–13). Simon, concerned about eating unclean meat and breaking the law, refused to do so in his vision. He was told, "Do not call anything impure that God has made clean" (10:15). After seeing the faith of Cornelius, a Gentile, and others (10:17–48), Peter later understood this vision to mean that "God does not show favoritism but accepts men from every nation who fear him and do what is right" (10:34–35). Peter later reported to the church in Jerusalem about his experience, and they too understood that Gentile God-fearers could come to Christ (11:18).

The spread of the Gospel continued as Christians went everywhere preaching the Gospel (11:19–30). Persecution began at the hands of Herod Agrippa I, the grandson of Herod the Great. "He had James, the brother of John, put to death with the sword" (12:2). He arrested Peter, who was freed miraculously (12:3–19). This part of the account ends, however, with the death of Herod (12:23) and the statement that "the word of God continued to increase and spread" (12:24). Not even the power of Rome could stop the good news of Christ.

Into the World Beyond (12:1—28:31)

Now, in the account of Acts, the mission to the Gentiles becomes the focus and occupies the rest of the book. To fulfill Christ's commission to be witnesses "to the ends of the earth" (1:8), the disciples needed to be on such a mission. The twelve apostles, however, were not the principal figures in the mission. That task fell to Paul and his colaborers.

Earlier, Barnabas had brought Saul to Antioch to help with the work there (11:25–26). For the first time the disciples received the designation "Christians," probably a name leveled in derision by nonbelievers against the disciples. From this point on Antioch became the principal headquarters of mission operations to take the gospel to the Gentiles. Two dominant churches existed by this time, at Jerusalem and at Antioch. The Jerusalem church concerned itself primarily with work among the Jews, while the church at Antioch sponsored and supported the work with the Gentiles.

By the leadership of the Spirit, the church at Antioch sent Saul and Barnabas on a mission (13:1). This was the first of those travels commonly referred to as the three missionary journeys of Paul. Paul traveled on more than the three mission journeys, but they are a good way to discuss some pivotal activities of the Apostle. The references for reading about the three missionary campaigns are in Acts: first journey, 13:1—15:35; second journey, 15:36—18:22; third journey, 18:23—21:16. After these Paul returned to Jerusalem, where

he was arrested and initially tried (21:17—23:30). Then he was taken under guard to Caesarea (23:31—26:32) and, finally, to Rome (27:1—28:10). Acts ends with Paul in Rome (28:11—31). There, although under house arrest, he preached the Gospel "without hindrance" (28:30–31).

The First Missionary Journey (13:1–15:35)

The first journey had marked success as people responded favorably to Paul and his colaborers. The work was done in southern Asia Minor, in cities such as Derbe, Iconium, and Lystra. Both Jews and Gentiles were the focus, but Paul's mission task force realized more clearly that the primary thrust of their work was to be toward the Gentiles (see 13:44–48). They encountered Jewish resistance, especially to the Gentiles' inclusion into the people of God on the basis only of their acceptance of Christ. Even Jewish Christians in Jerusalem feared that the law had been disregarded in the conversion of the Gentiles.

Church leaders addressed these concerns at a *Jerusalem conference* described in Acts 15:1–35). Paul and others argued for the inclusion of Gentiles into the church, and thus into the people of God, without regard to the observance of circumcision or other Jewish laws. This position prevailed, and the decision of the conference in essence was that a person did not have to meet regulations of the Jewish law before becoming a Christian.

The Second Missionary Journey (15:36—18:22)

The second missionary journey again included areas of Asia Minor and Macedonia and Achaia (Greece). Also, Paul wrote the first letters of which we have record, 1 and 2 Thessalonians, on this journey. Cities such as Philippi, Thessalonica, and Athens received visits and ministry from the missionary band. At Philippi, the jailer became a Christian (16:22–34). Telling his story helped Luke show the universality of the gospel—that the way of Christ is open to everyone. The jailer was not a Jew, a Samaritan (those who held some common beliefs with the Jews), a proselyte, or a God-fearer. He had no orientation to the God of Israel or to the law, yet he became one of God's people by his faith in Christ (16:31–34). Likewise, Paul preached an outstanding sermon at Athens (17:22–31); and in that philosophical context far removed from Judaism, some believed. By such accounts as these, Acts shows that barriers between people and God and people and people continued to fall as many responded to the gospel.

The Third Missionary Journey (18:23—21:16)

On this journey the mission team headed by Paul followed a route that took them to cities close to the coasts of the Mediterranean and Aegean Seas. During these travels Paul wrote 1 and 2 Corinthians, probably Galatians, and Romans.

One prominent event that represents some of the experiences of this journey happened at Ephesus. Paul preached in the synagogue, and a number of people became disciples of Christ. Later, a silversmith named Demetrius aroused people against the mission team. Demetrius made silver shrines for the goddess Artemis, a local fertility goddess whose Roman name was Diana. Her image resided in the Ephesian temple.

Demetrius convinced people that those responding to Christ discredited the great

Prison at Philippi where, according to a local tradition, Paul, Silas, and Timothy were imprisoned. The crypt-like structure was originally a Roman cistern. *Biblical Illustrator* Photo/David Rogers.

goddess (19:23–27), although his interest was in his business of selling the shrines. His words caused an uproar, and only by the insistence of the city clerk (19:35–41) was order restored. The acceptance of Christ by citizens of Ephesus changed things radically for them, cutting across economic and religious practices that brought them rejection at times. Nonetheless, even in the face of rejection, they believed. Acts gives us some insight into the radical changes in life and society whenever the gospel is preached, then and now.

Paul's Arrest and Imprisonment (21:17—26:32)

Paul returned to Jerusalem, and soon was arrested at the instigation of Jews who opposed him. On more than one occasion during the hearings for his case, Paul gave witness to Christ. An attempt was to be made on his life (23:12–15), but the "son of Paul's sister heard of this plot" (23:16) and relayed the information to Paul. When informed of the plot, the Roman commander sent Paul to Caesarea under the guard of a detachment of soldiers. The Romans wanted to protect him because he was a Roman citizen.

Even while a prisoner at Caesarea, Paul had opportunity to proclaim Christ before Festus, a Roman governor of the region, and Herod Agrippa II, the great-grandson of Herod the Great. During the process Paul, on the basis of his Roman citizenship, appealed to have his case tried before Caesar (25:10–11). This meant that he had to be sent from Caesarea to Rome.

In Prison at Rome (28:14–31)

After an eventful journey by land and sea (27:1—28:13), Paul arrived in Rome. Fellow Christians met him to give him encouragement. Acts pointedly describes Paul's situation there: "For two whole years Paul stayed there in his own rented house and welcomed all who came to see him. Boldly and without hindrance he preached the kingdom of God and taught about the Lord Jesus Christ" (28:30–31). Paul was under house arrest but had considerable freedom to meet with people. Interestingly, in the Greek text, the last word in the text is the word translated *unhindered*. No barrier, not even imprisonment, can ultimately hinder the spread of the Gospel.

FOR STUDY AND REVIEW

IDENTIFY:

Proselyte
Saul
Stephen
Cornelius
Philip
The Jerusalem conference
Ethiopian eunuch
Demetrius
God-fearer
Artemis (Diana)

QUESTIONS FOR CONSIDERATION

1. What is the purpose of Acts?

2. Was the experience with the Holy Spirit at Pentecost the first time the Holy Spirit came? Was this the first acquaintance of the disciples with the Holy Spirit?

3. What Jews received the first persecution after the death of Stephen?

4. What was the significance of Simon Peter's vision about the sheet?

5. Where were the disciples first called "Christians?"

6. What were the two dominant churches in the account in Acts? What was the mission of each?

7. What are the Acts references for the three missionary journeys of Paul?

8. Name some cities visited during each of the three missionary journeys.

9. What letters did Paul write on the second journey. On the third?

10. What is the significance of Acts ending with the word "unhindered" or "unhinderedly"?

FOR FURTHER READING

Bruce, F. F. "Acts of the Apostles." *The International Standard Bible Encyclopedia.* 33–47.

Polhill, John B. *Acts.* Volume *26, The New American Commentary*, Edited by David S. Dockery (Nashville: Broadman Press, 1992).

Stagg, Frank. *The Book of Acts: The Early Struggle for an Unhindered Gospel.* Nashville: Broadman Press, 1955.

ENDNOTES

1. Hans Conzelmann, *The Theology of St. Luke*, trans. Geoffrey Buswell (New York: Harper & Row, 1961).

2. Ibid., 16–17.

3. This is the basic thrust of Frank Stagg's thesis, to which I am indebted for the idea of the church breaking through barriers, in *The Book of Acts: The Early Struggle for an Unhindered Gospel* (Nashville: Broadman Press, 1955). For an excellent discussion of the purpose and themes of Acts, see John B. Polhill, *Acts* in *The New American Commentary*, vol. 26, ed. David S. Dockery (Nashville: Broadman Press, 1992), 55–72.

4. Marion L. Soards, *The Apostle Paul: An Introduction to His Writings and Teaching* (New York: Paulist Press, 1987), 22.

5. F. F. Bruce, *Paul: Apostle of the Heart Set Free* (Grand Rapids: William B. Eerdmans Publishing Company, 1988 reprint), 128–129.

13

The Apostle Paul: His Life and Letters

Background

Paul was born in Tarsus. Acts 22:3 reports Paul saying, "I am a Jew, born in Tarsus of Cilicia, but brought up in this city." "This city" means Jerusalem. Some disagreement exists about the meaning of "brought up." Does this mean that Paul's family moved from Tarsus to Jerusalem when he was a child or that he was educated in Jerusalem? Strong arguments exist for both positions.

Little is known of Paul's physical appearance, although it has occupied some discussion at times. An apocryphal work entitled *Acts of Paul*, which really cannot be depended on for historical accuracy, says that Paul was "a man of little stature, thin-haired upon the head, crooked in the legs, of good state of body, with eyebrows joining, and nose somewhat hooked"[1] A persistent physical problem evidently plagued him. He referred to "a thorn in my flesh" that even his impassioned prayer did not alleviate (2 Cor. 12:7–9). Perhaps Paul had bad eyesight, for in Galatians 4:12–15 he seems to connect an illness (4:13) with the Galatians who out of their devotion to him would have "torn out" their eyes and given them to him. Nonetheless, no certainty exists as to the explanation of Paul's thorn in the flesh and exactly what

he meant by the Galatians' willingness to give him their eyes.

Education and Influences

Whether Paul grew up in Jerusalem or went there later as a student, Jerusalem strongly influenced his educational preparation. But other influences in his early life are evident. At times he reflected an unusual familiarity with Greek thought, such as his references to what Greek poets said (Acts 17:28; 1 Cor. 15:33; Titus 1:12), and his style of writing in Greek reflects a fairly strong Greek education in that regard. Five major influences helped shape the Paul we meet in the New Testament: Pharisaic Judaism, Hellenism, the revelation of Jesus Christ, Christian teaching and tradition, and his experience as missionary and apostle.[2]

Paul, or Saul, however, was a Hebrew first and foremost in thinking and action (see Acts 22:3; 26:5; Gal. 1:14; Phil. 3:5–6), a heritage about which he expressed pride. He was of the tribe of Benjamin and named after the best-known figure of that tribe, Saul, the first king of Israel. His Roman name was Paul. He was born of Hebrews, which meant that neither of his parents were proselyte Jews. A Pharisee, Paul's belonged to a group that placed heavy emphasis on the law and led to his legalistic approach to relationship with God before his conversion to Christ.

According to Acts 22:3, Paul received his formal education in Judaism under Gamaliel. Gamaliel had been educated by his grandfather, Hillel. Hillel advocated a form of Judaism more open and liberal than his major counterpart, Shammai. Shammai was very conservative and more exclusive in his approach to Judaism. Paul's advocacy for the inclusion of Gentiles had its roots in some of the teachings of Hillel, who was in favor of evangelizing Gentiles into Judaism.[3] Indeed, Paul probably was a Jewish missionary before he became a Christian missionary. As explained earlier in reference to Acts 9, Saul, or Paul, possibly saw Christianity as a real threat to his proselytizing, an effort to win Gentiles to Judaism, for synagogues outside of Israel.

Conversion

Paul's conversion experience, which was also an event of revelation (Acts 9:1–19; 22:3–16; 26:9–17; 1 Cor. 9:1,16; 15:8–11; Gal. 1:15–16), was the pivotal event of his life. The Paul of pre-conversion experience was very different from the Paul of post-conversion. If nothing else could be said about the difference except by his own testimony that he was a persecutor of the church who became its apostle, that would be enough to state the radical change in Paul's life. But in addition, he turned away from his Pharisaic teaching, with its emphasis upon law-keeping as the way to renew and save Israel to salvation through grace by faith in Jesus Christ.

Before Paul's conversion, Jesus was not for him the Messiah, but a pretender to that title. Other messianic pretenders came along, but these had been rejected too. Afterthe cru-

cifixion Jesus was definitely not a candiate for Messiah, (the crucifixion was a stumbling block for Paul, 1 Cor. 1:22–25). The experience of the living, resurrected Christ, via Paul's own personal encounter, changed all that. "He understood for the first time that the crucifixion of Jesus was not a sign of God's displeasure toward the crucified one, but rather the unfathomable act of God's saving love in giving up his Son . . . (Rom. 5:6–10; 8:31–32; Gal. 2:20)."[4]

Paul understood this act of salvation toward him as an act of love by God. Paul had no merit to bring to God since he had persecuted the church and since by that action he had missed altogether the will of God in Jesus Christ. Paul's classic statements about this love are, "But God demonstrates his own love for us in this: While we were still sinners, Christ died for us" (Rom. 5:8) and "The life I live in the body, I live by faith in the Son of God, who loved me and gave himself for me" (Gal. 2:20).

Out of his conversion and revelation experience near Damascus, Paul received his commission to ministry. He was to preach Christ among the Gentiles. He was the apostle to the Gentiles, a mission in which he was not alone, for many others worked alongside him. People such as Barnabas, Timothy, Titus, John Mark, Luke, Lydia, Aquila and Priscilla, and others were among those who were fellow-laborers with Paul in the gospel. Paul gave much credit to them in what they accomplished in their combined ministries, and we probably should take more note of their work ourselves. Although we often quote from Paul's letters about interpretations and views, his fellow workers held and taught similar or the same views. Through their combined efforts they planted many churches over much of the Roman Empire.

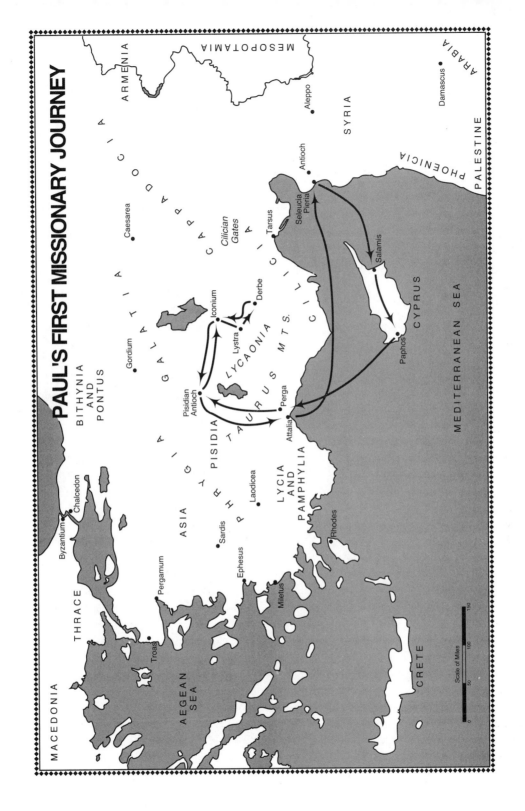

PAUL'S FIRST MISSIONARY JOURNEY

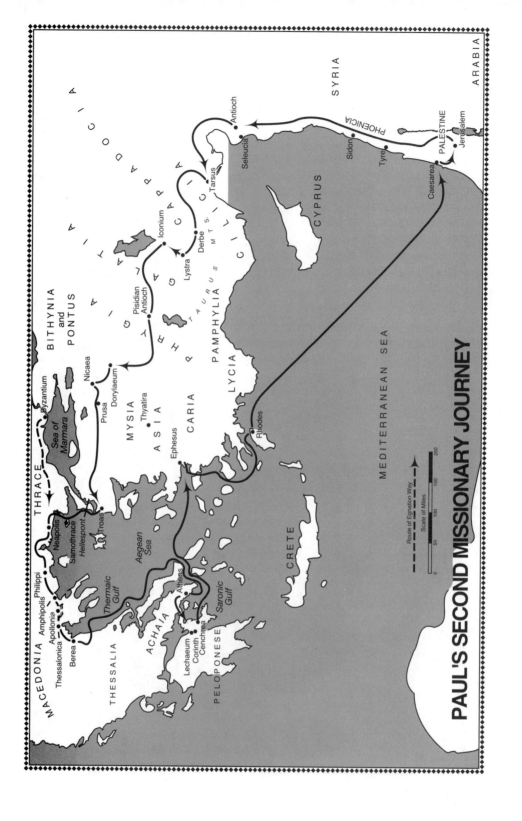

PAUL'S SECOND MISSIONARY JOURNEY

ARABIA

SYRIA

Antioch

PHOENICIA

Seleucia

Sidon

PALESTINE

Tarsus

Tyre

Jerusalem

Caesarea

CYPRUS

CILICIA

CAPPADOCIA

GALATIA

Iconium

Derbe

Lystra

Pisidian Antioch

TAURUS MTS.

PAMPHYLIA

LYCIA

BITHYNIA and PONTUS

PHRYGIA

Nicaea

Dorylaeum

Prusa

MYSIA

Thyatira

ASIA

CARIA

Ephesus

Rhodes

MEDITERRANEAN SEA

THRACE

Byzantium

Sea of Marmara

Hellespont

Samothrace

Neapolis

Troas

MACEDONIA

Philippi

Amphipolis

Apollonia

Thessalonica

Berea

Aegean Sea

Thermaic Gulf

THESSALIA

ACHAIA

Athens

Lechaeum

Corinth

Cenchrea

Saronic Gulf

PELOPONESE

CRETE

Route of Egnatian Way

Scale of Miles

0   50   100   150   200

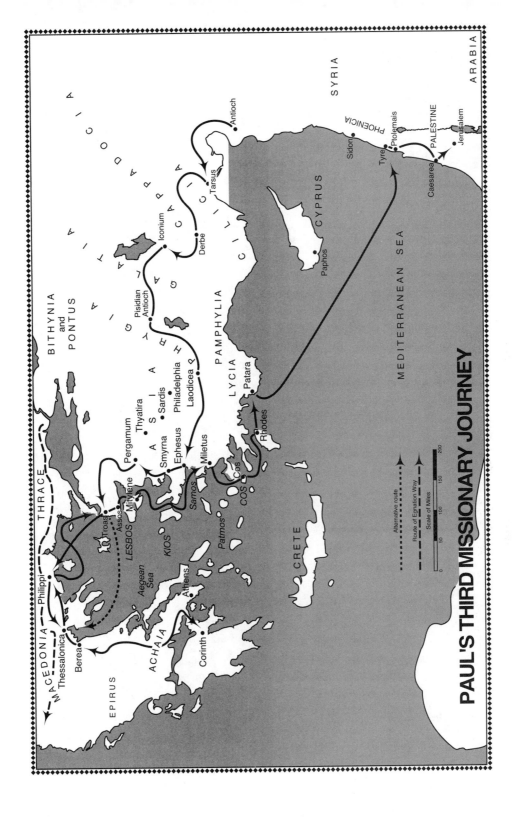

PAUL'S THIRD MISSIONARY JOURNEY

Alternative route

Route of Egnation Way

Scale of Miles

0   50   100   150   200

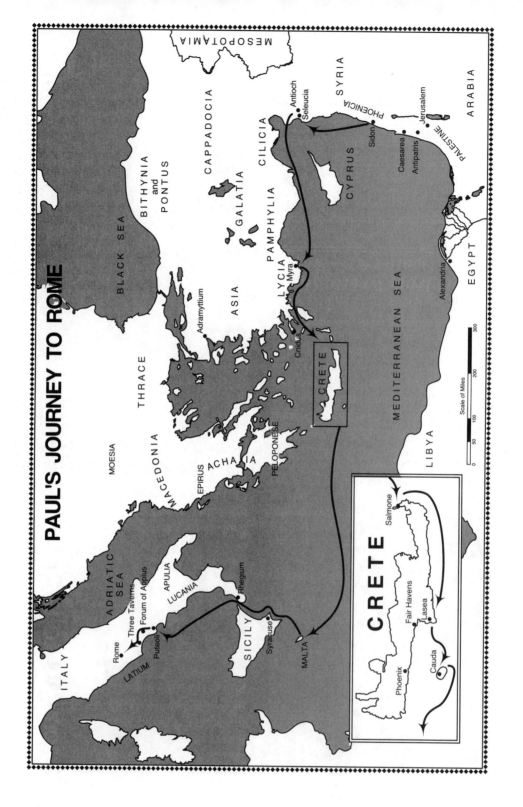

PAUL'S JOURNEY TO ROME

MESOPOTAMIA

SYRIA

ARABIA

Antioch
Seleucia

PHOENICIA

Sidon

Jerusalem

Caesarea
Antipatris
PALESTINE

BITHYNIA
and
PONTUS

CAPPADOCIA

CILICIA

CYPRUS

GALATIA

PAMPHYLIA

EGYPT

BLACK SEA

ASIA

LYCIA
Myra

Alexandria

Adramyttium

Cnidus

CRETE

MEDITERRANEAN SEA

THRACE

LIBYA

MOESIA

MACEDONIA

EPIRUS

ACHAIA

PELOPONESE

Scale of Miles
0 50 100 200 300

ITALY

ADRIATIC
SEA

APULIA

LUCANIA

Rhegium

SICILY

Syracuse

MALTA

Rome
Three Taverns
Forum of Appius
Puteoli
LATIUM

CRETE

Salmone

Phoenix

Fair Havens
Lasea

Cauda

Letters

Paul receives more attention as compared to his fellow workers not only because he was an outstanding leader but also because he was a letter-writer. He wrote letters to churches, usually because of some need in the churches to which he could contribute instruction or direction by means of a letter. Letters such as these these are termed "occasional" letters, because some occasion led to the writing of a letter.

Areopagus in Athens, where Paul was taken before the council, probably as a lecturer. *Biblical Illustrator* Photo/David Rogers.

Box 14: The Letters of Paul

Earlier Letter
   1, 2 Thessalonians

Church or Gospel Letters
   1, 2 Corinthians
   Galatians
   Romans

Prison or Captivity Letters
   Ephesians
   Philippians
   Colossians
   Philemon

Pastoral Letters
   1, 2 Timothy
   Titus

His letter-writing form was the Greek, which involved the name of the sender first, the name of the recipients or readers second, the expression of greetings third, the body of the letter fourth, and a closing, sometimes a benediction, last. After the greeting, the body of the letter usually begins with some expression of praise, thankfulness, or prayer for the readers.

Paul often "Christianized" the letter form, expanding upon the parts of the form with statements that communicate a message in themselves. For example, in Galatians 1:1, Paul identified himself as the sender or writer and then added information about himself that the readers needed to hear. He wrote, "Paul, an apostle—sent not from men nor by man, but by Jesus Christ and God the Father, who raised him from the dead" a message of particular importance because his opponents told the Galatian Christians that Paul was not acting according to God's will.

A Chronology of Paul's Life

Charting the chronological development of Paul's life is possible within a one- to four-year margin for most events. At least we have a good beginning point from which to work backward and forward in order to determine dates. The Delphi inscription, named after the place of its discovery, the ancient Greek town of Delphi, confirms the dating of Gallio as proconsul in the area from A.D. 51–52. Acts 18:12–18 shows that Paul was in Corinth and that he appeared before Gallio, which was either in 51 or 52. Correlating this information with the information of Paul's letters and Acts, we can set a reasonable range of dates for his birth, conversion, and the major activities in his life.

Date (A.D.)	Event
10–15	Birth
32–35	Conversion
47–48	First missionary journey
49	Jerusalem conference
49–52	Second missionary journey Writing of 1, 2 Thessalonians (and perhaps Galatians)
52–57	Third missionary journey Writing of 1, 2 Corinthians (perhaps Galatians) and Romans
57	Travel to Jerusalem with the offering; arrest, imprisonment
57–59	Imprisonment at Caesarea
59–60	Voyage to and arrival in Rome
60–62	Under house detention in Rome Writing of Ephesians, Colossians, Philippians, and Philemon
62–65	Pastoral letters written, 1, 2 Timothy, Titus
64 or 65	Death in Rome

The captivity or prison letters may have been written from Caesarea or Ephesus (see discussion in chapter 22), but Rome is still favored by many interpreters. As regards the death of Paul, we really have no direct information. Acts ends with Paul in prison at Rome, and the Pastoral letters only indicate a possible execution. Tradition has Paul being released from prison; making a trip to Spain; returning finally to Crete, Ephesus, and Macedonia; arrested again somewhere in Macedonia; imprisoned at Rome again; and martyred in Rome during the Neronian persecution against Christians.[5]

FOR STUDY AND REVIEW

IDENTIFY:

Tarsus
Occasional letters
Saul
Delphi inscription
Gamaliel

QUESTIONS FOR CONSIDERATION

1. What were the five major background influences in Paul's life?

2. Who was to be the focus of Paul's ministry according to his commission or calling?

3. What are the parts of a Greek letter form?

4. What are the categories of Paul's letters? Which letters belong to which categories?

5. What are the dates of the major events in Paul's life?

FOR FURTHER READING

Bruce, F. F. *Paul: Apostle of the Heart Set Free.* Grand Rapids: William B. Eerdmans Publishing Company, 1988.

Fitzmyer, Joseph A. *Paul and His Theology: A Brief Sketch.* 2nd ed. Englewood Cliffs, New Jersey: Prentice Hall, 1989.

Hengel, Martin. *The Pre-Christian Paul.* Philadelphia: Trinity Press International, 1991.

Plevnik, Joseph. *What Are They Saying About Paul?* New York: Paulist Press, 1986.

Scott, C. A. Anderson. *Christianity According to St Paul.* Cambridge: University Press, 1966.

Soards, Marion L. *The Apostle Paul: An Introduction to His Writing and Teaching.* New York: Paulist Press, 1987.

ENDNOTES

1. *The Acts of Paul, The Apocryphal New Testament,* ed. M. R. James (London: Oxford University Press, 1926), 273.

2. For a discussion of these areas of influence, see Joseph A. Fitzmyer, *Paul and His Theology: A Brief Sketch*, 2nd ed. (Englewood Cliffs, New Jersey: Prentice Hall, 1989), 27–35.

3. See John Drane, *Introduction the New Testament* (San Francisco: Harper & Row, 1986), 248–49.

4. Joseph Plevnik, *What Are They Saying About Paul?* (New York: Paulist Press, 1986), 20.

5. For a discussion of evidence for Paul's release from prison, journey to Spain, and death, see F. F. Bruce, *Paul, Apostle of the Heart Set Free* (Grand Rapids: William B. Eerdmans Publishing Company, 1988), 441–55.

14

Romans: The Righteousness of God Through Christ for Salvation

Writer

Paul was the writer of the letter to the Romans. Although Romans begins and ends like a letter, the body of material reads more like a theological treatise, for Paul did not deal with one problem after another or answer questions of the recipients. Indeed, at times he seemed to give a synopsis of what he had learned about Christ and the application of Christ to some burning issues in his career to that point. Paul wrote the letter from Corinth near the end of the third missionary journey, A.D. 56–57. His amanuensis or secretary was Tertius (16:22), and Phoebe likely carried the letter to Rome in Paul's behalf (16:1).

Readers

The recipients of the letter were the saints in Rome. *Saints* was another name for disciples of Christ and did not in any sense designate a superior class of Christians as compared to others. Determining the composition of that church in Rome is difficult, however. Probably the best conclusion is that the church had both a Jewish (see 2:17; 3:1; 4:1; 7:1; 9—11; 16:3,7,11) and Gentile constituency (see 1;5,6,13; 11:13; 15:7–12), with the

Jewish constituency in the minority. The Gentiles were familiar with Judaism and the Jewish law; otherwise they could not have understood some of what Paul wrote. Perhaps, then, some of the Gentiles were God-fearers or had been proselytes in Judaism before becoming followers of Christ.

As influential as the Roman church became in early history, it is likely that no apostle founded it. Simon Peter and Paul have been suggested as the founders of the church. However, Simon Peter was still in Jerusalem around A.D. 49, at the Jerusalem Council (Acts 15), and a church existed in Rome before then. Too, Paul did not mention Peter in his letter. If Peter had been the leader of the church, Paul certainly would have greeted him or referred to him as a matter of courtesy and diplomacy to the leader and the church. Finally, when Paul arrived under arrest in Rome in Acts 28, no mention of Simon Peter is made, an unlikely situation if Simon Peter were in Rome as the leader of the church. On the other hand, Paul was not the probable organizer of the church in Rome. His letter addresses the church without the intimacy of one who was instrumental in its beginnings (see 1:10,13; 15:22).

Other options for the church's beginnings include Jewish Christians converted at Pentecost (Acts 2) who returned to Rome and began the church. Another suggestion is that converts from missionary work in Asia Minor, perhaps both Jews and Gentiles, eventually made their way to Rome and established a church. Since Rome was the center of almost everything in the Roman Empire, many people migrated there for work and other purposes. This third suggestion best explains the beginning and the composition of the church.

Message

As previously indicated, Paul did not seem to be addressing particular needs of the congregation. The message he delivered was of a nature to apply to Christians generally in almost any city or situation. We will discuss the message of Romans in terms of purpose and theme. Sometimes purpose and theme of a New Testament writer are tied so closely together that in a survey no need exists to distinguish between the two. For Romans, brief separate discussions of the two should be helpful.

What was Paul's *purpose* for writing to the Romans? One possibility is that he wrote to prepare the church to defend itself against the Judaizers who gave the Galatian Christians such troubles. Paul did establish that Christ alone by grace alone is the way of salvation, but this is not his comprehensive purpose. Neither did he name the troublesome Judaizers in a direct way, which one would expect if that were his purpose in writing. What seems certain is that Paul's battles with the Judaizers and others had sharpened his theology and message for all Christians, and he wrote against that background. But again, combatting an opposing movement does not surface as the central purpose in Romans.

Did he write to prepare the way for further missionary journeys beyond Rome all the way to Spain (15:23–24), and in visiting Rome on the way to encourage the church there? A secondary purpose certainly included these intentions, but Paul went to a great deal of trouble and said many things he did not have to say if those were his intentions. Why write all that he did if he were going to Rome to tell them anyway?

Paul told the Romans that he was going to Jerusalem, and after that he planned to come to Rome first, then Spain. He was going to go to Jerusalem to deliver the offering taken by churches in Macedonia and Achaia for the poor in Jerusalem (15:23–29). Why was the offering so important?

Malcolm Tolbert[1] suggested that Paul originally had planned to go to Rome, but changed his mind in order to take the offering. The offering was vital, and Paul saw his personal deliverance of the offering as very important—as a significant bridge builder between the Gentile and Jerusalem churches. In other words, he saw a golden opportunity to build the oneness of the church, a oneness directly related to the heart of the gospel and vitally important to the Christian mission to a diverse world.

Evidently his change of plans might have been detrimental to his relationship to the Roman church if he had not explained. Therefore, he reassured them that he wanted to come and see them. Indeed, he had planned to visit many times, but was thwarted (1:10–13). He also affirmed to them, possibly concerned that they might question his commitment at that point, his continuing dedication to the Gentile mission (15:14–30). Too, he stated that he was "not ashamed of the gospel" (1:16), perhaps anticipating that some at Rome might think he was unsure that his gospel would work in Rome.

But Paul also knew that he risked his life if he went to Jerusalem for some leaders there

Roman Forum as seen through one of the Barrel-vaults of the Arch of Septimius Severus. *Biblical Illustrator* Photo/Ken Touchton.

wanted his death. Therefore, he wrote the letter to the Romans in place of a visit which might never take place if he indeed did meet with death. Such a purpose would explain the rather sweeping nature of the content of the Roman material, constituting as it does something of a last statement of his presentation of the gospel.

The *theme* of the letter is in 1:16–17 and may be stated for our purposes as "salvation by God's righteousness granted through Jesus Christ to those who believe." People cannot generate right standing with God, which constitutes a saved status, by their own righteousness. Rather, by their faith in Jesus Christ people receive and stand in God's righteousness. God imputes His righteousness to believers; righteousness cannot and does not have to be earned by works. Paul restated the theme a little differently in 3:21–22: "But now a righteousness from God, apart from law, has been made known, to which the Law and the Prophets testify. This righteousness from God comes through faith in Jesus Christ to all who believe."

Paul was not "ashamed" of this gospel (1:16). By *ashamed* he did not refer to timidity or fearfulness about sharing the gospel. Rather, he meant that the gospel would not shame him. That is, the gospel would do, accomplish, what the gospel said it would do; it would not fail anywhere to do the work of salvation in those who believed. After all, the gospel was "the power of God for the salvation of everyone who believes" (1:16), and that gospel would not shame Paul by failing to save someone who believed.

With this background of purpose and theme in mind, we turn our attention now to a survey of the message of Romans. Structurally, after the introduction (1:1–17) and before the closing (15:14—16:27), the message may be divided into two broad parts: the

message of salvation by the righteousness of God, chapters 1:18—11:36; and practical applications arising out of this message of salvation (12:1—15:13). A survey of Romans by sections of material will aid in developing an understanding of the content.

Introduction (1:1–17)

Paul followed the Greek letter-writing format, but greatly enhanced the sections, obviously adding weight to his identity (1:1) and to the description of the gospel he proclaimed as well as the authority for proclaiming it (1:4–6). The body of the letter begins with his customary thanksgiving for his readers and his prayers for them. He reminds them of his desire and intentions to visit, and then states the theme of his letter as discussed above.

All Need the Righteousness of God for Salvation (1:18—4:25)

First, Paul established that the Gentiles need salvation. They cannot excuse themselves from this need by appealing to a lack of understanding, for "God's invisible qualities . . . have been clearly seen, being understood from what has been made" (1:20). They have the law "written on their hearts," and their consciences also bear witness to God (2:14–15). So the Gentiles need salvation by God's righteousness in Jesus Christ.

The Jews had an advantage, because they had the "very words of God" (3:2). But in Romans 3:10–18, Paul quoted loosely, in a rabbinic manner, from a string of Old Testament passages (Pss. 5:9; 15:1; 36:1; 53:2–4; 140:3; Isa. 59:7–8)[2] to support his contention that the Jews were under sin. Paul claimed that "all have sinned and fall short of the glory of God" (3:23). He used Abraham as an example in chapter 4, to point out that Abraham's relationship with God came by faith, not by works of the law. Those who have been justified, made right, or declared not guilty with God by God through their faith, both Jew and Gentile, are the children of Abraham. Being a child of God is not based upon relationship to law but upon justification through the righteousness of God, which comes through faith in Christ Jesus (4:16–25).

Freedom from Wrath, Sin, Law, and Death (5:1—8:39)

Anders Nygren, in his influential commentary, points out that chapters 5—8 present what the person who has been made righteous is free from.[3] Chapter 5 shows that a person is free from wrath (5:9). Some people perceive God's wrath as anger, which boils over into destructive action. A state or condition of existence of separation from God, by a person's own choice, more nearly describes what Paul meant by wrath. A condition of being over against God and His purposes of salvation is best described as a condition of wrath in which a person exists. God's justification by His righteousness through the faith of a person frees one from that wrathful condition.

Chapter 6 emphasizes that a Christian is free from sin (6:18). That is, Christians are free from the power of sin which previously determined their existence. Perfection, absence of failure or particular sins, is not the issue here. The issue is existence. To be under the power of sin is to have one's life determined by the goals and destinies of sin.

Paul showed that God's justification frees one from that power of sin—the reason that a Christian will not deliberately sin against the grace of God (6:1–2). People who are justified do not have the goals and motivations of the power of sin determining life. Believers cannot act out what they are not. They are dead to sin; something dead, the motivation and the will to live in an existence that has the goals of evil, cannot live itself out in a person's life (see 6:6,11,15–19).

In chapter 7 Paul established that a person is free from law. Trying to determine whether Paul described a pre- or postconversion experience (7:14–25) has made this chapter difficult to interpret. Again, viewing the chapter as a description of two existences, one with God and one apart from God, is probably the best approach to take for survey consideration. To be apart from God is to be in the body of death (7:24), but to be justified is to be in life. Paul saw the law as having a positive effect in that it shows or convinces people that they are in a state of sin. But the law has no power to deliver; it condemns, and in that condemnation people know their need. As Paul indicated, a person in such state of relationship to the law does not have the power to do what is right ultimately (7:14-15). So a person exists in a state of condemnation, under the power of a law which condemns but does not deliver. But freedom is in Christ: "Who will rescue me from this body of death? Thanks be to God—through Jesus Christ our Lord!" (7:24–25). As Paul said in Romans 8:1, "Therefore, there is now no condemnation for those who are in Christ Jesus."

Chapter 8 tells of a last and great freedom, freedom from death. Much of the chapter discusses those who "do not live according to the sinful nature but according to the Spirit" (8:4). Where the *New Interna-*

tional Version translates "sinful nature," the *New Revised Standard Version* translates "flesh." The Greek word actually means "flesh," but the NIV translators attempted to capture Paul's meaning here rather than the actual word. Translating from another language often requires translating to get the sense of something rather than finding a word to word equivalent that may not give the sense.

However, "flesh" as the translation does offer the better contrast here with "Spirit," because the idea is not that people have two natures within them. Rather, Paul was talking about two existences that can be embraced, life in the flesh or life in the Spirit. Life in the Spirit is life in Christ. In this existence is life in which the "law of the Spirit of life" sets people "free from the law of sin and death" (8:2). The existence in the flesh, or sinful nature, is the existence of death. The whole person is meant in either case.

Of course, we are torn between the two existences at times, but to those who belong to Christ, life in the Spirit is determinative of life-style. Those who have their minds set on the Spirit seek and do what the Spirit desires. "To set the mind on the flesh is death, but to set the mind on the spirit of life and peace" (8:6, NRSV). Still, we are torn by the cares and troubles of this world. But in those God "works for the good of those who love him" (8:28). He can accomplish the most with those who love Him because they are the ones most responsive to His work in their lives.

Even physical death is not an ultimate catastrophe for God. Paul affirmed that God is for us; nothing can separate us from Him, not even death (8:31–39). Indeed, nothing separates us "from the love of God that is in Christ Jesus our Lord" (8:39). The kind of love Paul meant here is a living relation-

ship. Death does not stop that living relationship, and since it is a living relationship, one who belongs to God in Jesus Christ lives.

The Problem of Israel's Rejection (9:1—11:36)

Chapters 9—11 almost could stand by themselves, although they are related to the first eight chapters. Perhaps they were a sermon preached by Paul. C. H. Dodd even suggested that Paul may have had a sermon manuscript with him as he wrote Romans and inserted it as an important part of his argument.[4] The chapters deal with the problem of Israel's rejection as the people of God, while at the same time the Gentiles become the people of God.

The argument of these chapters is difficult to develop in the limited space we have here. Paul's statement should not be pressed too far, as for example to work out an elaborate doctrine of predestination or election that includes God's electing some to be relegated to eternal destruction without regard to their choice. The context should be given full consideration, especially the fact that Paul employed here the diatribe method of communication in which the questions of an imagined objector, or "straw man," are met and answered.

Generally, the main emphases of the argument are clear. Chapter 9 establishes that God has the sovereignty and consequently the right to choose whom He will without being answerable, of course, to anyone. For some Israelites would reason, however, that if Gentiles are called the people of God simply on the basis of faith, without conformity to the demands of the law by which they might participate in the promise to Abraham that his descendants would be God's people, then Israel has been rejected and God has gone back on His promise. Paul answered this objection by an appeal to God's sovereignty. God may choose whomever He wishes to choose.

But Paul does show in chapter 10 that Israel's status has the possibility of change (10:1). Their problem, and hence the reason for their rejection, is that they sought a righteousness of their own and not God's righteousness (10:3). Paul reminded his readers that "God did not reject his people" (11:2). Indeed, Paul himself, "an Israelite . . . a descendant of Abraham, from the tribe of Benjamin" (11:1) was not rejected.

Practical Application (12:1—15:13)

Chapter 12 begins with the word *therefore* (12:1) which marked the transition from what Paul had written to what he was about to write. The sentence may be paraphrased in this manner: "Because of what I have written up to this point, you are therefore encouraged to do the following." Chapter 12, then, begins a section of practical application of the way of righteousness in life. Dedication to the will and service of God (12:1–2) and service in the church (12:3–7) characterize the way of righteousness. Christians are to work at healthy and redemptive relationships inside and outside the church (12:9–21). Love

Reconstruction of the colosseum (72-80 A.D.) where some of the persecutions of Christians may have occured. Note the posts at the top for stringing the velarium—a canopy for shading and protecting spectators from the elements. *Biblical Illustrator* Photo/Bill Lata/Museum of Oman civilization at Eur (2/29).

toward one another, responsible conduct in business, meeting others' needs, and returning good for evil are part of a life dedicated to God in Christ.

Another encouragement to right living is that followers of Christ should obey the governing authorities (13:1–6). Paul rejected violent revolution against the Roman government, something advocated by radical Jewish groups and into which Christians must not be drawn. Of course, Paul did not advocate submitting to the state or to other governing authorities whenever that submission conflicts with the will of God for life. If Paul had believed that, he would not have been imprisoned.

In addition, Paul plead for tolerance among believers (14:1–23). Some he characterized as weak and some as strong. The strong were those who felt no need to observe certain days or certain dietary rules, while the weak felt that such observance was necessary (14:5–6). Paul placed the burden for responsibility upon the strong, appealing to them not to do those things that would cause the weaker brother to stumble (14:15). Rather, all should "make every effort to do what leads to peace and to mutual edification" (14:19), or the building up of the church. Paul completed the discussion about the weak and the strong in 15:1–13.

Paul's Conclusion (15:14—16:27)

As he continued in chapter 15, Paul told of his mission work (15:14–22). He stated his desire to go to Spain after he has taken the offering to Jerusalem (15:23–29). The trip to Jerusalem, however, will be precarious, so he admonished the church at Rome to pray for him. Concluding his letter, Paul sent a number of greetings and encouragements (16:3–24), then closed with a beautiful benediction.[5]

FOR STUDY AND REVIEW

IDENTIFY:

Tertius
Phoebe
Saints
Ashamed (1:16)
Weak and strong (14)

QUESTIONS FOR CONSIDERATION

1. What are the suggestions as to the establishment of the church at Rome?

2. What was Paul's purpose in writing Romans?

3. What is the theme of Romans, and what does it mean?

4. What freedom does each of the chapters 5—8 emphasize?

5. What are the meanings of *flesh* and *Spirit?*

FOR FURTHER READING

Barrett, C. K. *A Commentary on the Epistle to the Romans. Harper's New Testament Commentaries.* Edited by Henry Chadwick. New York: Harper & Row, 1957.

Carson, D. A., Douglas J. Moo, and Leon Morris. *An Introduction to the New Testament.* Grand Rapids: Zondervan, 1992: 239–57.

Songer, Harold S. "Romans." *Holman Bible Dictionary.* 1202–07.

ENDNOTES

1. The discussion about the offering and the purpose of Romans as being written in place of a visit is mainly that of Malcolm O. Tolbert in his unpublished doctoral dissertation, "The Purpose of Romans," New Orleans Baptist Theological Seminary, 1962.

2. C. H. Dodd, *The Epistle to the Romans, The Moffatt New Testament Commentary* (London: Hodder and Stoughton, 1960), 48.

3. These are categories or chapter titles delineated by Anders Nygren, *Commentary on Romans*, trans. Carl C. Rasmussen (Philadelphia: Fortress Press, 1967), 191–349. My discussion is indebted somewhat to his treatment.

4. Dodd, *Romans*, 149.

5. Manuscripts exist with the doxology in several places, which normally marks the end of the letter. This has led some to say that chapters 15 and 16 were not part of the original letter, and others to say that 16 was not a part of the original. For a discussion and suggested resolution for the ending of Romans, see D. A. Carson, Douglas J. Moo, and Leon Morris, *An Introduction to the New Testament* (Grand Rapids: Zondervan, 1992), 245–47.

15

1 and 2 Corinthians

Writer

In 1 Corinthians Paul identified himself and Sosthenes as the senders of the letter (1:1), while 2 Corinthians identifies Timothy as the co-sender of the letter (1:1). Paul was the author of each, but he rightly gave affirmation to his co-laborers who worked as he did in the establishing of churches and preaching the gospel. They, too, dealt with discouragement and problems as well as sharing the joys of the victories in Christ.

We sometimes think of Paul as the lonely pioneer almost single-handedly planting the gospel over much of that world, but the truth of the matter is that Paul's efforts would not have been successful without the coworkers and churches who supported them. Paul occupies our attention because he was the leader of the mission to the Gentiles, and he also wrote the letters which reveal to us the rich information about the mission efforts.

He was in Ephesus when he wrote 1 Corinthians, probably about A.D. 55. He wrote 2 Corinthians from Macedonia around A.D. 55–56. These two letters were part of the significant correspondence of Paul during his third missionary journey.

The letters designated 1 and 2 Corinthians are not the only letter contacts Paul had with the Corinthians at Corinth. Consider the following list of correspondence contacts with the Corinthians:

1. Previous letter: This letter is mentioned in 1 Corinthians 5:9. It is called "previous" because Paul wrote the letter prior to 1 Corinthians.

2. A letter from the Corinthians: Paul refers to this letter in 1 Corinthians 7:1. By this means, the Corinthians raised questions to which they wished him to respond.

3. First Corinthians, written from Ephesus.

4. A "painful" or "tearful" letter, so called because of Paul's language in 2 Corinthians 2:1–9; 7:8.

5. Second Corinthians, which may in itself be a composite of two or more letters.

Readers

Corinth had a reputation for wickedness. It was an important and wealthy city of trade; nevertheless, the Romans destroyed it in the second century B.C. Julius Caesar rebuilt the city in the latter part of the first century B.C. The new city was made up of retired soldiers, freedmen, Jews, and others from all over the empire. The wicked reputation of the city seems to have come mainly from the old city, but from a reading of 1 and 2 Corinthians

Lachaeum Road looking south toward Corinth. Agora with Acrocorinth in the background. *Biblical Illus-trator* Photo/David Rogers.

alone we can determine that evil influences were intense.

The church was Gentile, and converts came into the church from a wide variety of backgrounds and religious experiences. That variety in no small degree encouraged the difficulty and complexity of problems in the church at Corinth. Members of the church had little if any preparation for living the Christian life, unlike those churches composed of God-fearers, proselytes, and Jewish converts. Paul, therefore, had to deal with basic moral, church, and theological matters.

Through 1 and 2 Corinthians, present-day readers have the opportunity to see a church in a Gentile setting. A cursory reading of these materials reveals a church faced by many problems. Paul's relationship with them varied from cordial to strained as one crisis after another arose from within to threaten the church. However, he brought positive guidance to bear upon the problems within the church at Corinth. As a result we have Christian teaching about ethics, theology, and ecclesiology (the nature and practice of the church). We can appreciate the Corinthians, while being sympathetic and regretting the difficulties with which they dealt, because we can learn from their problems and how Paul answered them. The modern church needs the ethical, theological, and ecclesiological information found in the Corinthian corre-spondence..

1 Corinthians: The Nature and Unity of the Church in Christ

Paul went to Corinth on his second missionary journey and began teaching immediately in the synagogue there. While some of the Jews believed, leaders and others of the synagogue rejected his witness. He continued his work through the home of Titus Justus, a Gentile who lived next door to the synagogue (Acts 18:7). Although Paul met resistance, the work went well and a struggling church began with even the synagogue ruler and his family becoming Christians (Acts 18:7–8).

A bonus of the whole experience was Paul's introduction to Aquila and Priscilla, two Christians who became pivotal workers in the ongoing mission to the Gentiles. A husband and wife team, they were Christian Jews. Whether they became Christians under the influence of Paul or not is uncertain. They were tentmakers and effective missionaries who seemed to have an excellent grasp of the Christian faith. For example, Priscilla and Aquila took the gifted Apollos aside to instruct him more accurately in the faith (Acts 18:24–26). A church met in their home, which put them in a natural leadership position (1 Cor. 16:19).

After leaving Corinth, Paul wrote the "previous letter," of which we have no copy. Some think that a portion of that letter appears in 2 Corinthians 6:14—7:1. However, no certainty exists for this except that the subject matter in 1 Corinthians 5:9–13 and 2 Corinthians 6:14—7:1 bear some similarities. Also, 2 Corinthians 6:14–7:1 does seem to be somewhat independent of the materials around that section.

Later Paul heard from "Chloe's" people (1 Cor. 1:11). Chloe, a woman, evidently was a leader at either Corinth or Ephesus. People from her household came to see Paul, bringing reports of party divisions at Corinth. Later Stephanas, Fortunatus, and Achaicus arrived to visit Paul (1 Cor. 16:15–18). One of the two groups brought a letter from the Corinthians which raised several issues calling for response from Paul. He responded to the oral reports and the Corinthian letter with First Corinthians. The church, plagued with problems (see box), needed Paul's firm guidance. The problems presented challenges to the nature and unity of the church.

Box 15: Problems Reflected in 1 Corinthians

1. Factions (1:10–17; 3:5–15)
2. Worldly wisdom (1:18–31; 2:6—3:4)
3. Unethical conduct (5:1—6:20)
4. Marriage and celibacy (7:1–40)
5. Idols (8:1—11:2)
6. Actions of women leaders (11:3–16)
7. Lord's Supper (11:17–34)
8. Spiritual gifts (12:1—14:40)
9. Unbelief in the resurrection (15:1–58)

The Challenge of Factions (1:10–17; 3:5–15)

The problem of factions, or parties, courses throughout the Epistles, because each of the difficulties divided the Corinthians along lines of opinions or actions. Some identifiable parties did exist: the parties of Paul, Apollos, Cephas, and Christ (1:12). While the distinctiveness of parties is unclear, the names by which they identified themselves may give some clue because of the particular emphasis and background of each leader claimed by the separate parties.

The party of Paul perhaps claimed freedom from the law, or freedom from regulation of conduct, to the extreme. On the other hand, perhaps the Cephas (Simon Peter, Cephas is the Aramaic name) faction overemphasized the law. The Apollos party may have placed emphasis upon human wisdom as an approach to the gospel. Speculation about the Christ party is more difficult. Were they the self-righteous group, placing themselves in a position of superiority over against the other parties?

Paul attacked this party division by asking three questions: Is Christ divided? Was Paul crucified for you? Were any of you baptized in the name of Paul? (1 Cor. 1:13). The answer to all three questions, obviously, was no. The point is that the church exists in Christ. The church was brought into being by Christ because Christ died for them, as being baptized in His name indicated. Paul, as he developed later in his letter, really believed the church to be the body of Christ. To be divided into parties is to mutilate the body of Christ. If you entered a room, and you found parts of a body strewn around the room, how would you react? Your reaction would be no less than horror at such a grotesque sight and treatment of a human body.

No less grotesque is a church that splits itself into factions or parties and thus mutilates the body of Christ. With our heavy emphasis upon individualism in our society, it is difficult for us to be sensitive to the *corporate personality* of the church. The church manifests the corporate person of Christ. The church is not *like* a body; it *is* the body of Christ. If I hurt a member of the church, I am actually attacking the body of Christ. We should remember that when Paul, or Saul, persecuted the church, Christ asked him, "Saul . . . why do you persecute me?" (Acts 9:4). As Paul attacked Christians in various

ways, he actually attacked Christ. If we took the church as body of Christ seriously enough, our church problems could be solved without grotesque divisions and party spirit.

The Challenge of Worldly Wisdom (1:18–31; 2:6—3:4)

Paul was an intellectual who could be as theological or philosophical as he needed to be in order to communicate with his audience. Consider Acts 17, where he presented a strong witness to a group steeped in philosophical background. That his witness was effective is evidenced by the fact that some believed (Acts 17:34). What he spoke against at Corinth is the exaltation of a human wisdom to a place of prominence that displaced "Jesus Christ and him crucified" (2:2). To claim to have superior knowledge, placing oneself in superiority over fellow Christians, was an attitude and position directly opposite to Christ and Him crucified. Christ by his self-giving served the church, and so should the Christians of Corinth serve. Self-exultation is directly contrary to Christ and consequently directly contrary to the true nature of the church.

The Challenge of Unethical Conduct (5:1—6:20)

The city of Corinth was famous as a center of immoral behavior. "To live like a Corinthian," a proverbial Mediterranean saying arising out of the reputation of the old city of Corinth, denoted life loosed from moral restraints. Such conduct still existed in Corinth. Sexual immorality was rampant. Sacred prostitution, in relation to Aphrodite, the love goddess, was practiced. Evidently, some of the converts from the immoral Corinthian environment misunderstood Paul's emphasis upon freedom in Christ as freedom to do as one pleased.

Manifestations of sexual immorality crept into the Corinthian church. A man lived with his father's wife, his stepmother (5:1). Also, some were frequenting prostitutes (6:15–16). Paul urged separation from those in the church who engaged in immoral sexual behavior. The man living with his stepmother was to be delivered to Satan (5:5). This was a deliverance from their midst (the church) to dramatize and emphasize the repugnant nature of his sin. The ultimate purpose of this action, however, was to bring the man to his senses so that he would separate himself from the evil and be ready for the coming of the Lord (5:5).

As regards other immoral sexual behavior, Paul stressed that Christians' bodies were "members" of Christ (6:15). Christ and the church are one. For Christians to join their bodies to some immoral behavior, such as an act of sexual immorality, was to engage the body of Christ in that behavior. Their bodies and the body of the church were temples of the Holy Spirit (6:19).

Another matter concerned Paul greatly. The Christians took one another to court in order to settle disputes between themselves (6:1). Living as members of Christ meant that they should be able to seek and know the right thing to do. The implication is that to live as those who belong to Christ meant that harmony and unity based in Christ's will would be achieved. To do otherwise was to present a destructive, negative witness to those outside the church.

Therefore, immoral behavior, whatever its form, dishonors Christ. Such behavior denies who a believer really is. Immoral behavior eventuates in disrespect for another person. Disrespect for another person is disrespect for Christ.

The Challenge of Marriage and Celibacy (7:1–40)

Questions about marriage and celibacy arose in the Corinthian church. From Paul's discussion we learn that Paul answered in light of the expected immediate return of Christ. At this point he was not thinking of the possibility of a long interim period between the resurrection and the return of Christ. Paul's advice, therefore, was that everyone remain as they were (7:17). Consequently, he affirmed both celibacy and marriage. In light of the short time (7:29) until the return of Christ, freedom from distractions was to be preferred so that people could concentrate upon matters of the Lord (7:29–35). He felt that the single person had an advantage in this regard, but Paul did not count the married state to be less holy. A careful reading of the chapter reveals that he had a high view of marriage.

The Challenge of Idols (8:1—11:2)

Pagan worshipers who ate meat sacrificed to pagan deities believed they took in the spirit of the deity to whom the meat was sacrificed. Of course, followers of Christ understood that an idol was nothing and that there was only one God (8:4). In this new-found freedom, some followers of Christ ate meat left over from pagan rituals. Other disciples of Christ, however, rather immature in their faith, still perceived this as taking in the pagan deity. Paul warned that the practice, although he valued the freedom in Christ, might encourage a person weak in conscience to identify with the idol by eating the sacrificed meat (8:7). Also, a negative witness would be presented to outsiders. Paul was aware that people perceived his witness to Christ through the prisms of their backgrounds. He took that into consideration, for although he was free he became a "slave to everyone" in order that he might win them (9:19).

The Challenge of Certain Actions by Women Leaders (11:3–16)

Women found freedom in Christ. They sometimes did not know how to use that freedom in their context, a problem which the men had as well, as the matter of eating meat sacrificed to idols illustrates (see 8:1—11:2). Women who prayed or prophesied in that context with their heads uncovered put their reputations at risk. Respectable women did not appear outside the home with their heads uncovered. Prostitutes did. A head uncovered disconnected a woman from her husband. Consequently Paul emphasized the prevailing social wisdom and identity with the husband as head to protect the women's reputation and the witness they gave.

The Challenge to the Lord's Supper (11:17–34)

The Lord's Supper was a meal celebrated by the Corinthian church in a private home. The breaking of bread and the drinking of wine were the focal points of the meal. However, some participants arrived before others and turned it into a riotous party. The poorer

members who had to work longer arrived to little or no food.

Perhaps the early arrivals thought they celebrated the messianic banquet of the kingdom, but they missed what Jesus had told them to be. Their actions contradicted the basic meaning of the Lord's Supper, the self-giving of Jesus Christ. Paul reminded them of the Lord's commands (11:23–34). Indeed, the early arrivals acted selfishly. They were the ones taking the supper in an "unworthy manner" (11:27). To fail to meet your brother and sister at the table of the Lord on an equal basis and without concern and self-giving toward them was one way to take the meal in an unworthy manner.

The Challenge of Spiritual Gifts (12:1—14:40)

The church as the body of Christ has the means to function as a body, a living organism capable of accomplishing its purposes. The means were known as "spiritual gifts" (12:1). However, some people placed the gift of *glossolalia*, or tongues-speaking, as superior to all other gifts. Some pagan religions practiced forms of speaking in tongues, so the practice was not original to the Christian church. Perhaps some of the converts brought the practice with them when they came to Christ, giving it a particular Christian content and practice.

The attitudes of the tongues-speakers created disunity. Paul used the human body as a metaphor for the church to point to the reality of unity in Christ's body, the church. He wanted to demonstrate that there was variety in unity. The tongues-speakers wanted uniformity, but uniformity and unity are not the same. Variety can exist in unity, but not in uniformity. A variety of gifts existed in the church, and one gift was not to give a person reasons for feeling superior over someone who had a different gift. As Paul later emphasized in chapter 14, however, the gift of prophecy is more useful for building up the church than speaking in tongues.

The temptation of the church always is to take one experience of faith and make it normative for everybody else. The tendency of the church is to move toward uniformity and stifle variety and creativity which arise from the dynamic of the Holy Spirit. Some in the church at Corinth submitted to that temptation.

We do need to remember that the real spiritual gift of the Spirit to the church is the person. In fact, the first line of 12:1 can be translated, "Now concerning spiritual persons. . . ." Each person has abilities and characteristics which the Holy Spirit transforms into use for service to and through the church. The person is the gift to the church. All members, with all their variety of abilities and characteristics, are equally important to the functioning of the body.

The greatest gift, which everyone has or can have, is the gift of love. The kind of love spoken of here is *agape*. Paul reserved this noun to refer to the love which has its origin in God and is expressed, known, and experienced through Jesus Christ. Indeed, the positive love that Paul described in chapter 13 is a word portrait of Christ. For what *agape* (love) is, Christ is. It is a self-giving love.

Paul stressed in chapter 12 that every gift is to be used for the common good (12:7)—that is, for the common good of the church. A gift exercised without *agape* as the motivation misses the mark of being for the common good (13:1–3). Members needed to live out who they were in Christ out of love for their brothers and sisters in Christ.

Paul continued his discussion of spiritual gifts in chapter 14 by focusing upon two of the

The bema at Corinth, located in the center of the central row of shops. Includes the remains of the foundations.

speaking gifts, tongues-speaking and prophecy. To many people the word *prophecy* means the activity by which someone predicts the future. Actually, prophecy occurs whenever someone proclaims the will of God to a given situation. The predictive element in prophecy in the Old Testament is limited, and the prophets got into trouble not for predicting but for telling the will of God to people in a given situation. Prophecy is inspired preaching.

Throughout chapter 14, Paul showed the superiority of prophecy over tongues-speaking. Prophecy builds up the church (14:3), gives a clear message (14:6–12), is valuable for instruction (14:19), is a witness to outsiders (14:24), and lends itself to order (14:33,40). Paul did not disallow tongues-speaking, but he saw it as having little value for the church, and his conditions for the exercise of the gift virtually relegate it to a matter of private experience and practice.

The Challenge to the Resurrection (15:1–58)

Some of the Corinthians discounted the resurrection altogether. At the heart of the gospel, however, is the resurrection of Jesus Christ. Paul stressed that if there were no resurrection of the dead, then there was no need to preach the resurrection of Christ. Also, if Christ himself was not raised, then faith in Christ was valueless (15:12–19). "But Christ has indeed been raised from the dead," Paul affirmed (15:20). He enumerated the witnesses to the resurrection, which, of course, confirmed his own testimony (15:3–11).

Paul did not accept the Greek idea that a person had a soul which survived death in a bodiless existence. Neither did he find the idea of a revived corpse acceptable. He explained the resurrected body as a spiritual body. A person really dies and is really resurrected. The resurrected existence is not a bodiless existence, but the whole person in a spiritual-body existence. While he did not elaborate on the exact nature of the spiritual body, Paul did successfully counter the Greek idea and the idea of a revived corpse.

Final Instructions and Greetings (16:1–24)

First Corinthians concludes with a number of instructions and several greetings. At the time of this writing, Paul and his fellow-workers were in the process of collecting an offering among the Gentile churches for the Jerusalem needy. He gave instructions about this matter (16:1–4). After other instructions, Paul concluded the letter with a heart-warming benediction to this much-troubled church: "The grace of the Lord Jesus be with you. My love to all of you in Christ Jesus. Amen" (16:23–24).

2 Corinthians: Reconciliation Through Christ

Despite Paul's best efforts in writing 1 Corinthians, the church did not make progress in unity. Indeed, hostility toward him increased. He made a painful visit to Corinth (2 Cor. 2:1), which did not seem to accomplish much. He then wrote a "painful" or "tearful" letter (2 Cor. 2:1–9; 7:8) to them. Some interpreters feel that the painful letter may be contained in chapters 10—13 of 2 Corinthians. The letter shifts tone at that point, and the content reflects a situation in which Paul used stern words in the midst of great tension. Chapters 10—13 certainly reflect a painful relationship.

Titus perhaps delivered the painful letter to Corinth. Having left Ephesus, Paul went to Troas, where he expected to meet Titus (2 Cor. 2:12–13). Titus did not arrive, so Paul went into Macedonia where Titus finally caught up with him (2 Cor. 7:6). The painful letter and Titus's efforts evidently led to a change of attitude on the part of the Corinthian Christians. Consequently, from Macedonia Paul wrote 2 Corinthians with its strong note of reconciliation in chapters 1—7. This letter allows us to look into the inward Paul in particular detail. We see his anxiety, pain, anger, determination, and relief as he struggled to guide the Corinthian church.

Second Corinthians has three major sections. Chapters 1—7, the first major section of the letter and generally understood as the section reflecting reconciliation, takes us through the range of emotions, as in chapter 2 for example. Paul told about his painful visit (2:1), his affliction and anguish of heart in writing the painful letter (2:4), his anxiety (2:13), and then his exhilaration in the triumph which Christ gives (2:14). Paul shared his struggles with the church at various places in chapters 1—7, and in the process he proclaimed a victorious Christ as well as affirming the Corinthian believers.

Chapters 8—9 discuss the offering for Jerusalem and the Corinthians' support of the effort. Paul encouraged liberal, sacrificial giving on their part. He used other Gentile churches as examples to encourage generosity. Churches of Macedonia, for instance, had given sacrificially and joyfully (8:1–5). Of course, pivotal to the whole matter of giving for others was the self-giving of Christ (8:9). Paul fully expected the Corinthians to give sacrificially, pointing out to them that they would be blessed in the process (9:6–15).

The tone changes in chapters 10—13. Paul reflected on the criticism directed against him. He is bold when away from them, but humble when present with them (10:1), his critics claimed. Paul quoted them as saying, "His letters are weighty and forceful, but in person he is unimpressive and his speaking amounts to nothing" (10:10). By such criticisms Paul's opponents attacked the Corinthians' trust in him.

Although his opponents' identity is uncertain, they preached another Jesus (11:4). They were "super-apostles" (11:5), evidently presenting themselves with rather forceful and impressive expression as being much superior to Paul. Paul defended himself, being forced to boast of his own commitment, sacrifice, and service. Indeed, the "things that mark an apostle . . . were done among" them (12:12). In this way Paul defended the authenticity of his work and his apostleship. Despite the tough language arising out of obvious conflict, he closed his letter with a generous benediction, pronouncing grace, love, and fellowship upon them.

FOR STUDY AND REVIEW

IDENTIFY:

Aquila and Priscilla
Glossolalia
Agape
Prophecy
Corporate personality of the church

QUESTIONS FOR CONSIDERATION

1. What are the places and dates of writing for 1 and 2 Corinthians?

2. What are the correspondence contacts Paul and the Corinthians had with each other?

3. What were the problems of the church at Corinth?

4. What were the identities of the four factions (1 Cor. 1:12), and what beliefs might have distinguished each party?

5. How did Paul deal with the party division (1 Cor. 1:13)?

6. What actions by the Corinthians dishonored the Lord's Supper?

7. Why is prophecy superior to speaking in tongues?

8. What are the major divisions and content of 2 Corinthians?

FOR FURTHER READING

Barrett, C. K. *A Commentary on the First Epistle to the Corinthians. Harper New Testament Commentaries.* Edited by Henry Chadwick. New York: Harper & Row, 1968.

_____. *A Commentary on the Second Epistle to the Corinthians. Harper New Testament Commentaries.* Edited by Henry Chadwick. New York: Harper & Row, 1973.

Drane. *Introducing the New Testament.* San Francisco: Harper and Row, 1986: 313–26.

Martin, Ralph P. *2 Corinthians.* Volume 40, *Word Biblical Commentary.* Edited by David Hubbard and Glenn W. Barker. Waco: Word, 1986.

❖ 16 ❖

Galatians: Freedom in Christ

Writer

Where Paul was when he wrote to the Galatians is difficult to determine. Possible places of the origin of the letter are Ephesus, Macedonia, Antioch, and Corinth. Difficulties in dating the Epistle range from the belief that it was Paul's earliest letter, written around A.D. 48, to the belief that Paul wrote the letter shortly before he wrote Romans, around A.D. 56–57. The issues of origin and date are really tied to considerations as to the destination of the letter, or where the readers lived to whom Paul wrote.

Readers

In the third century B.C., Gauls invaded Asia Minor and eventually occupied a territory in the northern area named Galatia. By 25 B.C., the territory came completely under Roman rule. The Romans expanded the territory to include a portion of Central and Southern Asia Minor and made a new Roman province. They named the province Galatia.

Was Galatians addressed to churches in the territory of Galatia or to churches in the province of Galatia? Those who believe Paul addressed churches in the territory hold to what is called the *North Galatian Hypothesis*

(or *Territory Hypothesis*). Those who hold to an address for the readers in the Roman province hold to the *South Galatian Hypothesis* (or *Province Hypothesis*). While the destination of the letter does not affect its message, the location of its readers significantly impacts a reconstruction of Paul's life as the information about Paul in Acts and in Paul's letters, especially Galatians, are placed together.

Those who favor a North Galatian destination note that Paul visited the territory on his second missionary journey (Acts 16:6) and again on his third missionary journey (Acts 18:23), which means that Paul did missionary work in this area. Also, only people of the territory of Galatia, according to ancient records, referred to themselves as "Galatians." Soards points out that *galatai*, namely Galatians, in Greek is a variation of *keltai*, the name for Celts.[1] On the other hand, people in the province, of a diverse national and ethnic heritage, would not refer to themselves by the same name. Opponents to this position claim that the references to Paul's North Galatian visits indicate nothing about churches or mission work; he simply traveled through this area.

Proponents of the South Galatian hypothesis emphasize that Acts states plainly that Paul did missionary work in the southern

143

part of the Galatian province. Too, when Paul referred to groups of churches, he referred to them in terms of their Roman provincial location (1 Cor. 16:19; 2 Cor. 1:1; 8:1). Addressing the churches in Galatia was the best way to address all the churches in Asia Minor.

Involved in a final decision about the readers is determining the relationship of the visits to Jerusalem mentioned by Paul in Galatians as compared to the number of visits Paul made as recorded in Acts. Acts records five visits to Jerusalem (9:26; 11:30 and 12:25; 15:4; 18:22; 21:17), while Galatians mentions two visits (1:18; 2:1). How do these visits coincide with each other, or do they? The most important question is whether Paul wrote Galatians before or after the Jerusalem Council visit of Acts 15.

The visits can be reconciled, but reconciling them has generated extended and diverse opinions. One solution is to distinguish between the visits Paul mentions in the letter and the visits described in Acts. Paul was not interested in recounting all of the visits—only those which showed that he was not dependent upon anyone in Jerusalem for his authority to be an apostle and to preach his message to the Gentiles. The records of visits would correspond then as follows:

Visit 1 (Acts 9:26)   =   Galatians 1:18

Visit 2 (Acts 11:30; 12:25) =   Paul does not mention

Visit 3 (Acts 15:2-4)   =   Galatians 2:1

Paul does not mention the later visits to Jerusalem according to this arrangement, but he does mention a second visit to Galatia (Gal. 4:13), which probably corresponds to Acts 16:1–6. So Paul could have written from Corinth around A.D. 51–52 (at the close of his second missionary journey) or A.D. 54–55 from Ephesus (during his third missionary journey). Both of these dates would support the South Galatian hypothesis, although the North Galatian hypothesis would fit with the later date as well.

Another solution is seen in this correspondence of visits:

Visit 1 (Acts 9:26)   =   Galatians 1:18

Visit 2 (Acts 11:30; 12:25) =   Galatians 2:1

In this case Galatians would be written before the Acts 15:4 visit, which means that Paul wrote it before the Jerusalem Conference. This arrangement requires a dating of Galatians in A.D. 48 or 49, which would make Galatians the earliest letter of Paul of which we have a copy. If this date is correct, Paul wrote the letter, probably while at Antioch in Syria, to churches in Southern Galatia.

Neither of these arrangements answers all the questions or reconciles all the data.[2] Other proposed solutions exist. Whether written at the earlier or the later date, the message of Galatians remains the same—that of proclaiming across the centuries the liberty Christians have in Christ.

Message

Paul faced two problems when he wrote Galatians. First, opponents attacked his authenticity as an apostle, and he wrote to defend his apostleship. Second, the opponents of Paul preached a different gospel to the Galatians a different gospel, which some of the Galatian Christians followed (1:6). So Paul wrote to discredit their gospel and to defend the truth of the gospel of Christ (1:6–9,11–12).

Photo of west side of reconstructed Pergamum altar, taken from the porch looking out toward the northern projection, *Biblical Illustrator* Photo/David Rogers/British Museum.

At the heart of what the preachers of a false gospel advocated was the observance of certain laws (4:21; 5:4), including circumcision (5:2–6; 6:12) and the keeping of certain days, months, seasons, and years. Apparently these were times of Jewish ritual and legal observance. Evidently, the false gospel view was that Gentiles had to adopt and observe certain legal requirements before they could become Christians.

Interpreters ofter identify the opponents with the name *Judaizers*. Judaizers were those, probably exclusively Jews and not proselytes, who considered themselves to be loyal to the law and to Christ, both of which were necessary in their view in order to be part of being made right before God. How their concept of Christ related to their belief about the law is difficult to determine. Perhaps they looked upon Christ as the new interpreter of the law (in that sense a new Moses), and submission to the law as they perceived Christ to have taught it would make one right before God.[3]

Paul saw this as simply another form of legalism, an attempt to earn one's relationship to God rather than receiving it as a gift. The central message of Galatians is that justification is by faith alone (for examples, see 2:15–16; 3:2–3,11). Justification is right standing before God, where one is pronounced not guilty before God and finds full acceptance from Him and with Him.

With this great emphasis upon justification by faith alone, the letter to the Galatians has been pivotal to generations of Christians for understanding that salvation is not something one earns. Instead it is the relationship God gives to those who have faith in Jesus Christ. To say that salvation, or justification, is something that God gives is to speak of God's grace. Grace is God's gracious action toward us, in a way we do not earn or merit, to give us forgiveness, acceptance, and life. God offers all of this as a free gift. Our response, again, is not to merit or earn this in some way, but to live for Him by faith.

The message of Galatians is difficult to organize structurally. Paul's passionate presentation of the gospel is ruled by his interest in defending himself and keeping the Galatians out of the legalistic yoke of slavery. Nevertheless, unstructured developments can be followed in the letter (see box 16).

Box 16: An Outline of Contents

Salutation and greeting (1:1–5)
The Galatians' wrong choice (1:6–9)
Paul's defense of himself (1:10—2:14)
Justification by faith (2:15—4:31)
Freedom in Christ (5:1–26)
Practical instructions and benediction (6:1–18).

Salutation and Greeting (1:1–5)

Paul followed the normal letter-writing pattern but expanded upon it to speak to the Galatian problems. He was an apostle by the will of Jesus Christ and God the Father, not by human will (1:1), a charge his opponents brought against him. Despite the troubling situation caused by the Galatians, he still greeted them with "grace and peace" (1:3).

The Galatians' Wrong Choice (1:6–9)

Notice that no thanksgiving and assurances of prayer occur at this point the letter, as is true with other letters of Paul. He was angry at the Galatians and launched into a direct confrontation with them. He was "astonished" (1:6) that they so quickly departed from a gospel of the grace of Christ and turned to another gospel. In truth no other gospel exists, although some were preaching such. Paul emphasized the dangers of such preaching. The Galatians forgot the very foundation

of the gospel: the self-giving of Jesus Christ, an act of grace for the rescuing of those who believe (1:4,6).

Paul's Defense of Himself (1:10—2:14)

Paul's opponents accused him of preaching a gospel to please people, possibly because they believed he discarded the demands of the law and presented a non-demanding message that people could accept without much difficulty. By this initial confrontation with the Galatians, Paul demonstrated that he was not trying to please anyone (1:10). The gospel is not something made up. God gave it to him. None of the apostles—not even James, Peter, and John themselves—were the source of Paul's particular call by God or the content of what he preached (2:9). As for the law, he knew the law. Before his conversion, he had ardently subscribed to and defended the law (1:13–14). He had even persecuted the church which he now served. Christ changed all that and called him to preach among the Gentiles (1:16–17). His conflict with Simon Peter demonstrated the independence of his apostleship and his preaching from the influence of Peter or the Jewish leaders at Jerusalem (2:11–14).

Justification by Faith (2:15—4:31)

While Paul emphasized grace and justification by faith throughout, the heart of his passionate argument is in this section. The reported conflict with Peter gave him opportunity to stress justification by faith, because Peter's action of withdrawing table fellowship from the Gentiles affirmed the law, not justification by faith. Why Peter acted this way is a mystery. The representatives who came from Jerusalem (2:11–12) precipitated Peter's action.

Perhaps Peter feared how his having table fellowship with the Gentiles might play back in Jerusalem, but not so much with Christian Jews as non-Christian Jews. If so, the reason for his action is understandable although wrong. Perhaps he feared that his close fellowship with the Gentiles would cause Jews back in Jerusalem, whom he and others were trying to reach, to turn a deaf ear to the gospel of Christ. Consequently, the Jewish mission and all that he and his fellow workers were trying to do at Jerusalem would be undermined.[4]

Paul showed that this action did not affirm but denied the gospel. Jewish Christians should know that the law is not necessary for justification, because if the law justified (made them not guilty before God and placed them in right relationship to God) they would have no need to accept Christ by faith for their own justification. Indeed, "if righteousness could be gained through the law, Christ died for nothing!" (2:21).

As Paul continued his argument, he confronted the Galatians once again, even calling them "foolish" (3:1) for their departure from what they knew to be true (3:1–5). He pointed to Abraham as an example, Abraham's belief, not his law-keeping, made him righteous before God (3:6). The law had not yet been given. Paul appealed to other Old Testament examples and contexts to make his point: the "book of the Law" (1:10–16); the promise to Abraham and his seed and the identity of the true heirs of Abraham (3:15—4:20); and an argument based upon the slave woman and her son and the free woman and her son (4:21–31).

Kneeling Satyr (about 200 B.C.). From Pergamon in Greece. The satyr kneels before a twisted tree trunk. *Biblical Illustrator* Photo/David Rogers/Nelson Gallery of Art.

Actually no one has advantage or privilege over anyone else in access to God; with God people are not divided into special classes or races. Paul made this great statement: "There is neither Jew nor Greek, slave nor free, male nor female, for you are all one in Christ Jesus" (3:28). All belong to God in Jesus Christ equally; all potential believers have equal access to belong to Christ through faith. With God, human beings stand on level ground. This is the reality of equality that Paul learned from Christ in his conversion experience (1:13–16), for no works of merit of Paul, who persecuted the church of God, caused God to love him, God just loved him (2:20).

Freedom in Christ (5:1–26)

People, because they are not self-sufficient or gods, are going to be in bondage to something. They can bind themselves to their own illusion of self-sufficiency, to religion, to some philosophy or movement, or even to the work they do or the status they have. The only bondage that really gives freedom is the bondage to Jesus Christ. Christ takes away from a person that which robs of life and gives to a person that which is life. "It is for freedom that Christ has set us free." (5:1).

Paul had in mind the demands of the law, which become a "yoke of slavery" if one submits (5:1). The law can point out failure and make a demand that a person not have such failure, but the law has no power to forgive, restore, and accept. Therefore, the law is a constant source of condemnation. Although in the Christian church we know that salvation comes as a free gift, composed of both forgiveness and restoration, we can have our own set of rules and regulations which becomes to us a "Law" by which we try to earn God's favor. Paul's letter reminds us of God's grace and justification freely given to us for our relationship to Him.

In Paul's view, law was not bad (see Rom. 7:7–20). Law does show us our inability to deliver ourselves from bondage and our need to turn to a deliverance that is freely given, one we do not have to merit or earn. Does this mean that standards of right and wrong do not apply? Of course not. For those in Christ, right living is a function of the faith and love relationship they have with God in Christ.

Paul emphasized that doing the law in some supreme sense, such as being circumcised, is not a matter of importance in the Christ relationship. He wrote, "The only thing that counts is faith expressing itself through love" (5:6). He further wrote, "The entire law is summed up in a single command: 'Love your neighbor as yourself'" (5:14). Right living, therefore, arises from within a person out of the faith-love relationship in Christ.

If believers are in Christ, they are in the "Spirit." If they are not in Christ, they are in the "sinful nature" (5:16). Again, the actual word for "sinful nature" is the Greek word *sarx*, which literally means "flesh." However, this is not flesh as substance but as a kind of existence that people are in when apart from Christ. To be in the Spirit is to be in an existence in relationship to Christ. Out of the flesh existence flow destructive things: "sexual immorality, impurity and debauchery; idolatry and witchcraft; hatred, discord, jealousy," and so forth (see 5:19–21). Out of the Spirit existence flow positive, life building and life-enhancing things: "love, joy, peace, patience, kindness, goodness, faithfulness," and so forth (see 5:22–23). To be in the flesh is slavery, to be in the Spirit is freedom.

Practical Instructions and Benediction (6:1–18)

Paul encouraged the Galatian Christians to some specific practical applications of living out their lives in Christ or in the Spirit. They should restore a person who has fallen, carry each other's burdens, and act responsibly themselves (6:1–5). They should remember that what a person sows is what he will reap. Since this is true, they should not become weary in doing what is good, for the harvest of the good will come (6:7–10). Again, Paul warned them not to give heed to the false teachers (6:12–16). He closed the letter with an emphasis on grace: "The grace of our Lord Jesus Christ be with your spirit" (6:18).

FOR STUDY AND REVIEW

IDENTIFY:

Judaizers
Grace
Justification

QUESTIONS FOR CONSIDERATION

1. What are the possible places of the origin of Galatians and the possible dates for the writing of Galatians?

2. Who were the opponents of Paul? What did they preach?

3. What are the North (territory) and South (province) hypotheses? What are some of the factors supporting each hypothesis?

4. What are two patterns to making the Jerusalem visits of Acts correspond to the Jerusalem visits recorded in Galatians?

5. What distinction is made between "Spirit" and "flesh" in the discussion of Galatians 5?

FOR FURTHER READING

Carson, D. A., Douglas J. Moo, and Leon Morris. *An Introduction to the New Testament.* Grand Rapids: Zondervan Publishing House, 1992: 289–303.

Cole, R. Alan. *Galatians.* Rev. ed., *Tyndale New Testament Commentaries.* General editor Leon Morris. Grand Rapids: William B. Eerdmans, 1989.

Kümmel, W. G. *Introduction to the New Testament,* translated by H. C. Kee. Revised and enlarged ed. Nashville: Abingdon Press, 1975: 294–304.

ENDNOTES

1. Marion L. Soards, *The Apostle Paul: An Introduction to His Writing and Teaching* (New York: Paulist Press, 1987), 57.

2. For a survey of the possibilities of destination and date, see Donald Guthrie, *New Testament Introduction,* 3rd. ed. rev. (Downers Grove, Illinois: InterVarsity Press, 1970), 450-65.

3. Soards, *Paul,* 61.

4. F. F. Bruce, *Paul: Apostle of the Heart Set Free* (Grand Rapids: Eerdmans, 1977), 176–77.

Ephesians: The People of God in Christ

The Prison Epistles

Ephesians is one of four letters (Ephesians, Philippians, Colossians, and Philemon) of Paul known as the prison Epistles. The content of each indicates that Paul wrote them in prison. The place of origin for the prison letters is uncertain. In fact, Paul may have written from two different places. Two imprisonments in the life of Paul are certain, Caesarea (Acts 23:33; 24:27) and Rome (Acts 28:16). A third possible place for imprisonment is Ephesus. Although a direct statement about Paul being in prison at Ephesus was not made, Paul did write about hardships there which might reflect imprisonment (1 Cor. 15:32; 2 Cor. 1:8–11).

Tradition supports Rome as the place of origin. But the primary difficulty with Rome as the site is the distance between Rome and the churches who received the letters. Philippians, for example, indicates at least four journeys to and from Paul's prison site and Philippi. Other journeys between the two places were anticipated by Paul, as indicated by the letter (Phil. 2:19,25). The distance would have made extremely difficult the journeys and anticipated journeys alluded to in Philippians. The Ephesus site for imprisonment is attractive as a possibility because of its proximity to Philippi. Still, Rome has the favored position as the site for the origin of the prison letters.

If written from Ephesus, the letters would be dated around A.D. 55–57; if from Caesarea, A.D. 57–59; if from Rome, 60–62. What is true without doubt, however, is that the prison letters give us, by words and the examples of Paul and the churches, a moving witness to Christ.

Writer

Paul had a rather long history in relation to Ephesus. On his second missionary journey he, together with Aquila and Priscilla, left Greece and went to Ephesus. While Paul went on to Antioch, Aquila and Priscilla remained there to continue the work (Acts 18:18–21). Paul returned on his third missionary tour (Acts 19:1), staying this time for three years (Acts 20:31). Ephesus became a center for Christian work in the area and was later associated with the apostle John and the Johannine writings.

Ephesians is one letter over which much discussion occurs about Paul's authorship. The discussion revolves around such questions as these: How are the differences from Paul's other letters in theological emphasis, vocabulary, and style to be explained? Since

Ephesians has such identity with Colossians, is it not likely that someone copied and used Colossians to communicate a message in the name of Paul? In answer, much vocabulary, theological emphasis, and style are the same as in Paul's other letters. Too, the argument about interdependence of the two could be used in favor of the apostle. Could such intricate relationship between two writings exist without the same writer?

In an effort to account for Ephesians in relation to the other letters of Paul, Goodspeed proposed an interesting theory. He suggested that Ephesians was written after Paul's death to serve as a cover letter for a collection of Paul's letters made around A.D. 90. Part of the reason for his suggestion is that Ephesians does gather up a number of important Pauline emphases revealed in other letters.[1] However, the traditional position of Pauline authorship is strong, the letter was probably written by him from Rome between A.D. 60–62.

Readers

While some translations of the Bible, following some Greek manuscripts, indicate that the recipients were the Ephesians, other translations, following other Greek manuscripts, omit the reference to the Ephesians in 1:1. How are these two manuscript traditions to be explained? The letter lacks the personal contact usually associated with letters to one specific church. Perhaps it was a circular letter, a copy of which was to be carried from church to church, or several copies circulated among several churches. If so, the name of the recipients might have been left blank, with the name of the church to be filled in whenever the letter made its way to a particular congregation. Or perhaps it was simply a general letter, with a copy of the letter being identified with the Ephesian church at a later date so that the title and the name of the recipients became identified with the church at Ephesus.[2]

Ephesians very much parallels Colossians, and Paul may have developed some of the themes sounded in Colossians more completely in order to serve a more general audience. Because of its close affinity with Colossians, some think that Ephesians, without an actual identity of the readers in 1:1, may have been the letter to the Laodiceans referred to in Colossians 4:16. In any case, the letter is general in tone, designed to address several churches with its message. The readers were Gentiles.

Message

Christ in His Church and the church in Christ may serve as the overall message of the letter. Some of the loftiest thought in the New Testament on Christ in relationship to His people is found here. Christ is unequivocally the exalted head of all things as well as head of the church (1:22). This reality issues in the reality of oneness with God and oneness with each other, a major emphasis throughout Ephesians. The letter has a salutation (1:1–2), two major sections (1:3—3:21 and 4:1—6:20), and a conclusion (6:21–24). A doxology (3:20–21) denotes the division between the two major sections, although both sections have some common themes. For our purposes, we will emphasize the oneness with Christ in the first major section and the oneness Christ's people have with each other in the second major section.

The Oneness with Christ (1:3—3:21)

After a brief salutation, Paul praised God for what He had done in Jesus Christ (1:3–14). He wrote of the security that believers have because God chose them (1:4,11). Through Christ they experienced grace, forgiveness, redemption, and knowledge of the "mystery of his will" (1:7–9). *Mystery*, a word related to the mystery religions where only those initiated knew the secrets of the religion, is a word Paul adapted to special use. The mystery is really an open secret. God made plain His purposes for all to see if they will see. The mystery made known is God's purpose "to bring all things in heaven and on earth together under one head, even Christ" (1:10). This mystery has much meaning and many applications as the letter affirms, because involved in this open secret is the total revelation of God in Jesus.

Expressions of thanksgiving and prayer follow. The prayers in the readers' behalf include petitions that they will understand the blessings they have in Christ. Christ is head (1:22) of the church, His body. Ancient physiology viewed both life and the thinking processes as residing in the head. Christ, therefore, as head of His body, the church, gives life and direction to the church.

Since Christ acted to give life to the church, Paul reminded his Gentile readers that they were made alive to become one with God's people, both Jews and Gentiles (2:1–22). Out of diverse people, divided and hostile to one another much of the time, God made in Christ Jesus "one new man" (2:15). The expression "one new man" means "one new humanity." God has made, therefore, a new people in this world, which is the church, composed of Jews and Gentiles.

Ephesians confronts us with the lofty nature and place of the church. We may think certain political, institutional, or economic structures are first in the hierarchy of structures. Actually the church is a living community, made alive and given direction by Christ, and it is the most strategic "society" in the world. As Christ makes the church by people's response to Him in faith, barriers of alienation and hostility among humanity fall. The significance of this reality for our divided and warring world is obvious.

The phrase "in Christ," which takes the form of other expressions such as "in him" and "in Christ Jesus," is important to Paul's thought. The phrase has basically three connotations.

First, "in Christ" connotes a mystical sense by which the people of God know their identity and nature. In this sense Christ is in them and they are in Christ, something like our being in the air and the air being in us.

Second, to be in Christ is to be in the eschatological age. That is, Christ's people are in the last age of existence inaugurated and determined by Christ. "Last age of existence" does not refer to a chronologically determined countdown of time, but to a time of existence whose nature, purpose, and destiny are determined by God in Jesus Christ.

Third, many times Paul used "in Christ" to mean "in church." Of course this is not a reference to a church building, denominational structure, or church organization. Rather, the church is the body of Christ, and the people who belong to Christ make up His body. Identifying the church as body is more than metaphor here, for the church really is the visible body of Christ in this world when it acts in accord with His will.

Statuette of a ram found at the altar of the temple of Artemis at Ephesus. *Biblical Illustrator* Photo/David Rogers/Ephesus Museum.

A statement about Paul's relationship to the mystery (3:1–13), a prayer for the readers (3:14–19), and a benediction (3:20–21) close the first major section of the letter. Paul emphasizes that the mystery of God was "made known" to him "by revelation" (3:3). The mystery, again, is that God makes a diverse people into one people in Jesus Christ (3:6). Paul was a servant dedicated to spreading this good news, a privilege granted to him by God's grace (3:7). The prayer is primarily for the readers to know the strength and love they have in Christ, and the benediction affirms the blessing of the One who "is able to do immeasurably more than all we ask or imagine according to his power that is at work within us" (3:20).

One With Each Other (4:1—6:20)

In the second major section, Paul gave attention to the church living out its relationship to Christ in the world. The church should be characterized by oneness and service (4:4–16). The church is one body with one hope, one Lord, one baptism, and one God and Father (4:4–6). Within this one body people have different functions of service, "some to be apostles, some to be prophets, some to be evangelists, and some to be pastors and teachers" (4:11). These are leadership functions "to prepare God's people for works of service" (4:12). In other words, the whole church, including the leaders, is a body of servants or ministers.

The church also should live as people who belong to Christ in matters of everyday conduct. Since they have been made new (4:20–23), they have "put off" (4:25), as one would put aside an old garment, falsehood, stealing, unwholesome talk, bitterness, and other sinful actions and attitudes. They also are to put on new actions and attitudes, such as speaking truthfully, sharing with the needy, building others up, and being kind, compassionate, and forgiving (4:25–32).

The church is to live a life of love in imitation of God as He is known in Christ (5:1–2), which imitation excludes all pagan practices (5:3–20). They are no longer children of the darkness, darkness representing evil, but of light (5:8). Family relationships should be determined by mutual commitment to one another, as is true in the relationship between Christ and his body (5:21—6:9). Also, those in Christ should be prepared for moral warfare (6:10–20). Preparation consists of putting on the "full armor of God" (6:13–18).

Notice that *none* of the weapons mentioned—truth, righteousness, peace, salvation, word of God—are weapons of violence. In a world of violence, where most things were determined by the mightiest sword, Jesus never advocated identity with or use of violence. Paul understood that as well. Remember, before becoming a disciple of Christ, Paul used violence against his enemies, the church of Jesus Christ. After meeting Christ, he never advocated any weapon but the truth of Christ against his enemies. Like his Master, Paul never called for taking up violence as a means for accomplishing the objectives of Christ.

Finally, the letter closes with personal notes (6:21–24). Tychichus is recommended as a source of information about Paul's situation. In the meantime, Paul prayed for his readers to be blessed with peace, love, faith, and grace.

FOR STUDY AND REVIEW

QUESTIONS FOR CONSIDERATION

1. What are some of the issues as regards the authorship of Ephesians?
2. What is the difficulty in determining the recipients of the letter (1:1)?
3. What is the overall message of Ephesians?
4. What is the meaning of "mystery" (1:7–9)?
5. What does "in Christ" mean?
6. What is the function of leadership (4:11–12)?
7. How does one prepare for moral warfare? Are Christians to use violence in this warfare?

FOR FURTHER READING

Barth, Markus. *Ephesians. Anchor Bible.* Volumes 34A and 34B. Edited by W. F. Albright and D. N. Freedman. Garden City, New York: Doubleday, 1974.

Harrison, F. F. *Introduction to the New Testament,* rev. ed. (Grand Rapids: Wm. Eerdmans Publishing Company, 1982), 331–40.

Martin, Ralph P. *Ephesians, Colossians, and Philippians. Interpretation.* Edited by

James L. Mays. Atlanta: John Knox Press, 1991.

ENDNOTES

1. Edgar J. Goodspeed, *An Introduction to the New Testament* (Chicago: University of Chicago, 1937), 222.

2. For a discussion and alternative possibilities, see C. Milo Connick, *The New Testament: An Introduction to Its History, Literature, and Thought,* 2nd ed. (Encino, Calif.: Dickenson, 1978) 320.

✣ 18 ✣

Philippians: Joy in Christ

Writer and Readers

Acts 16 tells of Paul's vision of a man from Macedonia whose request was, "Come over to Macedonia and help us" (Acts 16:9). In responding to that call, Paul eventually went to Philippi, on his second missionary journey, and a church resulted from the work. This church, the first to be founded on European soil, became one with which Paul had a warm, enduring relationship. The members seemed to accept his authority and authenticity as an apostle, quite unlike some at Galatia and Corinth. No need existed for him to defend himself since they accepted him and obviously cared for him (see 1:3–11; 4:1,10–20).

After Paul's imprisonment, the church kept in contact with him. He had ministered to them; now they wanted to minister to him. They collected an offering for him and sent it by Epaphroditus. The church expected Epaphroditus to remain and assist Paul, but he became ill. Paul sent him back to Philippi with this letter to the church (2:25–30).

Message

Paul wrote the letter to share his appreciation for the Philippians and to thank them for their gift and ministry, to explain Epaphroditus' recovery from illness and calm their fears about his well-being (2:26), and to affirm Epaphroditus' success in carrying out the church's ministry to Paul. In addition, he dealt with certain matters troubling the church.

Introduction (1:1–11)

After addressing and greeting the Philippians, Paul gave an expression of thanksgiving for them, as he did for other churches in other letters. However, this expression is one of the strongest among the thanksgivings of Paul and is characterized by joy. *Joy* or *rejoicing* surface at other points in his message to the Philippians. Consequently, joy is the keynote of the letter.

Paul's View of His Imprisonment (1:12–30)

Paul put his imprisonment in perspective. Of course, he wanted to be released (1:19), but more important was that his imprisonment serve to advance the gospel of Jesus Christ. He was ready to die for the cause or to remain alive.

Forum and Agora at Philippi looking east showing the southern row of shops and the large rectangular pavement area of the Forum. *Biblical Illustrator* Photo/David Rogers.

Service in Christ (2:1–18)

In this section, verses 5–11 form the centerpiece of this letter. Paul presented Christ's self-giving service for the Philippians to see and follow. Because of the rather formal nature of the statement, this may have been an early Christian teaching that Paul learned from witnesses before him. It is a hymn to Christ, so called because of its rhythmic and poetic qualities. The hymn gives the whole history of Christ, beginning with His preexistence through His exaltation, with God ultimately bestowing upon Him the "name that is above every name" (2:9).

A major point is that Christ "did not consider equality with God something to be grasped" (v. 6), instead He became a human and a servant at that (v. 7). Contrary to what human beings normally do (attempt to deny their humanness and make themselves into gods or God), Jesus was a human being. He reversed the action of Adam, who attempted to become a god and denied his humaness. Christ became a servant. A moment's reflection on that reality should evoke appreciation. God in Jesus Christ, the ruler of all things, becomes a servant in order to serve those over whom He is sovereign.

Paul's Plans for Timothy and Epaphroditus (2:19–30)

Paul hoped that he would be able to send Timothy to them, apparently to help and encourage them in their ministry. That Paul thought highly of Timothy is obvious. He followed his affirmation of Timothy with information and commendation of Epaphroditus. Epaphroditus' assignment was to be of assistance to Paul, so Paul indicated that Epaphroditus accomplished his task. He certainly did not want the Philippians to think Epaphroditus failed in his mission as he planned to send Epaphroditus back to them.

Warnings about Legalism and Lawlessness (3:1-21)

Evidently the Judaizers, by means of their legalistic approach to Christianity, tried to influence the church at Philippi. Paul described them as "mutilators of the flesh" (3:2), a reference to circumcision. They probably taught that the Philippians had no assurance of salvation unless they engaged in circumcision and some other Jewish prerequisites contained in the law.

But Paul pointed out that if that had anything to do with determining one's relationship to Christ, he would have met the requirements with ease. He was circumcised, a Hebrew, a Pharisee, and a keeper of the law (3:4–6). However, through faith in Christ, he did not have to generate a righteousness of himself (3:8) in order to please God, efforts which he considered futile anyway in comparison to gaining Christ through faith (3:7–8). So he warned the Philippians to avoid these teachers. They were not advocates of the gospel.

Many people today find strength for daily living in particular statements made in Philippians. In 3:12–14 Paul compared his Christian pilgrimage to an athletic race. As an athlete in a race will lose if he always looks back, so the Christian must forget the past, refusing to live in or by the past, and strain "toward what is ahead" (3:13). Paul's prize was Jesus Christ. This gave direction to his life in the present and moved him toward the ultimate fellowship with his Lord in the resurrection (3:14). Again, Christians today are called to follow Christ, who gives the right direction to the race we are in. As we look to our destiny, we know we are headed to fulfillment of life in an ultimate sense in our own resurrection.

Conflict and Encouragement (4:1-23)

Euodia and Syntyche, two women in the church, had a running feud for some reason. Paul appealed to them to "agree with each other in the Lord" (4:2). To move the focus from themselves to Christ was the one possibility for unity. To so move the focus meant that they put the concerns of Christ before their own concerns.

The rest of this chapter includes encouragement and thanksgiving. Paul urged the Philippians to rejoice (4:4) and to keep the true and honorable (4:8–9). He himself rejoiced in their concern for him and their partnership in the work (4:14–20). Again, many Christians today have found Paul's words particularly helpful. His injunction to "rejoice!" (4:4) encourages us to have an attitude of appreciation for life and what God is doing in us and around us. Too, after telling of his own struggles and suffering, Paul stated, "I can do everything through him who gives me strength" (4:13).

Some people think, unfortunately, that if they believe this enough, their fears, problems, or obstacles will go away. Problems or our own limitations do not usually go away. When they do not go away, people may fix blame upon themselves in some way because they have not merited the strength of Christ by having enough faith. This makes a legalistic transaction out of Paul's statement.

Negative circumstances do not always go away, but we are able to cope, overcome, or accomplish victory in the face of challenge because Christ is with us. His strength aids our strength. Therefore, we have the courage to go ahead, even bringing our fears and feelings of inadequacy along with us. That kind of encouragement to courageous Christian living is prominent in Philippians. Having given affirmation to the church who encouraged him so much, therefore, and having accomplished his purposes for writing, Paul closed the letter with his characteristic warm benediction (4:23).

FOR STUDY AND REVIEW

IDENTIFY:

Epaphroditus
Joy
Hymn to Christ
Euodia and Syntyche

QUESTIONS FOR CONSIDERATION

1. What was the history of Paul's relationship with the Philippians?
2. What is the overall message Paul intended to communicate in the letter?
3. What were the Judaizers preaching?
4. Of what significance to Christians today is Paul's illustration of himself running a race?

FOR FURTHER READING

Caird, G. B. *Paul's Letters from Prison.* Oxford: Oxford University Press, 1976.
Hawthorne, Gerald F. *Philippians. Word Biblical Entaries.* Edited by David Hubbard and Glenn W. Barker. Waco, Texas: Word, 1983.

19

Colossians: The Sufficiency of Christ

Writer

Some interpreters doubt that Paul wrote this letter, for many of the same reasons as mentioned in the discussion about of Ephesians. Colossians parallels Ephesians closely in content, which has led to the rejection of one or the other or both as being Pauline. The theology, vocabulary, and style, at some points, seem to be uncharacteristic of Paul. The nature of the heresy confronting the Christians at Colossae has been a reason for attributing pseudonymous authorship for Colossians. The heresy, the argument goes, could not have reached the level of development shown in the letter, by Paul's time, but would require a date late in the first century; or, more probably, the first half of the second century.

More recent opinions reflect that a greater variety and development of ideas existed in the first century than previously thought possible.[1] The letter itself says that Paul, along with the support of Timothy, wrote the letter (1:1). Any argument brought against that claim has an argument of equal weight to counter, so the traditional position of Pauline authorship has wide acceptance among scholars.

We have no record that Paul ever visited the city. Epaphras, one of Paul's fellow workers, probably was the person who evangelized the area (1:7). Tychicus delivered the letter from Paul to the Colossians (4:7-8).

Readers

The letters of Philemon and Colossians are related. Colossians addresses the congregation as a whole, and Philemon addresses an individual within the congregation (see Col. 4:7–8,17; Philem. 2,8–12). Consequently, Paul had two sources of information about the church, Onesimus and Epaphras. Both came to Paul for different reasons while he was in prison.

Paul learned from them of a false "philosophy" (2:8) that threatened to lead the church away from the reality of Christ. The philosophy gave central place to cosmic powers; these were angelic beings that were worshiped and believed to possess the fullness of God (see 1:16; 2:8,9,18). In addition, certain legalistic and ascetic elements belonged to the philosophy (2:20–23). Some interpreters identify the philosophy as "incipient Gnosticism," or Gnosticism in its beginning stages, because they believe a defined Gnosticism developed only in the second century.

Adherents of Gnosticism (See Chapter 6 for a fuller discussion), a term from modern times to designate certain ill-defined philosophical ideas of the first and second centuries, perceived all matter to be evil, including the human body. Spirit and matter were incompatable, thus creating a dualism in which spirit was over against matter. Through secret or special knowledge (*gnosis*, the Greek word for knowledge, hence the designation Gnostic or Gnosticism) revealed by Jesus himself, the spirit of a person could free itself from evil matter and find its home among the cosmic, angelic beings. Such developed Gnosticism probably was not present at Colossae when Paul wrote.

Other interpreters identify the false philosophy of Colossians as a ritualistic Judaism tempered by ascetic and dualistic tendencies. Withdrawal from the evil world as much as possible would represent ascetic influences (2:20–23). Seeing the world as divided into good spirit and evil matter would represent the dualistic tendencies. Regardless of the exact identity of the philosophy, it confronted the Colossian Christians with beliefs and ideas popular in much of Greek culture and in some people of Jewish background.

Message

Paul had an answer for them: Christ. Christ is supreme, not simply one among elemental spirits of the cosmos. Christ is the unity of all things, including humanity and creation. Christ is indwelling presence, and He is the wisdom and knowledge people need. The message of Paul to the Colossians is that in every way Christ is sufficient; nothing needs to be added to their relationship with Him to make right their relationship with God.

Introduction (1:1-14)

After a brief salutation Paul gave thanks for the Colossians, having heard and learned of their faith, love, and witness. He told them specifically of his prayers for them and ended the section by trumpeting the redemption in Jesus Christ, which prepares the way for the primary thrust of his letter.

The All-Sufficient Christ (1:15–20)

These verses constitute the high-water mark of the letter. They are called by many interpreters a "hymn to Christ" because of their rhythmic and poetic structure. They contain a lofty statement about Christ and should be considered, although briefly, in their several elements. Christ is:

1. "the image of the invisible God" (1:15). He is not image in the sense of a reproduction or likeness, but in the sense of essence. Therefore, we can know who God is by knowing Christ. Knowledge of Him is the knowledge needed, not the so-called hidden knowledge of the errant philosophy.
2. "firstborn" (1:15). "Firstborn" does not mean the first among created beings and things, but first in the sense of having priority before all created beings and things.
3. creator (1:16). Just as Christ is God's expression of Himself in salvation, so Christ is God's expression of Himself in creation. In Christ we know God the Savior. In Christ, also, we know God the Creator. Matter and the created order are not evil, as adherents of the false philosophy at Colossae believed.
4. "before all things, and in him all things hold together" (1:17). Rather than the fragmented universe pictured by the heresy, Christ unites all things in harmony. His superiority "before all things" is prominent in this hymn.

5. "the head of the body, the church" (1:18). The Christians at Colossae were to know themselves as in Christ and belonging to Him. As head, Christ gives the church life and direction.

6. "firstborn from among the dead" (1:18). Here again is the emphasis upon Christ's priority, not first in order of happening or appearance, but over all things by virtue of His resurrection. He has all power and authority, even power over death.

7. the "fullness" of God (1:19). All the revelation of God is contained in Him. He is not, as the false philosophy might teach, one of the angelic beings of partial revelation standing among a hierarchy of beings between God and humanity.

8. Reconciler (1:20). In His unifying work, Christ removes estrangement existing between God and all things. He reconciles (makes them come together) them to God. Of course, human beings are the focal point of this reconciling work.

In this brief hymn, Paul struck at the heart of the false philosophy. The created order is not evil, divided up by the war between spirit and matter and fragmented by the influences of principalities and powers or angelic beings. Human beings have been and are separated from God by their own evil deeds (see 1:21). Nevertheless, they are made one in Christ through faith. But the really dominant fact of this hymn is that Christ is sufficient, and He is the only One who is sufficient for the world's salvation.

The Reconciling Work of Christ (1:21—2:7)

Paul emphasized the reconciling work of Christ to the church. Though they were previ-

ously separated from God by their evil deeds (1:21), Christ removed their estrangement from Him. Paul's ministry among them in itself was part of that reconciling work of Christ (1:24–29). Paul wanted the church to know unity in Christ (2:2) and to remain firm in their faith (2:5), "rooted and built up in him, strengthened in the faith" (2:7).

Christ's Sufficiency for Status Before God (2:8—3:4)

Elements of the false philosophy surface in this discussion along with Paul's responses. He contrasted human tradition as the truth about God with that of Christ and stated the incarnation (God becoming human by virtue of the union of the human and divine in Christ Jesus) in his own way. He said, "For in Christ all the fullness of the Deity lives in bodily form, and you have been given fullness in Christ, who is the head over every power and authority" (2:9).

Since the church members have the fullness of God by being in Christ, Christ is the source of their knowledge and conduct. Therefore, they do not need to take their status of relationship with God on the basis of someone telling them they should be circumcised (2:11–12) or what they should "eat or drink" (2:16) or what special days they should observe (2:16,20–23). They are safe and secure with Christ and can concentrate on the "things above" (3:1).

Right Living in Christ (3:5—4:6)

Although Paul dealt with the Colossians' relationship to Christ against a theological and philosophical backdrop, he did not neglect speaking of the practical implications of that relationship. Since Christ is who He is and since they are in Him, certain attitudes and actions result. Some things should be put out of their lives, such as "sexual immorality, impurity, lust, evil desires and greed" (3:5). In addition, they must "rid" themselves of "anger, rage, malice, slander, filthy language," and lying to each other (3:8–9).

Other things should be "put on" according to their new nature in Christ, such as "compassion, kindness, humility, gentleness and patience," and forgiveness (3:12–13). Family relationships and master-slave relationships are to be dominated by love and service to one another (3:18—4:1). Christians' concern is to be exercised for those outside the community as well. They are to pray for an open "door" so that Paul may be able to proclaim the "mystery of Christ" to others (4:3). They also are to act graciously toward outsiders (4:5–6). Being in Christ, consequently, is a way of life the church follows in its daily conduct.

Final Greetings (4:7–10)

Personal notes bring the letter to a close. Tychicus, who brought the letter from Paul to Colossae, could fill them in about Paul's personal affairs. Also, Onesimus brought the Philemon letter (or perhaps Tychicus had the responsibility to deliver that one as well) and traveled with Tychicus. After conveying greetings from Aristarchus, Mark, Jesus who is called Justus, Epaphras, Luke, and Demas, Paul sent greetings to others. Obviously he had many contacts and much help while he was in prison.

In addition, he encouraged the Colossians to read the letter to the Laodiceans. Ephesians or Philemon may have been that letter,

although certainty is beyond our grasp at this point.

FOR STUDY AND REVIEW

IDENTIFY:

Epaphras
Incipient Gnosticism
Ritualistic Judaism

QUESTIONS FOR CONSIDERATION

1. What were some of the elements of the false philosophy?

2. What are the elements of the "hymn to Christ," and what do they mean?

3. What connections do Tychicus and Onesimus and the letters of Ephesians, Colossians, and Philemon have with each other?

FOR FURTHER READING

Bruce, F. F. *Paul: Apostle of the Heart Set Free.* Grand Rapids: Eerdmans, 1977: 407–23.

Caird, G. B. *Paul's Letters from Prison.* Oxford: Oxford University Press, 1976.

Martin, R. P. *The Epistles of Paul the Apostle to the Colossians and Philemon.* Grand Rapids: Eerdmans, 1960.

ENDNOTE

1. For discussions, see Everett F. Harrison, *Introduction to the New Testament*, rev. ed. (Grand Rapids: Wm. B. Eerdmans Publishing Company, 1982), 326-28; F. F. Bruce, *Paul: Apostle of the Heart Set Free* (Grand Rapids: Eerdmans, 1977), 408–12; for opposing view see

Marion L. Soards, *The Apostle Paul: An Intro-duction to His Writing and Teaching* (New York: Paulist Press, 1987), 139–42.

20

Philemon: In Christ, All Are Family

Writer

Philemon is related closely to Colossians, so it is discussed here rather than after Titus. As Paul gave his closing greetings in Colossians, he said that Tychicus, who is delivering news from Paul, will fill them in on other questions they have about Paul. Then Paul related that Onesimus is coming with Tychicus, and he identified Onesimus as being one among the people of Colossae (Col. 4:7–9; compare with Philem. 12). Also, some of the same names appear in both letters: Epaphras (Philem. 23; Col. 1:7), Aristarchus (Philem. 24, Col. 4:10), and Archippus (Philem. 2; Col. 4:17).

Both letters mention that Paul was in prison (Philem. 1, 9; Col. 4:3, 10, 18), so Paul wrote them from the same place, probably Rome, at the same time, probably around A.D. 60–62. However, we cannot be sure about the place and time, for a good case can be made for Ephesus, around A.D. 55–57 (see the discussion "Prison Epistles" in chapter 17).

Readers

Paul addressed Philemon, Apphia, Archippus and the church "that meets in your home"
(1:2). The relationship of these individuals is uncertain. Were they all of one family, with Apphia being the wife of Philemon and Archippus their son? Or was Apphia the wife of Philemon and Archippus a leader in the church, perhaps its pastor? If Archippus were the leader or pastor, Paul included him and the church in the address as additional support for his instructions for Philemon to treat Onesimus, the returning slave, as Paul asked. Was Philemon the leader or pastor and Archippus the slave owner? If so, Philemon and the church were to encourage Archippus to deal with Onesimus graciously.

The last position is that taken by the New Testament scholar John Knox, who proposed that Archippus was the slave owner. Paul did not know Archippus, so Philemon and the church were enlisted by means of the letter to work with Archippus on this matter. Hence, Paul addressed Philemon and the church. Philemon was a leader among the churches around Colossae. In actuality, Philemon was the letter identified as the "letter from Laodicea" (Col. 4:16). Colossians 4:17 says, "Tell Archippus: 'See to it that you complete the work you have received in the Lord.'" Knox viewed this ministry that Archippus was to complete as that of treating Onesimus as described in the letter to Philemon.[1]

Another part of Knox's hypothesis also is interesting. In the early part of the second century, a man named Onesimus was bishop at Ephesus. Knox identifies this Onesimus with the runaway slave of the Philemon letter. He further proposed that Onesimus collected Paul's letters, put them together, and wrote Ephesians in the name of his teacher, Paul, as a cover letter for the Pauline collection.[2] Knox's position, carefully developed on the basis of information available, ultimately requires a leap from the evidence to the conclusion; but it is a plausible position to consider because of his treatment of the evidence.

Message

The message of Philemon is that a runaway slave, Onesimus, should be forgiven and accepted back as a brother in Christ (16). To this end Paul addressed the church as well, for the church needs to be involved in dealing with Onesimus.

Onesimus, who evidently took money from his master (18) and ran away, eventually made his way to Paul. Again, the place of Paul's imprisonment could have been Ephesus or Rome. But Ephesus was close to Colossae, so it seems more likely that the slave made his way further from home to Rome. Perhaps while there he became destitute and eventually sought out Paul for help. His under house arrest and able to receive visitors (Acts 28:30), took Onesimus in. Under Paul's influence, Onesimus became a follower of Christ (10).

Paul is sometimes criticized for not attacking the institution of slavery. While he did not attack the institution, his insistence upon receiving Onesimus as a brother (16) is the principle that destroys the institution. Also,

Paul may have wanted Onesimus to stay and to continue to work with him (13). But Roman law required that a runaway slave be returned, so Paul needed action from Philemon to free Onesimus to service. The play on words in verse 20 may support this idea. The word *benefit* in the Greek, *onaimen*, sounds much like Onesimus. When Paul wrote, "I want some benefit (*onaimen*) from you," he may have been saying, "I want Onesimus from you." Not only would this request free Onesimus from slavery, it would free him for service for Christ.

If Knox is right and Onesimus, bishop of Ephesus, was the Onesimus of Philemon, this may in part explain how this intensely personal letter was preserved. A letter of freedom would be important to the person whose freedom it earned. Indeed, without knowing all the details, we see from this small letter how the gospel makes brothers and sisters out of all and transforms all into family. Could our society or any society need this message more? As Paul wrote to the Galatians, "There is neither Jew nor Greek, slave nor free, male nor female, for you are all one in Christ Jesus" (Gal. 3:28).

FOR STUDY AND REVIEW

QUESTIONS FOR CONSIDERATION:

1. What are the possible relationships of Philemon, Apphia, and Archippus to each other?

2. What is the message of Philemon?

3. What is John Knox's explanation about the collection of Paul's letters?

FOR FURTHER READING:

Bruce F. F. *Paul: Apostle of the Heart Set Free* (Grand Rapids: Eerdmans, 1977), 393–406.

Harrison, Everett F. *Introduction. to the New Testament,* rev. ed. (Grand Rapids: Wm. B. Eerdman Publishing Company, 1982), 328–30.

Knox, John. *Philemon Among the Letters of Paul.* London: Collins, 1960.

ENDNOTES

1. John Knox, "The Epistle to Philemon: Introduction and Exegesis," *The Interpreter's Bible*, ed. George A. Buttrick, 11 (New York: Abingdon Press, 1955), 562–63.

2. Ibid., 557–60.

21

1 and 2 Thessalonians: Life in the Light of Christ's Return

Paul had a vision in which a man from Macedonia entreated him to "come over to Macedonia and help us" (Acts 16:9). Following this summons, Paul and his fellow missionaries eventually arrived in Macedonia. They proceeded to Philippi and then on to Thessalonica. Situated on the "Via Egnatia," the vital highway that linked the East with Rome, Thessalonica was the capital of the Roman province of Macedonia. Thessalonica also had an excellent harbor for sea trade. Therefore, this city of influence in the area, on a major land route and possessing a significant harbor, was a strategic place to preach the gospel and begin a church.

Both Jews and Gentiles responded to the preaching of the gospel, making some of the Jewish leaders in Thessalonica angry and jealous. The Jewish leaders incited a riot. The situation grew so intense that friends secreted Paul and his fellow missionaries out of town.

The missionaries went to Berea and then on to Athens. At Athens Paul sent Timothy back to Thessalonica to check on the young church's welfare. Paul then went to Corinth. Timothy met him there and reported on the church, reporting both good news and bad news. The young church remained faithful even in the face of persecution and rejection. But some difficulties existed also, and Paul wrote his first letter in response to Timothy's good and bad news.

1 Thessalonians: Writer and Readers

From Corinth, then, around 50 A.D., Paul wrote to the young church at Thessalonica. He again expanded upon the Greek letter-writing form. Notice the recipient or reader part of the form as he identified them not simply as the "church of the Thessalonians," but the church of the Thessalonians "in God the Father and the Lord Jesus Christ" (1:1). That identity, stressing their security in God and Jesus Christ, was for a church experiencing local pressures of rejection. Also, they had insecurities about their status in relation to the coming (sometimes referred to by the Greek word, *parousia*) again of Christ. As people who were in God the Father and the Lord Jesus Christ, they could be sure of their security. As will be evident from our discussion, however, Paul had to answer specific questions about the matter of Christ's *parousia* to further reassure them.

Message: Gratitude and Reassurance (1:1—3:13)

The letter has two major sections, 1:1—3:13 and 4:1—5:28. In the first major section, Paul was thankful for and reassuring toward the Thessalonians. He gave thanks for the Thessalonians' faithfulness (1:3–10). In fact, they had become models for believers in Macedonia and Achaia (1:7), turning from idols to "serve the living and true God" (1:9) and to await the coming of Christ from heaven (1:10).

In chapter 2, Paul dealt with attacks against himself. His enemies probably were some of the Jewish leaders who succeeded in inciting the riot. They accused Paul of heresy, deceit, and greed, among other things. Some traveling teachers and missionaries of different philosophies and religions in that day went from place to place preying upon the good hospitality of people. Not only did they secure hospitality; they also took offerings. When they got as much for themselves as they could, they went to another place. Other teachers and missionaries were not interested in selfish gain but in getting their message out. Christian missionaries, therefore, had competition in some places where they worked.

Paul's detractors accused him of acting like unscrupulous traveling teachers, and he defended himself and his fellow missionaries. They spoke "as men approved by God to be entrusted with the gospel" (2:4), so they would not speak with "error or impure motives" (2:3). They did not look for the praise of men nor did their work serve as a "mask" for "greed" (2:5). They endeavored not to be a burden to them—that is, in terms of support; most of their support came from themselves (2:7–9).

Paul reassured them that he and his friends had not ceased to be concerned about them (2:17–19). They were his "joy," his "crown" (2:19). He reminded them that they had been warned to expect persecution. After being separated from them by that persecution, Timothy was sent back to encourage the church and to return to Paul with a report about their status (3:1–10). He recounted these facts to help stabilize the young church, struggling as it was to maintain its faithfulness. Paul and his fellow missionaries certainly had not forsaken them.

Guidance Given and Questions Answered (4:1—5:28)

The second major part of the letter focuses upon guidance for the church and questions asked by the new congregation. Paul called for them to live "in order to please God" (4:1). They were to avoid "sexual immorality" (4:3). They were to practice brotherly love (4:9–10) and be responsible in their work and conduct (4:11–12).

Paul then turned to two major questions the church had. Family members and friends of the Thessalonian Christians had died. Since these persons would not be present at the return of Christ, what would happen to those who were "asleep" (4:13–18)?

Paul's answer was not about the status or state of existence of those who died, but of their relationship to Christ when His *parousia* initiates the consummation of all things. Statements in the New Testament indicate immediate relationship with the Lord at death (Mark 9:4; 12:26–27; Luke 16:19–31; 2 Cor. 5:1–10; Phil. 1:23). Other passages seem to indicate that the union with the Lord will not occur until the resurrection, as in this passage under

Arch of Galerius at Thessalonica (303 A.D.) on the Eqnatian Way. Built to commemorate the victories by the emperor Galerius over the Persians in Mesopotamia and Armenia. *Biblical Illustrator* Photo/David Rogers.

discussion. In Philippians, both views seem to be put forth: to die is to be with Christ (1:23), but the "day" of Christ is in the future (1:6).

Paul seemed to present both views in 1 Corinthians 15:20–28, 49–54, as contrasted with 2 Corinthians 5:1–10. Frank Stagg suggests that the difference in the two Corinthian passages is attributable to the difference in emphasis.[1] In other words, Paul spoke to a particular need in terms of the actual event of the return of Christ and that moment of the event in the first case (1 Cor. 15:20–28), and more to what happens in the immediate aftermath of death in the second case (2 Cor. 5:1–10). To be away from the earthly "house" is to be at hom,e with the Lord. Of course, we

know that God is not bound by time, and sometimes the New Testament writers were concerned not with chronology but with event and reality (as in 1 Cor. 15:20-28).[2]

Ample evidence exists in the New Testament that neither time nor death separates us from a real, living relationship with God in Christ. As in Romans 8:39, nothing separates us from the love of God in Christ, and God's love is a living relationship which overcomes death. Death cannot keep a person from that living relationship of love with God. Therefore, relationship with God in Christ is immediate after death.

The second question the Thessalonians asked about concerned the time of the return of Christ (5:1–8). Paul answered with illustrations. He reminded them that the "day of the Lord will come like a thief in the night" (5:2). Of course, Paul did not mean that Jesus was a thief or that he would be sneaky. He meant that just as a thief does not announce his time of arrival for robbing someone, neither does Jesus announce His coming. Likewise, just as the birth of a baby does not occur until the sudden onset of birth pains, so Jesus return is sudden and unannounced. But Paul reassured them. Since they are children of the "day" (5:5), whether it is physically day or night, they would know whenever Christ's return occurs. Since they would know whenever the return happened, they really had no need to fret about it, especially about missing the return.

The letter ends with several encouragements and practical instructions. They were to respect their leaders (5:12–15). Paul admonished them to such practical everyday living as being "joyful always" (5:16), praying "continually" (5:17), and holding "to the good" (5:21). He concluded with prayer and blessing for the church.

2 Thessalonians: Writer and Readers

Soon after the first letter, Paul found it necessary to write another letter to the Thessalonians. What he wrote in the first letter and what he had taught previously was misunderstood by some of the readers at Thessalonia. Or perhaps there was deliberate distortion which caused misunderstanding. Evidently a forged letter circulated among the Thessalonians, attributed to Paul and his fellow missionaries by opponents, which gave incorrect information about the *parousia* of Christ (see 2:1–2).

Since the second letter has so much similar material to the first, some interpreters see this as a letter written much later by someone other than Paul. Differences in tone, vocabulary, and concepts, especially about the return of Christ, are reasons given for concluding Paul was not the author.

These variations should be expected from a person writing amid the urgency of his work in constantly changing situations; and many similarities of style, vocabulary, and tone do exist between the two letters. Also, he used an *amanuensis* (3:17) or secretary, which might account for some of the variations. Finally, the letter itself gives evidence that Paul, Silas, and Timothy were the originators of the letters, with Paul taking the lead in expression—as is obvious from his being named first (1:1) and his reference to writing in his own hand (3:17).[3] So Paul and his companions, around A.D. 50, sent a second letter from Corinth to the Thessalonian Christians.

Message

Chapter 1 contains the usual salutation, greeting, and thanksgiving, as well as a word about future judgment. The chapter closes with a prayer by the apostle.

In addition to the statement about the forged letter, chapter 2 deals with several matters related to the return of Christ. The "man of lawlessness" (2:3) will be revealed before the Lord's coming. This person has been variously identified. Some interpreters see him as the antichrist. Others simply think Paul referred to Satan, the epitome of evil. Still others define the evil one here in terms of a Roman ruler. Of course, whoever or whatever he is, the reality of Christ brings into bold relief that which is really the antichrist, the evil one, or Satan, so that there is no doubt about him when Christ returns. Christ's return illuminates, to those who belong to Him, things as they really are (see again Paul's reference to those of the "day" in 1 Thess. 5:4–5).

The "one who now holds [lawlessness] back" (2:7), also has been variously identified. God, the Roman government, and even Satan have been suggested as the restraining power Paul meant. Whatever the identity, those who "refused to love the truth and so be saved" (2:10) were the victims of the lawless one and Satan.

As indicated by Paul's discussion in chapter 2, as was also true in portions of 1 Thessalonians, the Thessalonian Christians were confused and insecure about the return of Christ. They had an intense expectation that Christ was coming immediately. They still had not learned to temper that expectation with the sovereignty of Christ and allow that the coming of Christ might be longer than they could calculate. Part of Paul's purpose in writing them was to comfort and reassure them. They were not going to make a mistake and miss it; nor, of course, would Christ fail to make Himself known to them. Basically, Paul reassured them that when Christ came there would be no doubt that He had arrived.

In chapter 3 Paul dealt with some nagging practical problems arising out of their misunderstanding of Christ's *parousia*. Some, in the expectation of Christ's return at any moment, thought it unnecessary to continue working at their jobs. Having used up all their resources, these people became a burden on the rest of the church. Paul says, in effect, that they should go back to work (3:6-10). In addition, these people, with time on their hands, began to involve themselves in matters concerning other people. They became "busybodies" (3:11) and caused problems and conflicts within the church. Again, they were to go

back to work, which would keep them from interfering with others.

Paul closed the letter by writing with his "own hand" (3:17). Up to that point he had dictated the letter to a secretary, but he now took the pen in hand so his readers would know that it was he who wrote rather than a forger (see 2:2).

FOR STUDY AND REVIEW

IDENTIFY:

Parousia
Man of lawlessness
One who holds back the man of
   lawlessness
Amanuensis

QUESTIONS FOR CONSIDERATION

1. Why was Thessalonica a strategic place to preach the gospel?
2. Where was Paul when he wrote 1 and 2 Thessalonians? When did he write the letters?
3. What were the two major questions discussed in reference to 1 Thessalonians 4—5? How did Paul answer them?
4. In 2 Thessalonians, what had some people done in regard to their vocations? What problems did this cause?

FOR FURTHER READING

Jewett, Robert. *The Thessalonian Correspondence.* Philadelphia: Fortress Press, 1986.
Marshall, I. Howard. *1 and 2 Thessalonians.* Grand Rapids: Eerdmans, 1983.
Morris, Leon. "1 Thessalonians." "2 Thessalonians." *Holman Bible Dictionary.*

Nashville: Holman Bible Publishers, 1991, 1338–42.

ENDNOTES

1. Frank Stagg, *New Testament Theology* (Nashville: Broadman, 1962), 323.

2. The reader may be interested in the detailed study of time by Mathias Rissi, *Time and History*, trans. Gordon C. Winsor (Richmond: John Knox Press, 1965).

3.For opposing views and discussion see D. A. Carson, Douglas J. Moo, and Leon Morris, *An Introduction to the New Testament* (Grand Rapids: Zondervan Publishing House, 1992), 343–46; and Marion L. Soards, *The Apostle Paul: An Introduction to His Writing and Teaching* (New York: Paulist Press 1987), 131–37.

22

1 and 2 Timothy and Titus

In 1779 Paul Anton gave the designation "Pastoral Epistles" to 1 Timothy, 2 Timothy, and Titus as a group.[1] The title helps to distinguish them from the other Epistles of Paul. The title also designates the content of the three letters as pastoral in nature, since Paul gave instructions to two young pastors about their leadership in the churches under their charge. However, the content is not so neatly categorized. "First Timothy is most truly pastoral, and Second Timothy least so, with Titus occupying an immediate position."[2] Nothing demands that Titus be grouped with 1 and 2 Timothy, or that the two should be studied in close relationship with each other. They may not have been written at the same time; nor do they deal with the same situation.[3] Nonetheless, the designation is helpful in referring to the three letters. As far as the order of their writing, Titus probably came first and 2 Timothy last.

Few writings offer more discussions on authorship than do the Pastorals. Three major difficulties contribute to the wide range of opinions. First are the historical difficulties. We have no historical record of Paul's being released from prison which could put Paul in a time framework to write the letters, although 2 Timothy reflects a situation with Paul in prison. The other letters of Paul can be placed, and fairly accurately chronologi-cally, into the framework of the information in Acts, but not the Pastorals. Some interpreters feel that Paul never left prison in Rome, eventually suffering martyrdom there.

A second difficulty is connected with church organization. Paul's instructions in 1 Timothy reflect a rather developed church organizational structure. For such structure to exist, some believe that a period of time after Paul's death must be allowed for the writing of the letters so church structure would have opportunity to develop.

A third difficulty focuses on vocabulary and style. Over one-third of the words in the Pastorals are not found in Paul's other writings. Some vocabulary is not used as Paul did in other letters. For example, the word faith in the Pastorals refers to accepting a body of doctrine rather than the dynamic relationship between believer and Christ. Critics also point to the absence of the aggressive, emotional style of writing reflected in other letters of Paul.

Each of the difficulties has received involved and detailed responses by proponents of Pauline authorship. As regards the historical difficulties, Paul stated in Romans 15:28 that he intended to go to Spain. The house arrest of Paul recorded in Acts 28:30, where he received visitors in his own rented house, does not seem a threatening situation in which martyrdom would result. Also, earlier, after examining him, neither Festus nor Agrippa found him deserving of imprisonment or death (Acts 25:25; 26:32). Later writers, such as Eusebius, Jerome, and Chrysostom from the third and fourth centuries, express a tradition that the authorities released Paul from prison and that he did go to Spain. This historical situation would allow for a second imprisonment. Too, the Pastorals themselves are evidence for a release and second imprisonment.

Developed church structure is present to a degree in the pastorals. However, the leadership roles discussed were not foreign to Paul (1 Tim. 3:1–13). In Philippians 1:1, Paul greeted bishops and deacons, reflecting a church order there, although he gave no indication in the rest of the letter about the degree of its development. That such church development as reflected in the Pastorals could occur by A.D. 60–68 is not inconceivable.

The difference in vocabulary and theological meaning from the other letters of Paul evokes several explanations. An *amanuensis* could have taken some liberty in expressing Paul's dictation, or an editor could have used fragments of Paul's writing and added editorial styling and vocabulary of his own. Too, the particular situations would have called for Paul to use different vocabulary and different theological emphases to discuss and answer the problems. Finally, different vocabulary and style could be explained by Paul's use of traditional material already accepted by the churches in composing these three letters.

The above information leads interpreters to develop different positions on authorship. First, some say the Pastorals are pseudonymous, indicating that a writer later than Paul assumed his name. In that period of history, unknown writers sometimes assumed the name of a famous person in order to give their writings weight and authority. Second, others would say the letters are fragmentary as regards authorship. A disciple of Paul took authentic fragments of Paul's writing and edited his words into them to make a composite message. Still others take an *amanuensis* view, with Paul's secretary, after dictation, being allowed a rather free hand in composition. Fourth, the traditional view is that Paul is the author, having written the letters between A.D. 62 and 65. Three out of four of these views give direct authorship to Paul in some way. After all considerations, much weight of evidence exists for direct or indirect authorship of Paul for the three letters.[4]

1 Timothy: Affirmation of the Truth in Christ

Writer

The letter reflects a situation in which Paul left Timothy in Ephesus, in a place of leadership, after a period of ministry the two engaged in there. The place of origination for the letter is uncertain, but somewhere in Macedonia seems to be the most likely location, a conclusion drawn from 1:3. The time of writing is difficult to determine, but probably a date between A.D. 63 and 67 is a good possibility.

Readers

Timothy was the primary reader, but certainly he shared the contents with the church. He was a trusted friend and fellow-laborer to Paul in the Gentile mission. Often a representative for Paul in the work, (see 1 Cor. 4:17; Phil. 2:19) and consequently an itinerate missionary, he now had, according to the letters, primary responsibility for the church at Ephesus.

Message

Paul encouraged Timothy in his ministry, urging him to remain faithful and giving him instruction about dealing with false doctrine and matters of church organization and practice. After the salutation, Paul admonished Timothy to be responsible for seeing that teachers reject heresy and teach sound doctrine (1:3–20). Elements of church organization then receive attention (2:1—3:13), followed by further instructions pertaining to Timothy's leadership of the church (3:14—6:19). The letter closes with final instruction to Timothy and a benediction (6:20–21).

ralistic in regard to religion. Since Ephesus was so eclectic in religious and doctrinal choice, the church needed to be strengthened in its resistance to aberrant belief and practice.[5]

In giving Timothy instruction, Paul appealed to his own personal experience as a person who previously held to unbelief (1:13–14), but Christ had mercy upon him and extended him grace. He referred to himself as the worst of sinners; Christ came into the world to save such as he (1:15). Out of his personal example Paul directed the focus on Christ, for Christianity is bound up with the person, Jesus Christ, before it is bound to a systematic expression of doctrine. All doctrines must ultimately pass the standard of the Person who has been revealed to us.

Heresy and Sound Doctrine (1:3–20)

The identity of the particular heresy is uncertain. Certain elements of false teaching surface in the letter. The false teachers give attention to myths and genealogies (1:4; 4:7), they teach the law without understanding (1:7), they advocate asceticism in forms of forbidding marriage and partaking of certain foods (4:3), and they evidently put a great emphasis upon their brand of knowledge (6:20). The myths and genealogies may point to Jewish elements in the false teaching, while the emphasis upon knowledge and asceticism may reveal Gnostic connections.

Probably the false doctrine was syncretistic, incorporating elements of more than one belief system. Ephesus was well known for its openness to receiving different religions and appropriating them into relationship with one another. The city was a valuable trade center, so it is understandable that Ephesus was plu-

Elements of Church Organization (2:1—3:13)

Practical matters in light of the church's situation at Ephesus come into view in this section, perhaps offering in regard to women some of the most difficult interpretative challenges in the New Testament. Matters of worship receive attention, praying and teaching in particular. Women, here, are to be silent and are not to teach and have authority over men (2:11–12). Such admonition contrasts with 1 Corinthians 11:5, which acknowledges that women prophesy and pray in church, as long as they cover their heads. Prophesying referred to inspired utterance much as we refer to inspired preaching today.

Some scholars in recent works regulate this instruction (2:11–12) to the particular situation at Ephesus.[6] After intensive study of backgrounds, they note that some women in Ephesus, through the influence of the mother-goddess cult there, advocated supremacy of

Arch of Septimius Severus (203 A.D.) with corner of Mamertine prison at extreme right. Paul may have been imprisoned in the Mamertine. *Biblical Illustrator* Photo/Ken Touchton.

women over men. The same kinds of attitudes, brought into the church by converts from the cult may have been the specific problem addressed in Timothy. If the explanation is accurate, the instruction that women keep silent operated only in that historical situation concerning the specific problem of a mother-goddess cult influence.

Further instructions included practical matters about church leaders (3:1–13). "Bishops" (or the word may be translated "overseers" indicating those in leadership), "deacons," and "women" are to live exemplary lives within the community. The emphasis is upon practical aspects of Christian character. Converts who came out of the pluralistic religious society of Ephesus needed

to understand clearly that some of the practices they previously regarded as right could no longer be so. "Women" (3:11) may refer to the wives of the deacons or may be a reference to an order of servants or deaconesses at Ephesus. The issue is that the church, those who have been redeemed into Christ, are called to live by the moral commitments of Christ Himself.

Additional Instructions to Timothy as Leader (3:14—6:19)

These instructions include matters of asceticism (4:1–16) and relationships to members, widows, elders, and slaves (5:1—6:2). False teachers again come under attack (6:3–10), some of whom evidently attempted to gain some wealth from their relationship to the church (6:5). Among other things, Timothy is to "fight the good fight of the faith. Take hold of the eternal life to which you were called when you made your good confession in the presence of many witnesses" (6:12). After warning about riches (6:17–19), Paul encouraged Timothy to faithfulness once again (6:20–21). The letter closes with a simple benediction, "Grace be with you" (6:21).

The first letter to Timothy calls for Christian character in ministry and in the church. A double standard, one for Christian leadership and one for the church as a whole, was not Paul's intention. Leadership in a context without much moral direction was on his mind. Seeking financial gain, status, or power reflects base motivations. Service in the name of Christ, out of the character which Christ builds, is the basis for service.

2 Timothy: Faithfulness to Christ

Writer and Reader

This letter names Paul as the writer and Timothy as the recipient (1:1–2). Paul's worst fears, hinted at in 1 Timothy, have been realized, and he is once again in prison (4:8, 16). The letter supports Rome as the place of imprisonment 1:16–17). The most likely date for 2 Timothy is between A.D. 63 and 67.

Message

Paul urged Timothy to be faithful, to endure the difficulties, and to fulfill his calling as a preacher of the gospel. He foresaw the end of his own missionary career in martyrdom (4:6–8). The situation was made more difficult by Demas' desertion of the missionary enterprise (4:10) and by Alexander the coppersmith, who hurt Paul deeply (4:14).

Salutation (1:1–2)

The salutation is essentially the same as the salutation in 1 Timothy. The statement made in reference to Paul's apostleship is striking. He was an apostle "according to the promise of life that is in Christ Jesus" (1:1). In the light of the content of the letter in which Paul expected to be executed, the "promise of life" may be a particularly poignant statement. If that statement is directly related to his expected martyrdom, it expresses the faith of Paul that life is in store for him. Death will not have the victory (see 1 Cor. 15: 54–57).

Box 17: An Outline of Contents

Salutation (1:1–2)
A Personal Charge to Timothy (1:3—2:7)
A Charge for Correct Teaching and Practice (2:8—4:8)
Personal Requests of Paul (4:9–18)

A Personal Charge to Timothy (1:3—2:7)

Paul had deep appreciation for Timothy and reminded him that "God did not give us a spirit of timidity, but a spirit of power, of love and of self-discipline" (1:7). In the face of great challenges to the Christian faith and ministry, the young pastor could have been intimidated. Already seeing some desertion from the truth (4:10), Paul must have wanted to encourage Timothy to stay with his calling to service (1:8–9).

A Charge for Correct Teaching and Practice (2:8—4:8)

After reminding Timothy to "remember Jesus Christ, raised from the dead, descended from David," as preached in "my gospel" (2:8), Paul recommended certain attitudes and practices for Timothy as well as for others. Timothy was to present himself a "workman" who has no need to be ashamed and who rightly handles the word of truth (2:15), to "flee the evil desires of youth and pursue righteousness, faith, love and peace, along with those who call on the Lord out of a pure heart" (2:22), and to "continue" in what he has learned and firmly believed (3:14). He was to "preach the word, be prepared in season and out of season; correct, rebuke, and encourage with great patience and careful instruction (4:2). These charges involve Timothy's impact upon others who, through his ministry, would be challenged to follow Christ's way.

In poignant language, speaking of his death which seems imminent to him, Paul appears to be passing on the torch of responsibility to Timothy. Timothy was to "do the work of an evangelist" and fulfill his ministry (4:5). As for Paul, he states that he was at the point of being "poured out"—sacrificed (4:6). He has "fought the good fight, finished the race," and "kept the faith" (4:7).

Personal Requests of Paul (4:9–22)

Paul hoped Timothy could come to him before his death. He wanted Timothy to bring Mark with him and also to bring his cloak, books, and parchments. One wonders why

these specific items. How did the apostle use them in his last days? Unfortunately, we have no record of the last events in Paul's life.

Second Timothy pictures Paul under great stress, yet full of faith and courage although unsure about his survival (4:17–18). The letter closes with greetings and a benediction, and we have here the last recorded words of Paul available to us: "The Lord be with your spirit. Grace be with you" (4:22).

Titus: Standards for Serving Christ

Writer

Paul wrote Titus before 2 Timothy, and perhaps before 1 Timothy. For Paul to have written the letter, the date most likely would be the same range as for 1 and 2 Timothy, A.D. 63–67, with place of origin somewhere in Macedonia.

Reader

Titus had leadership responsibilities for the church at Crete. Titus, a Gentile, was an important fellow worker with Paul. Perhaps he became a disciple of Christ under Paul's witness, for Paul addressed him as "my true son in our common faith" (1:4). He often assisted Paul in his work in relationship to the churches (2 Cor. 7:6–7,13–16; 8:16–17, 23–24). The instructions are general enough in Titus so as to be read by or to the whole church.

Message

Titus' responsibility was to help the church "put in order what remained to be done" (1:5, NRSV). Competition from other kinds of evangelists made the work more difficult at Crete. While Paul did not give a specific identity for those primarily causing the difficulties, they were Jewish rivals of some sort, perhaps Judaizers. They emphasize, the letter says, "circumcision" (1:10), "Jewish myths" (1:14), and observance of the law (3:5, 9). These rivals to the gospel preached by Titus and Paul had been successful, as 1:11 confirms: "They must be silenced, because they are ruining whole households by teaching things they ought not to teach.

The young church at Crete was vulnerable, and Titus received a charge, in effect, to fight for the life of the church. Leaders and the church as a whole are called to hold to commitments and standards of conduct very basic to the life of any church. Chapter 1 deals with standards for elders or bishops and stresses the problems caused by false teachers; chapter 2 gives directions for basic instructions to the church; and chapter 3 deals with the church's relationship to challenges from the world around them.

Leaders in the church must have exemplary lives, reflecting high ethical standards (1:5–15). Titus himself could help by sound teaching and by proper relations to the various age groups and social groups within the church (2:1–15). In addition, Titus was to teach and to lead them in the application of practical ethical standards. Laziness, gossiping, quarreling, envy, hatred, and pursuit of wrong pleasures are not to have any part in the life of the church. Titus, rather, was to insist on "doing what is good" (3:8). The letter closes with an invitation for Titus to meet Paul at Nicopolis (3:12), with instructions for certain individuals (3:13–14), and final greetings (3:5).

Of course, we have no way of knowing whether the meeting at Nicopolis ever took place. This letter pictures Paul as a person of courage, involved with the church and its mission in the world, concerned about his friend, and anticipating further service for Christ in others as well as in himself.

FOR STUDY AND REVIEW

QUESTIONS FOR CONSIDERATION:

1. What are some of the difficulties involved in accepting Paul as author of the Pastoral Epistles?

2. What are some of the answers to the difficulties?

3. What were the characteristics and identity of the opponents alluded to in 1 Timothy?

4. What is the major message of each of the Pastoral Epistles?

5. What were Timothy and Titus to accomplish in their respective places of ministry?

FOR FURTHER READING:

Barrett, C. K. *The Pastoral Epistles. New Clarendon Bible.* Edited by H. F. D. Sparks. Oxford: Clarendon, 1963.

Fee, Gordon D. *1 and 2 Timothy, Titus. Good News Commentaries.* San Francisco: Harper & Row, 1984.

ENDNOTES

1. E. F. Harrison, *Introduction to the New Testament,* rev. ed. (Grand Rapids: Wm. B. Eerdmans Publishing Company, 1982), 350.

2. Ibid., 347.

3. See D. A. Carson, Douglas J. Moo, and Leon Morris, *An Introduction to the New Testament* (Grand Rapids: Zondervan, 1992), 359–60, for a concise discussion on the rela-

tionship of the three.

4. For contrasting arguments, see Donald Guthrie, *New Testament Introduction,* 3rd ed. rev. (Downers Grove, Ill.: InterVarsity Press, 1970), 584–622; and W. G. Kümmel, *Introduction to the New Testament,* translated by H. C. McKee, revised and enlarged ed. (Nashville: Abingdon Press, 1975), 370–84.

5. For excellent discussion of the background, see Sharon Hodgin Gritz, *Paul, Women Teachers, and the Mother Goddess at Ephesus* (New York: UP of America, 1991), 12–13, 31–43.

6. See, for example, Richard and Catherine Clark Kroeger, *I Suffer Not a Woman: Rethinking 1 Timothy 2:11–15 in Light of Ancient Evidence* (Grand Rapids: Baker, 1992).

❧ 23 ❧

Hebrews: The Superiority of Christ

Writer

Church tradition through many centuries has associated Hebrews with Paul's name. However, this tradition does not go back to the earliest centuries. Only after about the year 400, under Augustine's influence, was Pauline authorship widely accepted in the church, so earlier church leaders were reluctant to identify authorship with Paul.[1]

Even Luther and Calvin, leaders of the Protestant Reformation, doubted that Paul was the author. Few scholars today defend Pauline authorship. The stylistic and theological characteristics of Hebrews are so different from Paul's other writings that little connection of the book with his way of thinking is possible. And, indeed, Hebrews itself does not identify its author, for nowhere in the text is the writer mentioned. Therefore, the author of Hebrews remains anonymous.

Of course, attempts are made to deduce through textual and historical studies the writer's possible identity. Suggestions for authorship include Peter, Philip, Barnabas, Apollos, Luke, Priscilla, Aquila, and Clement of Rome.[2] None of these, however, offers even reasonable certainty for the identity of the writer. Nonetheless, some characteristics of the writer are certain. He knew Greek, for Hebrews is written in excellent Greek. He was well acquainted with Judaism, as evidenced by his knowledge of the temple functions and the priesthood. Also, he was very familiar with Hellenistic, or Greek, philosophy. In addition, he quoted from the Septuagint, the Greek translation of the Old Testament.

One would expect a Jewish writer of Palestine to quote from the Hebrew Old Testament rather than the Greek. This fact, plus the excellent Greek and knowledge of Hellenistic philosophy reflected in the book, points to the origin of the Book of Hebrews outside Palestine. The author probably was a Christian Jew of the Diaspora (those Jews away from the homeland) living in a context of strong Jewish and Hellenistic influences. Two of the most persistent suggestions as to the author's locale are Alexandria (Egypt) and Rome. Both of these major cosmopolitan cities had significant Jewish populations as well as strong Hellenistic influences.

Readers

The identity, location, and historical situation of the readers are as difficult to determine as authorship. The title, "Hebrews," was a later addition and not part of the older manuscripts. But the title does reflect a long-standing belief that the recipients were a group of Hebrews. As the reasoning goes,

185

only they could understand the references to the temple, the priesthood, and other Old Testament imagery. However, it should be noted that proselytes to Judaism, Gentiles who accepted the Jewish faith, could understand the Old Testament context as well. Nonetheless, that the author addressed a Jewish group is probable.

Where were the readers when they received the writing? Again, we cannot be certain. Rome, Alexandria, Colossae, Jerusalem, and other major cosmopolitan cities offer possibilities. The most persistent suggestion is Rome, which seems to be the place that best suits the content of Hebrews.[3]

Also, what was the status of the readers? Were they threatened with persecution and tempted to desert the faith because of the hardship of remaining Christian? Were they attracted again to Judaism, discouraged with Christianity for reasons other than persecution? Were they simply lazy, uncommitted, and unimaginative followers who were failing to embrace their missionary responsibilities? Or were they tempted to follow doctrines espoused by Jewish-Christian-Greek philosophical speculation? Did the author write to believers throughout the book, or did he write to nonbelievers in passages such as 6:4–8 and 10:26–31?

Major ideas emerge from interpreters' attempt to answer questions about the status of the readers:

1. The readers became disillusioned and were contemplating a return to Judaism. Their desire to return arose out of a limited understanding; the author answered their limitation with a developed presentation of the superiority of Christ.

2. The readers faced hardship and persecution as Christians, so they wanted to return to a more secure and a more accepted Judaism. The author wrote to warn them against falling from the faith. By presenting to them the superiority of Christ, he intended to win them to faithfulness in the face of their hardships.

3. The readers were lazy, neglecting their responsibility to participate in the world missionary enterprise to which they were called. The author wrote to warn them about their lack of faithfulness to the task and sought to give them a vision of the surpassing superiority of Christ in order to stir them to accept their mission to the world.

4. A Jewish-Gnostic philosophy, mixed with Christian elements, proved attractive to the readers. The readers lacked understanding, much as the Colossian Christians did as they faced the heresy there, about the superiority and sufficiency of Christ. The author sought to remedy that lack of understanding.

Message

The situation of the readers cannot be determined with absolute certainty. Faithfulness of the readers is the issue with which the author deals. Perhaps he addressed believers and those who had contemplated becoming believers. However, the positive message of Hebrews is the same to each situation suggested: the superiority of Christ and the finality and completeness of God's revelation and saving work in Him.

Christ's Superiority to Previous Revelation (1:1–3)

The first three verses contain a lofty Christology, in some ways similar to that in Philippians 2:6–11 and Colossians 1:15–20. Whereas in the past God revealed Himself and His will in many and creative ways, He now has expressed His ultimate and complete revelation "by a Son." Jesus is not just any Son, but the creator and "heir" of all things (1:2). That is, He is the beginning and the goal of all things. Also, He upholds "all things by his powerful word" (1:3), which means that he sustains that of which He is both beginning and goal. In addition, this Son "is the radiance of God's glory and the exact representation of his being" (1:3). Reflecting the glory and bearing the stamp of the nature of God mean that Christ is the essence of God Himself. Consequently, He is exalted to the "right hand of the Majesty in heaven" (1:3); He has established His power and authority over all things.

Christ's Superiority Over the Angels (1:4—2:18)

Some people of that time speculated about and believed in a hierarchy of angelic beings between creation and God. They believed that these had certain authority and powers. If this were the background against which the author wrote, then he probably countered some pre-Gnostic or beginning Gnostic philosophical speculation. However, we may have in the background the belief held by Jews and Christians of angels as part of the heavenly host of God. In any case, Christ is superior. Christ is the *One* to whom they should give their loyalty.

Christ's Superiority Over Moses and Aaron (3:1—4:16)

Moses and Aaron were the leaders of the Old Covenant. That covenant was made by God. But now God has made a superior covenant in Jesus Christ. Christ is the One in whom believers can find an eternal "rest" (4:1). The Sabbath pointed to an everlasting rest and represented fellowship with God, a day in which the people put other concerns aside to have undisturbed relationship with God. The eternal rest of the Sabbath was of the nature of that relationship to which the Sabbath pointed

That expectation was fulfilled in the Lord's Day Sunday. All the meaning of Saturday, the Sabbath, is caught up and fulfilled in Sunday, the Lord's Day, the day of the resurrection. It is in Jesus that humanity finds a "rest" which is eternal. The Lord's Day holds, therefore, a unique place in the theology and worship of Christians because Jesus has fulfilled the meaning and expectation of the Sabbath. Moses and Aaron and the Old Covenant could not give that, but Christ can. The New Covenant is superior. Therefore, the readers could turn to Christ and find help and deliverance (4:14–16).

Christ's Superiority Over the Levitical Priesthood (5:1—7:28)

Christ is the great high priest. He was appointed (5:5), but He was not of the order of the priesthood. He stands alone as the one and only high priest of God. He is like Melchizedek. When Abraham encountered Melchizedek, Abraham paid tithes to him. Melchizedek blessed Abraham (7:1–2). Both acts, paying tithes and being blessed, point to Melchizedek as the superior of Abraham. Also, Melchizedek had no "genealogy" nor beginning and ending of days (7:3). This does not mean that he actually had no father nor mother nor did not die, but as he is encountered in the Old Testament record (see Gen. 4:18–20) no genealogy, birth, and death are given for him. As far as the record goes, he stands in history as the one and only priest of his kind, and he is so forever. Therefore, Melchizedek is an illustration of who Jesus actually is. Jesus is the one and only priest of his kind, and He is priest forever. No other priest is needed. He is the priest who has now made sacrifice of a one and only kind, namely the giving of Himself. Consequently, no need exists for sacrifices to be offered "daily" as the priests did before, because the sacrifice Christ made is once for all and need never be repeated (7:27). His sacrifice is for the forgiveness of our sins and for our salvation.

Christ's Superiority Through the New Covenant and the New Sanctuary (8:1—10:18)

Both a better covenant and a perfect sanctuary are now established. Had the older covenant been sufficient, no need would have existed for the second (8:7). The tent or tabernacle Moses constructed was earthly. The earthly tent was only a "copy and shadow of what is in heaven" (8:5). Christ serves in the heavenly sanctuary, appearing "for us in God's presence" (9:24). That is, God meets believers in Christ, in whom He mediates the New Covenant and the new ministry on their behalf.

Obviously the author believed Jesus to be the ruler of all things since He had been given all authority over them. But note that the exalted Jesus Christ, supreme and superior, is the One who serves, who has given and continues to give in behalf of humanity.

Practical Responses to the Superiority of Christ (10:19—13:25)

Because all the author has said is true, believers should "persevere" (10:36) and not

"shrink back" (10:39). Faith should be their manner of life, as was true with the heroes of Hebrew history (11:1–40). With such a great cloud of witnesses about them, the readers should "throw off everything that hinders them" and "run with perseverance" the race before them (12:1). Jesus is the ultimate example to whom they are to look (12:2–3). Brotherly love, hospitality, and other practical ethical actions should be their manner of living (see 13:1–21). The author wanted them to be equipped with "everything good" so that they may do "his will" (13:21).

Hebrews is dramatic and timely. At its base the Christian faith is not about theological, philosophical, or ecclesiological systems. The Christian faith is not so much a religion as it is relationship to a person, Jesus Christ. Theology, philosophy, and ecclesiology are valuable and help us in our relationship with Christ, but we should never forget that the center and focus of true Christianity is the person, Jesus Christ.

FOR STUDY AND REVIEW

QUESTIONS FOR CONSIDERATION:

1. What must be taken into consideration in discussion of the author of Hebrews? What names are among those suggested as writers of the book?

2. What suggestions are offered as to the status of the readers?

3. What is the major theme of Hebrews?

4. In what ways is Christ superior as outlined in the discussion?

5. Who was Melchizedek and what was his significance?

FOR FURTHER READING:

Carson, D. A., Douglas J. Moo, and Leon Morris. *An Introduction to the New Testament* (Grand Rapids: Zondervan, 1992), 391–407.

Harrison, E. F. *Introduction to the New Testament,* rev. ed. (Grand Rapids: Wm. B. Eerdmans Publishing Company, 1982), 260–63.

McKnight, Edgar V. "Letter to the Hebrews." *Mercer Dictionary of the Bible.* 364–67.

ENDNOTES

1. W. G. Kümmel, *Introduction to the New Testament,* translated by H. C. McKee. Revised and enlarged ed. (Nashville: Abingdon Press, 1975), 392-94.

2. See Carson, Moo, and Morris, *Introduction,* 394-397; and Kummel, *Introduction,* 401-03.

3. C. Milo Connick, *The New Testament: An Introduction to Its History, Literature, and Thought,* 2nd ed. (Encino, Calif.: Dickenson, 1978), 345.

24

James: Faith in Christ Issues in Works

The "General Epistles" or "Catholic (or universal) Epistles" include James, 1 and 2 Peter, 1, 2, and 3 John, and Jude. They are called general or catholic for two reasons. First, most of them address a general audience, or were to be read by more than one church (although a few exceptions exist, such as 2 John). Second, as a group of letters, the title of general or catholic helps to distinguish them from the letters of Paul. These letters represent varieties of authors and circumstances; consequently, they compose a rich, varied witness to Christ and His church. We follow the canonical order and begin with James as the first general or catholic Epistle.

Writer

The identity of the writer is much debated. He called himself a "servant" of Christ and God (1:1). Three "James" in the New Testament may be considered. James, the son of Zebedee, is one. However, he died at the hands of Herod, probably around A.D. 44, a date prior to the writing of the Epistle. James, son of Alphaeus (Mark 3:17–18), is the second possibility, but no substantial connection between him and the book can be established. The traditional view is that this "servant" was the Lord's brother. If so, he was the leader of the church at Jerusalem and the

same person referred to in Mark 6:3 and Galatians 1:19, where James is identified as the Lord's brother.

Support for the traditional position comes from several points. The letter seems to have a strong Jewish tone with its emphasis upon ethical conduct. Although the letter is in Greek, the tone is that of the Old Testament. Indeed, the manner of instruction in James is not unlike that of a Jewish teacher applying Mosaic law to everyday life. The simple identification of the sender of the letter as James, "servant," suggests someone who needed little identification, someone like the Lord's brother, to write with authority and recognition to a wide audience. Also, similarity between the Greek of the speech made by James at the Jerusalem conference (Acts 15:13–21) and the Greek of this letter supports this James as author.

However, arguments against the Lord's brother as author are several. The author had an excellent command of Greek as reflected in the letter. Could the Lord's brother, who spoke Aramaic and who came from a Galilean peasant background, have written such excellent Greek? Although the Old Testament and the Law form the basis of the instruction given, the letter "repeatedly echoes Greek editions of the Hebrew Bible,

191

especially the book of Proverbs and later Hellenistic Wisdom books."[1]

Few references to Christ exist in the epistle, none personal, which one might expect from the brother of Christ. Too, this book of James was not accepted into the New Testament canon until late. Had the Lord's brother written it, would not the church have been eager to affirm it early in the development of the canon? In addition, the author did not identify himself as the Lord's brother.

With the inability to conclude without some doubt the traditional position of authorship, some interpreters simply say that an unknown James wrote the letter. Nonetheless, the letter gained its place in the canon because the early church finally concluded that it had apostolic connection or connection with the Lord's brother.

Therefore, the writer of the letter, who may very well have been the Lord's brother, was a Christian Jew well acquainted with Greek, shaped to some degree in his expression by Hellenistic influences. He wrote probably from a site in Palestine "prior to A.D. 62, the date of his death according to Josephus, or 66 according to Hegisippus' account contained in Eusebius."[2]

Readers

James addressed his readers as "twelve tribes scattered among the nations" (1:1), a

Ruins of the third-century synagogue at Capernaum. *Biblical Illustrator* Photo/David Rogers.

designation usually denoting the nation of Israel. The Jews of the dispersion were those who lived away from Palestine, who were "dispersed" from the homeland. However, those addressed here were Christians scattered throughout Asia Minor. While the audience intended may have been primarily Christian Jews, Christian Gentiles probably were among the readership as well. Since the author addressed a general audience, he wrote to meet the kinds of needs and challenges that faced churches in general. He also wrote to give practical instruction about the right kind of living God's people should do.

Message

James encouraged his readers in the trials and tribulations of life and challenged them to engage in right living. In this regard, evidently, some people professed faith, but their conduct did not correspond. In the admonitions "But be doers of the word, and not merely hearers who, deceive themselves" (1:22, NRSV) and "So faith by itself, if it has no works, is dead" (2:17, NRSV), James gave the heart of his message. The letter lacks an overall structure as the author moved from one subject to another, sometimes coming back to a previous emphasis to comment upon it once again. We will survey some of these subjects and seek the practicality of his instruction.

Living with Trials and Temptations (1:2–18)

The reality of life is that trials will come, and in those trials faith will be put to a test. James encouraged his readers to positive attitudes, making the bad trials of life turn to benefit. Meeting trials with joy, because a tested

faith works "perseverance," or patience, is one way of having a positive approach (1:2–4). This is not advice for Christians to seek trials, since trials come to life anyway. Neither is the instruction one in which the trials themselves are to be enjoyed; rather, the joy comes out of a faith applied to the difficulties of life in such a way that a person learns and grows. The author was careful to point out that God is not the source of temptation, of testing either by evil or toward evil, for "God cannot be tempted by evil, nor does he tempt anyone" (1:13).

James advocated the seeking of "wisdom" if anyone lacks wisdom (1:5), a statement modern readers should not construe to mean that praying for knowledge results in knowledge suddenly gained. When people seek wisdom they want the divine, or God's, viewpoint. Wisdom is a person's knowledge and life informed from God's viewpoint. Such "wisdom" can only come by faith, because faith in God leads to the divine perspective.

The doubter cannot possess the wisdom. The type of doubter here is one who is changing allegiances back and forth, a "double-minded" person (1:8). This does not mean a person cannot question, doubt, or examine the issues of faith. God is not afraid of our questions and doubts; and if we go to Him honestly, He will give us wisdom with our knowledge in order for us to cope or understand matters about which we question or doubt. Many questions will disappear as we engage in active service as discussed in the next section of the text.

Christian Action in the Church (1:19–3:18)

The author further encouraged his readers to put away evil (1:21), to be "doers of the word" (1:22), to control the tongue, and to "look after orphans and widows" (1:27 NRSV). James is the only book in the New Testament where religion is pointedly defined. In this case, a "pure and faultless" religion is one that ministers to widows and orphans (1:27). Widows and orphans represented the disenfranchised in society who had little power, position, opportunity, or means to change their lives.

James, continuing the same theme from the previous paragraph, argued for the recognition of the poor. In a society where people marked status by a person's wealth, the church was to make no such distinction by showing partiality to the rich man and disregarding the poor man (2:1–7). Today's Christians are called to be no less sensitive to the defenseless and the poor of society. The author inspired today's careful reader to go and do likewise, else we become hearers only (1:23). Works are the validating acts of faith (2:14–26). James left no room for someone simply to talk about good works and thus think that talking alone is faithful living. Real faith issues in good works.

Was James countering Paul, who emphasized that works did not save a person but faith did (Eph. 2:8–9)? After all, James said that "faith without deeds is dead" (2:26). But Paul expected Christians to do good works. Life in faith for Paul was life in the Spirit, which resulted in good works—gentleness, self-control, etc. (Gal. 5:22; see Gal. 5:16–26). Also, Paul himself went about doing good works. James was not equating works and faith but declaring as unauthentic a faith in God that does not result in good works for people in need. So no contradiction exists between James and Paul. In fact, James may have been writing to correct a misunderstanding of Paul's emphasis on faith.

Another of the validating works of faith is control of the tongue (3:1–12). Everyone knows what damage falsehoods, gossip, or degrading, abusive language can do. James rightly recognized the power of the tongue, saying, "The tongue is a small part of the body, but it makes great boasts. Consider what a great forest is set on fire by a small spark" (3:5). The tongue can be used for praise and also cursing (3:9–10). The tongue is not a power unto itself, operating by its own will since it expresses the character and motivations of a person. As a tree bears the fruit according to its nature (3:12), so words come out of a person's character. Having the right commitments leads to the kind of person and the kind of action which characterizes the community of faith (3:13–18).

Conduct Outside the Church (4:1—5:6)

James depicts the issues of right and wrong as engaged in the world outside the church.

In additional urging to ethical action, James warned about conflicts as evidenced in quarrels and fights, the answer to which is submission to God (4:1–12). No one should be boastful or prideful about the future, but should take cognizance of the fragility of life (4:13–17). One should say, "If it is the Lord's will, we will live and do this or that" (4:15), an attitude that reflects respect for the sovereignty of God and dependence upon Him. In addition, the author gave a strong warning about dependence upon and abuse of wealth (5:1–6).

Closing Instructions (5:7–20)

Patience in the face of suffering is the right way for the church to live (5:7–12). Certain actions exhibit and lead to such patience and endurance: having confidence in the return of the Lord (5:7–9), being patient and persevering as did the prophets and Job (5:10–11), and letting a "yes" mean "yes" and a "no" mean "no." Here James echoed the teaching of Jesus in Matthew 5:33–37. James' instructions parallel other teachings found in Matthew, especially in the Sermon on the Mount, such as joy in trials (1:2; Matt. 5:10–12) and being hearers and doers of the word (1:22; Matt. 7:24).[3]

Prayer should be a central activity of the church in order to minister to people's needs (5:13–18). Also, attention should be given to the person who wanders from the truth (5:19–20). Christians are responsible for one another.

FOR STUDY AND REVIEW

QUESTIONS FOR CONSIDERATION:

1. What are the possibilities for the authorship of James?

2. What is the major thrust of the message of James?

3. What is wisdom?

4. Was James in conflict with Paul over the matter of faith and works?

5. What are some of the validating works of faith?

FOR FURTHER READING

Martin, Ralph P. *James*. Volume 48, *Word Biblical Commentary*. Edited by David A. Hubbard and Glenn W. Barker. Waco, Texas: Word, 1988.

Wessel, W. W. "Epistle of James." *International Standard Bible Encyclopedia*, volume 2. 959–66.

ENDNOTES

1. Stephen L. Harris, *The New Testament: A Student's Introduction* (Mountain View, Calif.: Mayfield, 1988), 264.

2. E. F. Harrison, *Introduction to the New Testament,* rev. ed. (Grand Rapids: Wm. B. Eerdmans Publishing Company, 1982), 391; the Josephus reference is in his *Antiquities*, XX, ix, 1; the Eusebius reference is in his *Ecclesiastical History*, II, xxiii, 18.

3. For a list, see Donald Guthrie, *New Testament Introduction*, 3rd ed. rev. (Downers Grove, Ill.: InterVarsity Press, 1970), 743.

❦ 25 ❦

1 and 2 Peter and Jude

1 Peter: In Christ, A Living Hope

Writer

Christians in the northern portion of the province of Galatia faced persecution. They received a letter intended to help them in their struggle, a letter which became known as First Peter. For Simon Peter the apostle to have written the letter, the persecution under Nero (see under "Readers") is the most likely possibility, for the tradition of Peter's death during the Neronian persecution is very strong. First Peter 5:1–5 supports Simon Peter's authorship. Here the writer identified himself as an eyewitness of "Christ's sufferings" (5:1). His instructions to the leaders to "be shepherds of God's flock" echoed Jesus' admonition to Simon Peter in John 21:15–17 where Jesus charged Simon to care for the flock. So perhaps he wrote instructions here with an eye to that experience.

Objections to Petrine authorship are several. 1) For example, the vocabulary is too sophisticated and the Greek too polished to come from the hand of a rough fisherman. But the author himself pointed out that he was using a secretary (5:12), so the vocabulary and style might have been influenced sig-

nificantly by the secretary. 2) The persecution reflected must be either the Domitianic or the Trajanic persecution (see under "Readers"), making 1 Peter too late for Petrine authorship, for the persecution under Nero centered primarily in Rome and would not have spread to the northern province of Galatia where the recipients of the letters resided. Nonetheless, the tragic nature of the Neronian persecution was known in the provinces, and Roman soldiers or sympathizers of the Emperor might have put pressures on Christians in some of the provinces.

Those who reject Petrine authorship believe the letter is either pseudonymous or anonymous. If pseudonymous, the author wrote in Simon Peter's name some years after his death in order to give authority to the message conveyed or perhaps to convey the message that the author believed Peter would have written. If anonymous, some unknown author wrote the work and Simon Peter's name mistakenly became attached to it.

Ultimately, the objections to Simon Peter as author can be met with strong arguments. The text itself must be taken seriously, which names Simon Peter the author. The Author probably wrote from Rome, since "Babylon" in 5:13 is a cryptic reference to Rome, sometime during the Neronian persecution, A.D. 64–68.

Readers

The readers were Christians in the northern portion of the province of Galatia (1:1). The place names, however, might be a way of referring to Christians everywhere, or a reference to all of Asia Minor. The readers included Gentile and Jewish Christians. They were under persecution (1:6; 3:13–17; 4:12–19). Identifying the persecutor and his times probably best yields to the Neronian persecution (A.D. 64-68) rather than that of Domitian (A.D. 90–100) or of Trajan (A.D. 110–117). In some places during the first and second century, people viewed Christians as a strange and culturally unacceptable group. Consequently a low level of persecution would prove to be trying and disheartening for Christians. This kind of persecution could have spread to areas of Asia Minor during the Neronian persecution, although Nero directed his actions primarily against Christians in Rome.

The recipients were "strangers" (NIV) or "exiles of the Dispersion" (NRSV) in the world (1:1–2). The translation "exiles of the Dispersion" is a unique designation for the addressees. The expression usually referred to Israelites away from the homeland in areas outside of Israel. Obviously, Peter addressed Christians, or the church. Here, then, an expression normally used for Israel as the people of God refers to Christians, the church, as the Israel of God.

Message

The structure of 1 Peter may be viewed from the following outline: salutation and greeting (1:1–2); a living hope (1:3–2:3); the conduct of God's people, the church (2:4–4:19); a word to leaders (5:1–11); and final greetings (5:12–14). The church, the people of God, secure in the "living hope" provided

in Jesus Christ (1:3–4), is to stand firm in the grace of God (5:12). Standing firm requires a great moral commitment to righteousness for those who belong to Christ and who are committed to responding to suffering as He did.

The Living Hope (1:3—2:3)

What does one say to a people undergoing persecution to help them stand firm? A principal message communicated in 1 Peter is that of a "living hope" (1:3). Hope is the keynote of the Epistle. Peter urged them to rely upon their hope in Jesus Christ. Hope does not mean a vague wish or wishful thinking. In the New Testament, hope is an unrealized reality.

A legal will may serve as an illustration. Suppose a father writes a will in which he makes his daugher president and majority owner of his comany. This is the job she always wanted, the work of her dreams, and it can be hers when she finishes college. The job will belong to her without any doubt because her father has put it in the legal, binding form of a will to be activated upon her graduation. She has "hope," therefore, that her dream will be realized when she graduates from college. That is not a vague wish or wishful thinking on her part, for her father's will establishes a reality that cannot be undone by anyone but the father.

We can reasonably assume that the unrealized reality of her inheritance would impact her life in positive and life-enriching ways until that graduation. What her father willed her in love would inspire her, motivate her; indeed, the reality of that inheritance would in some degree be present already with her as she worked toward graduation. She would better endure the hard times of life because

Voltive Relief to Artemos and probably Apollo. At left of an altar, two men and two women stand in devotional attitudes. To the right, in the larger size of divinity, stands a young god with a staff in his hand and a veiled goddess with a crescent on her head. *Biblical Illustrator* Photo/David Rogers.

ahead of her was the reality of inheritance which promised her the fulfillment she had always wanted.

This illustration, although not perfect, is analogous to Peter's injunction about a living hope. His readers faced difficult and insecure times. Yet, one thing was certain: they would receive the eternal life and quality of life with the Heavenly Father which Jesus willed to them by virtue of His "resurrection . . . from the dead" (1:3). No one could take that inheritance away from them (1:4), and that toward which they hoped would never turn out bad. They had hope in their hands, unrealized reality, which would be fulfilled in due time. However, they had the reality already,

because that future blessed the present with direction, meaning, and strength. Also, God was with them already, a relationship that would grow and result in the fullness of relationship implied by the inheritance which awaited them.

They were to "set [their] hope fully on the grace" given to them (1:13). This hope, inheritance, salvation, and grace which Peter discussed with them was not without ethical content. In fact, they were to be "holy" in all they did (1:15). He was very specific, such as in these words: "Therefore, rid yourselves of all malice and all deceit, hypocrisy, envy, and slander of every kind" (2:1).

The Conduct of God's People, The Church (2:4—4:19)

Peter never departed from a strong moral emphasis in the letter. The description of God's people points toward their call to righteousness. Already designating them as "exiles of the Dispersion" (see earlier discussion), he used other terminology for the church normally applied to Israel of the old covenant. They were "living stones . . . being built into a spiritual house to be a holy priesthood, offering spiritual sacrifices acceptable to God through Jesus Christ" (2:5). These expressions indicate that the church is the new temple of God. In 2:9, the church is "a chosen people, a royal priesthood, a holy nation, a people belonging to God." That he was speaking not of Israel but of the church is evidenced by these words: "Once you were not a people, but now you are the people of God" (2:10). The church is now the Israel of God. The old, including the old Israel of God, has been caught up and fulfilled in and through Jesus Christ.

Again, the conduct of the people of God in an alien environment for the church is paramount. "Live such good lives," he wrote, "among the pagans that, though they accuse you of doing wrong, they may see your good deeds and glorify God on the day he visits us" (2:11). They were to be wise in their relationship to authority (2:13–21) and in family relationships (3:1–7). Too, they were to live in "harmony with one another" (3:8) and do good to those who were against them as well, for Christ did set such an example (3:13–22).

Peter appealed to them in their suffering to have the same "attitude" as Christ had in his suffering (4:1). Indeed, the "painful trial" (4:12) they suffered was a participation "in the sufferings of Christ" (4:13). Consequently, their suffering was not in vain, but that through which God could manifest His glory (4:14).

A Word to Leaders (5:1–11)

Leaders in the church were of great help in a persecution situation. Peter encouraged them to take faithfully their responsibilities of being "shepherds of God's flock" under their care (5:2). They were called to be servants and examples (5:2–4). "Young men" (5:5) could help the situation greatly by being responsive to the leadership provided. Peter made such affirmations because of God's power, a reality he pointed to when he wrote, "To him be the power for ever and ever. Amen" (5:11).

Final Greetings (5:12–14)

He closed the letter with reference to Silvana, his secretary, and sent greeting to the readers from the church of "Babylon," or Rome. Mark is included in that greeting which indicates that they were together in Rome (see discussion under authorship of the Gospel of Mark). His final words contained strength: "Peace to all of you who are in Christ" (5:12–14).

2 Peter: The Revealed Faith and Faithful Conduct

Writer

The letter names "Simon Peter, a servant and apostle of Jesus Christ" as the author. Some early church leaders reluctantly granted this letter canonical status, and great discussions have swirled about its authorship.

Works of different kinds appeared under assumed names, an accepted practice by many people during the period from approximately 200 B.C. to A.D. 200. For example, a writing named the *Testament of Moses*, or *The Assumption of Moses*, written at the beginning of the first century A.D., did not come from Moses. The author attributed Moses name to the writing to give it authority. Did someone close to Peter write in his name to express what he believed Peter would have wanted expressed in the situation of the readers? Some interpreters think so. A writing like this is a pseudonymous writing.

Early church leaders, such as Eusebius, had doubts about 2 Peter, so the letter did not always have support as being a part of the apostolic witness.[1] Too, Jude and 2 Peter have similar material. If Jude came before 2 Peter, as some think, then 2 Peter would have to be dated after the apostle's death. Also, the reference to a collection of Paul's letters (3:15) must point to a late writing of the letter, because Paul's letters were collected late in the first century. In addition, stylistic differences, such as a cumbersome style when compared with 1 Peter, and theological differences, such as a seeming difference in the view of the return of Christ as compared with 1 Peter, also are offered as objections.[2]

In support of Petrine authorship, some church leaders did favor its canonicity. As for as the relationship of Jude and 2 Peter, Jude could have used 2 Peter, or perhaps they both depended upon a common source. Stylistic similarities and theological similarities with 1 Peter exist as well. Counterbalancing arguments can be offered to the objections to Petrine authorship. Then, too, the epistle itself, as already indicated, names Simon Peter as author.

Readers

The letter does not identify the readers beyond this statement: "To those who through the righteousness of our God and Savior Jesus Christ have received a faith as precious as ours" (1:1). In 3:1 we read, "Dear friends, this is now my second letter to you." If this is a reference to 1 Peter, then they are the same readers named in 1 Peter 1:1–2.

Message

Three major sections form the brief letter. The first discusses Christian life and knowledge (1:3–21). The second section deals with false teachers (2:1–22), and the third deals with the return of Christ (3:1–18). The three sections are related, revolving around the challenge by false teachers to the faith as taught by the apostles, particularly as regards life in the light of Christ's return. Therefore, 2 Peter calls readers to remain true in both belief and conduct to the revealed faith, especially that which is true in the light of the Lord's return.

Christian Life and Knowledge (1:3–21)

The divine power of God in Jesus Christ gives everything needed "for life and godliness through . . . knowledge of him who called us by his own glory and goodness" (1:3). Human effort, or response of Christians to this gift of God in Christ, is expected. The readers should make "every effort" to add to their "faith goodness; and to goodness, knowledge; and to knowledge, self-control; and to self-control, perseverance; and to perseverance, godliness; and to godliness, brotherly kindness; and to brotherly kindness, love" (1:5–7).

Such knowledge of God in Christ and such a call to living are not of human origin (1:16), for the source is in Christ (1:16–18) and through witnesses who "spoke from God as they were carried along by the Holy Spirit" (1:21). Christians have the knowledge needed to live life for Christ in any situation if they honor both the knowledge received and the calling required.

False Teachers (2:1–22)

The false teachers were not identified enough for us to determine whether they were Gnostics or proponents of some syncretistic philosophy which included Christian elements. They did deny, as the letter says, "the sovereign Lord who bought them" (2:1), which is destructive in its impact upon them and upon those who listen to them. The remainder of chapter 2 makes plain that the false teachers will be held accountable for their teachings and actions, and judgment will come upon them.

The Return of Christ (3:1–18)

Evidently, some confusion and question existed among the readers about the return of Christ, here spoken of in terms of the "day of the Lord" (3:10)—a confusion and challenge caused in particular by the false teachers. Second Peter reminds readers that the last days will be filled with scoffers (3:3). But the timing of that coming is not determined by human agency or understood from limited human perspective, for "with the Lord a day is like a thousand years, and a thousand years are like a day" (3:8). God is sovereign over time, and that sovereignty impinges upon a given moment just as it does upon the totality of time however God determines totality. The

Christian is to watch, pray, and work. The author wrote, "So then, dear friends, since you are looking forward to this, make every effort to be found spotless, blameless and at peace with him" (3:14).

Jude: Remember the Faith Entrusted to the Saints

Writer

Here we depart from the order of the New Testament books. As already noted in the discussion of 2 Peter, the two are interrelated. For convenience, and also to keep in view the strong relationship Jude has with 2 Peter, Jude receives attention here rather than after the letters of John.

The distinguishing information given to the writer's identification includes "servant" and "brother of James" (1). The "brother of James" is more specific, but as to which James is meant involves the same discussion as that of the book of James (see under "Writer"). The traditional position is that Jude was the brother of the Lord (Matt. 13:55; Mark 6:3). We cannot be certain of this identity.

Some believe Jude to be a work written in the first part of the second century. One support for this conclusion is that the author seemed to be looking back upon the apostles from a long distance, as in the case of the faith "entrusted to the saints" (3). This statement seems to speak of faith as a body of belief rather than a dynamic relationship usually encountered in first-century Christian writings.

The relationship with 2 Peter is also a factor, with 2 Peter containing approximately 15 verses of Jude as well as other parallel statements and expressions.[3] Did Jude depend on 2 Peter, or did 2 Peter depend on Jude? Or did they both depend on a common source, such as a brief writing against false teachers in circulation when both letters were written?[4] All three positions find support from interpreters.

On the plus side, for Jude the Lord's brother as writer, is the Hebrew tone of the letter, much as we emphasized about the letter of James. The author showed acquaintance with Jewish writings, quoting from the *Assumption of Moses* (9) and the *Apocalypse of Enoch* (14). Too, in verses 17–18, the author seemed to indicate that the readers themselves heard the apostles, which would mean that such hearing occurred long before the second century, a time in which the Lord's brother could be the author. Also, the identification in the first verse provides evidence, although it is not conclusive because Jude is not identified enough for us to know without doubt who he is. Suggested dates range from A.D. 48 to A.D. 150. A date somewhere between A.D. 65 and 100 is more probable, although Eusebius seemed to indicate that Jude had died by the time of Domitian.[5] An earlier date, between 60 and 70, seems the most likely. If the position taken is that Jude is an unknown author, then the book could be dated as late as the first half of the second century.

Readers

The readers are "those who have been called" (1). Since this is a general letter, a general readership must have been in view. The readers did face false teachers whose beliefs threatened the churches.

Message

Jude wrote to encourage his readers to stand firm in the face of a formidable ethical and theological challenge to their faith. He urged them to "contend for the faith that was once for all entrusted to the saints" (3). The false teachers against whom they were to contend are not identified, although some interpreters suggest opponents who held a Gnostic-like philosophy. Their apparent moral laxness was one exprssion Gnosticism could take. They are godless and engage in immoral practices (4). They defile their bodies and reject authority, among other things. Indeed, the majority of the letter is a denunciation of the conduct of these false teachers, which indicates that the problem was serious.

But this small letter also has encouragement and affirmation. The readers received encouragement to "keep" themselves in God's love (21). They were to be "merciful to those who doubt" (22). The author closed with affirmation of the security they have in God as he placed the readers in God's care, the one who can keep them from "falling" (24). Consequently, he praised God as the one with "glory, majesty, power and authority, through Jesus Christ our Lord" (25).

FOR STUDY AND REVIEW

QUESTIONS FOR CONSIDERATION:

1. What are some of the arguments for and against Petrine authorship of both letters? Jude?

2. What are the three possibilities for dating the persecution reflected in 1 Peter?

3. What are the evidences in 1 Peter that the church is the new Israel, the people of God?

4. What is the keynote of 1 Peter? What is the meaning of "hope"?

5. What is true about time in relationship

to the "day of the Lord"?

6. What problems did the recipients of each of the three letters face?

FOR FURTHER READING:

Beker, J. C. "Second Letter of Peter." *Interpreter's Dictionary of the Bible.* 767–71.

Danker, F. W. "Epistle of Jude." *The International Standard Bible Encyclopedia.* 1153–56.

Green, Michael. *2 Peter and Jude.* Rev. ed. *Tyndale New Testament Commentaries.* Edited by Leon Morris. Grand Rapids: Eerdmans, 1987.

Harrison. *Introduction.* 394–437.

Leaney, A. R. C. *The Letters of Peter and Jude. The Cambridge Bible Commentary.* Cambridge: University Press, 1967.

ENDNOTES

1. Eusebius, *Ecclesiastical History*, III, iii, 1. See Michael Green, *2 Peter and Jude*, rev. ed., *Tyndale New Testament Commentaries*, ed. Leon Morris (Grand Rapids: Eerdmans, 1987), for a discussion about early church attestation of 2 Peter, 13–17.

2. See Donald Guthrie, *New Testament Introduction*, 3rd ed. rev. (Downers Grove, Ill.: InterVarsity Press, 1970), 773–90; and W. G. Kümmel, *Introduction to the New Testament* translated by H. C. McKee. Revised and enlarged ed. (Nashville: Abingdon Press, 1975), 416–434; for full discussions of objections and support to Petrine authorship.

3. Green, *2 Peter and Jude*, 23.

4. Ibid., 24.

5. Eusebius, *Ecclesiastical History*, III, xx, 1–2.

The Letters of John

The three Epistles associated with the name John are classed with the catholic or general Epistles. However, 1 John addresses specific problems in a specific situation, although these conditions may have been prevalent in more than one church. Both 2 and 3 John were personal notes to specific audiences. The three Epistles help to make up a greater body of literature known as the Johannine Literature. The other writings of this body of literature are the Gospel of John and Revelation.

Writer

Of these five writings, only one mentions the name John as its author, and that is the book of Revelation. Matters of authorship are the same as discussed in relationship to the Gospel of John, and a review of that section would help to put all five works of the Johannine Literature in perspective. But we will review the discussion here.

While some would suggest one author for 1 John and another for 2 and 3 John, enough similarities exist between the Epistles to make different authors unlikely. Whoever wrote 2 and 3 John probably wrote 1 John and the Gospel, or gave direction to their writing. The Epistles and the Fourth Gospel had the name of John associated with them quite early. Ire-

naeus quoted from 1 John 2:18–22 and stated that this was John's testimony in his epistle.[1] The Muratorian Canon, in existence around A.D. 170, refers to circumstances around the origin of the Gospel of John and alludes to John having written about the Lord in his letters.[2] The traditional position, therefore, agreeing with the titles of the writings as they appear in our Bibles now, is that John the apostle wrote all five of the books with which his name is associated.

As noted in our discussion of the Fourth Gospel, we do have specific information about John the apostle. He was the son of Zebedee and brother of James. They were fishermen. He was one of the three apostles upon whom Jesus depended the most, along with Peter and James. If he is the John of Revelation, we know that he lived to be very old and was exiled to the isle of Patmos during a time of persecution, probably between A.D. 90 and 100. Some interpreters believe that he is the "beloved disciple" of John 21:20-24, although this identification cannot be made with certainty.

Other scholars argue that John the apostle was not the writer. If the apostle did write the letters, more certainty would exist in identifying the letters with him in terms of the sautations. After all, as the reasoning goes, would not the apostle identify himself as such in a letter? Also, a strong tradition existed that John became a martyr not long after his brother James, who was put to death by Herod Agrippa (Acts 12:1–2). Mark 10:38–39 indicates that Jesus warned James and John that they would suffer martyrdom. Did this mean that they would die about the same time? Some think so. Nonetheless, these arguments are not conclusive. Perhaps no early definite identity of the writings with the apostle John was necessary, since the readers knew that John the apostle wrote to them.

One of the greatest challenges to Johannine authorship is the variety found in the writings themselves. Some characteristics, such as words and phrases and concepts, are missing in the Epistles when compared with the Gospel of John. Prepositional usage, adverbial participles, conjunctions, and certain idioms are missing. Also, ideas or expressions such as to save, to perish, to send, and a certain form of a word for *love* (*philein*) are not present. Neither does one find emphasis upon grace, peace, Scripture, and law in the Epistles as is true in the Fourth Gospel. So some interpreters conclude that more than one author wrote the various materials. However, the different times of the writings and the length and purpose of the Fourth Gospel in comparison with the Epistles could account for such differences if one author wrote the materials.

Some suggest that an elder named John wrote the Epistles. The writer did identify himself as the "elder" in 2 and 3 John. The ancient historian Eusebius quoted Papias, who seemed to allude to a well-known Christian leader named John the Elder, who in turn seemed to be distinguished from John the apostle.[3] Unfortunately, Papias' quote by Eusebius does not establish clearly that Papias meant two individuals instead of one.

Perhaps the elder and the apostle John were the same person.

Another suggestion is that the apostle John established a "school" of disciples whom he taught and trained. Some of these disciples, or perhaps one or several serving as editors, helped to organize and write the Gospel and the Epistles. Participation by several in the composing and editing process would account for the differences which occur.[4]

Another suggestion for authorship is simply a Christian named John. John was a common name, and perhaps the John of Revelation and of the Epistles and the Fourth Gospel was not an apostle, but a Christian witness about whom we know little. But writings found respect and usage as Scripture in the early church because their witness was directly connected to or directly from some apostle. The only way a "plain" John would likely find such respect and use of his writings was by the direct influence of someone like the apostle John, or being a member of the school of John if such a school existed.

Readers

The Johannine literature has long been connected with Ephesus. The letters probably went to congregations not far from Ephesus. The Gospel and the Revelation went to Christians in Asia Minor. Perhaps 1 John went to several churches that faced the same problems revealed in the letter. Nonetheless, some of the statements of the writer to his readers are so warmly personal that he seemed to have a particular group of people in mind.

Second John has specific addressees: "the chosen lady and her children" (1). She could have been a Christian lady and her children who provided influential leadership and stability in the church. At points he did seem to address a particular person, such as in verse 5. The last verse, "The children of your chosen sister send their greetings" (13), as well as the general tone of the letter, really suggest that he meant by "chosen lady" and "chosen sister" and their children the respective churches and their members.

Third John is a personal letter, the only one of the Johannine epistles. The addressee was Gaius (1), but the whole church was to hear the message, perhaps by having Gaius read the letter in the hearing of all.

1 John: Christ Jesus, Fully Human Son of God

The overall thrust of the message of 1 John might be stated this way: God has manifested Himself in Jesus, who was fully human and the Son of God, so that people may experience a fellowship of love with God and each other. The content of 1 John is difficult to organize into an orderly outline, because the writer moved from one instruction to the next and at times retraced his previous themes. He evidently intended to cover well the avenues of a heresy and its effects upon the people he loved. Alan Culpepper offered an interesting and helpful approach to delineating a structure in this first Epistle, based upon the statement "God is" (light, 1:5; righteous, 2:29; and love, 4:8). The major points of a structure following this theme are:

I.   The Prologue: The Word of Life (1:1–4)
II. Light Among God's Children (1:5—2:27)
III. Righteousness Among God's Children (2:28—3:10)
IV. Love Among God's Children (4:7—5:12)
V.   Epilogue (5:13–21)[5]

The recipients of 1 John faced a heresy that threatened to undermine faith in Jesus Christ. Heretical teachers in the church or churches taught that relationship with God came through special knowledge, love, and fellowship (1:6,2:3–9), as they defined knowledge, love, and fellowship. They denied that the human Jesus was the spiritual Christ (2:22–25), rejecting the historical Jesus who came in the flesh (4:2). They thought themselves to be above sin (1:8,10) and believed that they had special spiritual experiences which made them superior to others (4:1–6).

As might be surmised from this survey of their teaching, the false teachers caused problems for John's readers in three areas.[6] First, they created a theological problem by denying the humanity of Christ. In their view, if Christ were human, he would have to be evil, for to be human was to be physical, or material, and the material was evil inherently. To deny that the historical Jesus and the Christ were the same was to deny the historical basis of Christianity.

The opening verses (1:1–4) emphasize that the eyewitnesses have seen, heard, and touched that which was "from the beginning." Therefore, the eternal One did become flesh, or human, and the historical Jesus, the Christ, is a reality. The heretical teachers who claimed to be of Christ but denied his humanity lived a lie. In fact, they were antichrists. As John asked and answered, "Who is the liar but the one who denies that Jesus is the Christ? This is the antichrist, the one who denies the Father and the Son" (2:22, NRSV).

Second, since the false teachers thought themselves to have special knowledge and special spiritual experiences, they felt superior to others who were not as they were, which caused a fellowship problem. First John proclaims that Jesus is the source of knowledge (2:20, 21), and those who think they have fellowship with God and yet "hate" a brother are in the darkness (2:11). "Light" and "darkness" are notable themes in 1 John. To be in darkness is to be out of fellowship with God; to be in the light is to be in fellowship with God. Therefore, the superior attitudes of the heretical teachers which created tension and hostility within the church meant they were in darkness and out of fellowship with God.

The third problem was an ethical one. The heretical teachers believed that with their special knowledge, spiritual experiences, and fellowship with God, sin was not a factor for them. Since they denied the humanity of Jesus, they evidently held a belief that separated the physical, or material, from the spiritual. Their special knowledge, spiritual experiences, and fellowship with God were all spiritual, therefore, and had nothing to do with the physical. Since sin had to do with the physical, it really could not affect the spiritual.

They probably believed that all matter was evil, a philosophical world view prominent among Gnosticism in its incipient stages in the first century and developed stages in the second century. Since all matter was evil, and since the physical self was matter, a person was going to sin anyway. Nothing could be done about it; therefore, sin was not an issue. First John stresses the seriousness of sin (1:8–9, 3:4–10). In fact, anyone who "commits sin is . . . of the devil" (3:8). Christ, however, forgives sin, because sin needs to be forgiven (2:1–2; 3:5–6, 9).

Apparently the false teachers had Gnostic-like views. One form of Gnostic thinking was *docetism,* from the Greek word *dokeo,* which means "to seem." In this view, Christ was not really human, He only seemed to be. The heretics may have been so-called Christian Gnostics, who believed Christ to be the special revealer of special knowledge which only they understood, thus fitting aspects of the teaching of Jesus into their Gnostic-like systems of thought.

Another form of Gnostic-like thinking was that of Cerinthus, whose views may be reflected in the heresy 1 John combats. Irenaeus told of Cerinthus' views in *Against Heresies.*[7] Cerinthus taught that Christ came upon Jesus at his baptism but left him at his crucifixion. In this way the spiritual Christ was separate from the physical Jesus, so that the spiritual was not contaminated by the physical. Perhaps the false teachers were of the Cerinthus kind; but whatever kind they were, they denied the humanity of Jesus Christ.

God's love is a common denominator running throughout this message. God is light and He is righteousness, but a way of defining the content of that light and righteousness is "love." God does love, and those who have experienced His love return it to Him by loving others. John referred to *agape* (love) here, the self-giving love that we considered in relationship to 1 Corinthians 13. *Agape* is unique among all the loves and loving of humankind and has its origin in God. God's love is self-giving, always with the interest of the person loved at heart. Since God so loves us, can we not love one another with His kind of love?

2 John: Hospitality and Those Who Deny Christ

The "elder" stressed his love for his readers (1), and urged members to love one another (5). He warned them about the same deceivers singled out in 1 John, those who deny the humanity of Jesus Christ (7).

The author also raised the question of hospitality extended to the heretical teachers

(10–11). Hospitality was a sacred duty, once extended, to honorable people in the first-century world. This was true for Christian churches as well. They afforded lodging and meals for traveling preachers, missionaries, and teachers. Indeed, one of the important factors in the strengthening and spread of Christianity was the practice of hospitality among the churches. Without such support, those prepared to take the gospel to the world would not have been able to do so as quickly as they did.

The elder wanted his readers to understand that hospitality was not to be extended to the false teachers (10–11). Their duty did not include them; in fact, they were not even to greet them (10).

3 John: Opposition Within Christ's Church

Third John is the most intensely personal letter in the New Testament. The "elder" wrote to Gaius, a friend and fellow-laborer. Gaius was a member of a community of faith over which the elder had some influence. However, Diotrephes opposed the elder by resisting the elder's authority (9). One form of the resistance was refusal to "welcome the brothers," (10), who may have been representatives, or at least friends, of the elder. Diotrephes protected his authority with his group by keeping the elder's representatives out of the church.

On the other hand, Gaius received praise from the elder. Gaius and his friends welcomed the missionary brethren and ministered to them (5–8). Of course, welcoming them meant providing for them as befitted the requirements of hospitality. Another figure in this brief epistle is Demetrius. The elder also praised Demetrius, but did not identify him

beyond that point (12). He probably was the bearer of this letter to Gaius.

The epistle is brief because the author planned to make a visit soon after sending the letter (13). Obviously this was a different congregation than that of 2 John. The letter shows briefly some of the troubles of the church and reflects something of a developed church organization or ecclesiology, for the elder wrote as a leader in authority over the congregation. However, to see a bishop in a structured church hierarchy would make the church structure more formal than it was. In reality, the elder may have felt he had authority with the church simply because of previous association with them, a situation not unlike Paul's relationship to some of the churches he helped. The author kept his remarks brief because he planned to visit with them soon. Then he would speak with them directly (13–14). If we consider 1 John and the Gospel of John as reflective of the content which the elder wished to share with the congregation of 3 John, we can surmise that they had already, and would have when he visited them again, much knowledge about the Lord Jesus Christ.

FOR STUDY AND REVIEW

IDENTIFY:

Johannine Literature
Gaius
Diotrephes
Demetrius

QUESTIONS FOR CONSIDERATION:

1. Who are the possible authors of the

three letters and what are the reasons for supporting each?

2. What were the major problems created by the heresy as reflected in 1 John?

3. What are the different kinds of Gnostic-like approaches that may be reflected in 1 John? What did each approach propose about Jesus?

4. What was the concern in 2 John? What did the author recommend?

5. What was the problem in 3 John?

FOR FURTHER READING:

Marshall, I. H. "The Epistles of John." *The International Standard Bible Encyclopedia* 1091–98.

W. G. Kümmel. *Introduction* to the New Testament, translated by H. C. Mckee. Revised and enlarged ed. Nashville: Abingdon Press, 1975: 38–80. 435-52.

Stott, John R. W. *The Letters of John.* Rev. ed. *Tyndale New Testament Commentaries.* Edited by Leon Morris. Grand Rapids: Eerdmans, 1990.

ENDNOTES

1.   Irenaeus, *Against Heresies*, III, xvi, 5.

2.   F. F. Harrison, *Introduction to the New Testament*, rev. ed. (Grand Rapids: Wm. B. Eerdmans Publishing Company, 1982), 439.

3.   Eusebius, *Ecclesiastical History*, III, xxxviii, 3–7.

4.   See Raymond E. Brown, *The Community of the Beloved Disciple* (New York: Paulist Press, 1978).

5.   R. Alan Culpepper, "The Letters of John," *Holman Bible Dictionary*, (Nashville: Holman Bible Publishers, 1991), 808.

6.   These three problems are clearly stated in Malcolm Tolbert's book, *Walking with the Lord* (Nashville: Broadman Press, 1970), 9–19.

7.   Irenaeus, *Against Heresies*, I, xxvi, 1.

❧ 27 ❧

Revelation: The Victory and Reign of Christ

Writer

Contrary to the other books accredited to John, the author of the book of Revelation gave his name as "John" (1:1,4,9; 22:8). Determining which John is a challenge. Possible identifications include the apostle John, the Elder John, John Mark, an unknown Christian named John, or a person who wrote in John's name. The traditional position is that John the apostle wrote the book of Revelation. See the section on "writer" in the discussion of the Gospel of John and the epistles of John for more information about authorship of the Johannine Literature.

John was on the isle of Patmos when he wrote. The traditional interpretation is that he was banished there during a period of persecution of Christians. The setting of the persecution is somewhat difficult to determine. Two periods when persecution at the hands of Roman emperors occurred are dismissed because of their dates: the rule of Claudius (A.D. 41–54), considered to be too early for the writing of Revelation, and the rule of Trajan (A.D. 98–117), considered to be too late. Two other possibilities exist, the persecutions during the reign of Nero (A.D. 54–68), and during the reign of Domitian (A.D. 81–96).

Evidently Nero unjustly blamed Christians, perhaps as a way of hiding his own responsibility, for setting the fire that burned a significant portion of the city of Rome (A.D. 64). Christianity was not a recognized religion, and Christians were easy targets for affixing blame for the fire. Nero persecuted them severely, and executed many.

The rule of Domitian is the second suggestion for the setting of the writing. Historical evidence suggests that Domitian demanded to be worshiped as a god by his subjects, which Christians and Jews refused to do. Domitian's forces persecuted Christians in particular, which by the accounts in Revelation would have included martyrdom for many followers of Christ. Those who believe that the Domitonic persecution was the setting of Revelation I believe that John wrote the book between A,D. 91 and 96.

The difficulty in identifying John's writing with a Domitian-inspired persecution is that persecution of Christians by Domitian is difficult to support historically. The Neronian persecution, however, can be substantiated, so some interpreters opt for a writing date of A.D. 68 or shortly thereafter. The difficulty with the Neronian date, however, is that the severe persecution occurred primarily in Rome, whereas John seemed to depict a widespread persecution throughout Asia

Minor as well. Also, no evidence exists that Nero persecuted the Christians because they refused to worship him. Revelation apparently reflects that Christians refused to engage in emperor worship. For these and other reasons, most interpreters have favored the Domitian era for the origin of the book.

Another possibility for the setting of the writing is quite different. Gnostic-like philosophy became a formidable challenge to Christianity in the latter half of the first century. Perhaps John wrote to combat Gnostic-like ideas, teachings, and beliefs. In this approach, the struggle depicted in the highly intensive symbolism of Revelation is a struggle and victory against the evil represented in a Gnostic-type philosophy. Revelation, therefore, gives the special knowledge of the revelation of Jesus Christ as opposed to any special knowledge the Gnostics claimed to have about God and Jesus.[1] (See the discussion on Gnosticism in chapter 6 for more information.)

Again, however, the prevailing view is that the setting was one of political-religious persecutions at the hands of an emperor. This kind of setting seems to fit with the situation reflected in Revelation. Enough historical record exists to support a general persecution under Domitian, the setting and time of which seems to correspond to the content of Revelation.

Readers

The first readers of the Book of Revelation understood what they read, but interpreters have an especially hard time understanding what the readers understood. This has led to differing interpretations of Revelation. The book's name comes from the first word in its Greek text, *apocalypsis,* meaning a "disclo-

Colossal head and hand of the Roman Emperor Domitian, first century A.D., from Ephesus. *Biblical Illustrator* Photo/David Rogers/Archaeological Museum, Ismir.

sure," "unveiling," or a "revealing," hence the name *Revelation.* "The Apocalypse" is another title sometimes used for Revelation. What interpreters believe the writer unveiled, however, varies greatly.

One of the reasons that present-day readers have such difficulty understanding the book is because the author wrote in a style and thought form known as apocalyptic. This style of writing ceased about the second century A.D., so it has been a "dead language" for centuries. Revelation is the only apocalyptic book we have in the New Testament, while Daniel is the only fully apocalyptic book of the Old Testament. Some feel, therefore, that Daniel and Revelation should be interpreted together, which is unfortunate since each addressed different people at a different time in history with different messages. The fact that these two books appear in apocalyptic style does not mean that they have the same message.

Other apocalyptic books do exist outside of the New Testament. The Apocalypse of Abraham, Apocalypse of Noah, Apocalypse of Ezra, and the Books of Enoch are examples. From these and other writings we learn much about apocalyptic literature.

Apocalyptic literature has certain characteristics. Primarily, such literature is dualistic, eschatological, deterministic, and historically identified. It is *dualistic* in that the struggle of bad against good is depicted as a struggle of hell against heaven, of the present evil age against the righteous who await the age to come.

It is *eschatological*, a word referring to "last things," in the sense that apocalyptic literature sees humankind in the last age of existence. The length of the age is not precisely defined, but it is the last era of human existence that apocalyptic writing talks about.

It is *deterministic* in that the conflict and its consequences are inevitable; certain details of actions and consequenses therefore are inevitable. Consequently, apocalyptic material usually had a spirit of pessimism about it.

It is *historically identified* because authors wrote apocalyptic works at a particular time in history to a particular people with a message for them. Sometimes people interpreting the Book of Revelation do not take sufficient note that Revelation was written to a particular people at a particular time in history.

Apocalyptic writing had secondary characteristics as well. Symbols, visions, and images play important parts as means of communication. Numbers are important and are used to convey ideas and concepts (note box 18).

Box 18: Symbolic Meanings of Numbers

1 = unity, or the oneness of God
2 = companionship, added strength
3 = the divine number
4 = visible creation
6 = imperfection, incompleteness
7 = perfection, completeness
10 = human completeness
12 = organized religion or God's people

Multiples or combinations of these numbers have much the same significance as the primary number. The number 666 is an intensification of 6, indicating extreme evil, while 144,000 is the square of 12 multiplied by a thousand and represents a large inclusive number. Numbers so used were not for measurement but for conveying ideas in a very vivid way.

Many of the conflicting and varying interpretations occur primarily in reference to time. When? is the big question. When John was to write about what is "seen, what is now and what will take place later" (1:19), what time frame was meant? Four basic approaches to interpreting Revelation as regards time determine ultimately the direction of interpretation for most of the book. These are Preterist, Historical, Futurist, and Symbolic.

Preterist refers to viewing the events of Revelation as having taken place during and shortly after John wrote. The *Historical* approach sees the events as taking place at various times throughout history up to and beyond the present time. A *Futurist* approach, as the name implies, believes that most of the events of Revelation have yet to happen, perhaps in the very near future according to certain "signs" of the times. Finally, the *Symbolic* approach views time as depicted in Revelation as nonchronological, and the message of the book is one in which the nature of humanity and the nature of God are so well interpreted that any time in history always has the forces operating as they are depicted by John.

We tend to think of time exclusively as chronological time. However, "event" time also exists in apocalypticism, where events and their meanings are important, not the chronology of the events. Sometimes the same idea may be pictured as panoramic time, where one sees all the events at once without regard to chronology.

Message

As with any other book in the New Testament, we must keep in mind what the book said to the original readers. Certainly they were in a struggle, one involving severe persecution. Christ revealed the message to John. The message is one of the victory of Christ over evil, of the reign of Christ in which His followers participate, and of the judgment and destruction which comes upon evil. John wrote to encourage Christians who experienced a very difficult persecution because they identified themselves with Christ.

The structure of the Apocalypse is unique, grouping the message as it does in terms of the number seven. After the introduction (1:1–20), John addressed letters to seven churches (2:1—3:22). Next is the vision of heavenly worship (4:1—5:14). Then follows

what Milo Connick pointed out are seven visions with seven visions:

1. seven seals (6:1—8:6)
2. seven trumpets (8:7—11:19)
3. seven visions of the dragon's kingdom (12:1-13:18)
4. seven visions of worshippers of the lamb and worshippers of the beast (14:1—20)
5. seven bowls (15:1-16:21)
6. seven visions of the fall of Babylon (17:1—19:10)
7. seven visions of the end of Satan's evil age and the beginning of God's righteous age ((19:11—21:8)[2]

Introduction (1:1–20)

The revelation is given by God to Jesus Christ (1:1) for sharing with His servants. The revelation is called a "prophecy" (1:3), which leads some interpreters to conclude that this is a prophecy delivered in apocalyptic style. Prophecy did not function primarily to predict the future but to tell the will of God to a given situation. As a prophecy, therefore, the intention of the revelation was not to give a countdown of history, but to deliver a message to those undergoing persecution. This does not mean that application to the future and to our own human situation is not made, but made in the sense of other New Testament books. Other interpreters would take prophecy in a more predictive sense and apply most of the Apocalypse to future events.

The churches are introduced (1:11), and in the middle of them is the exalted Christ. The power, authority, and majesty of Christ are stated (1:17–18). He holds the churches and their angels (perhaps the pastors of the churches) in His right hand. His right hand is the hand of power, implying He has authority over the churches and is able to meet their needs.

The Letters to the Seven Churches (2:1—3:22)

The author focused upon seven specific churches located in western Asia Minor, but the churches may have been representative of all the churches who might read the Apocalypse. The pattern of the message to each church is much the same. Each church is identified, a review of the special characteristics of each church stated, the faithfulness or unfaithfulness of each expressed, and certain actions emphasized which each needs to take to remain or become faithful. In the context of persecution, churches needed this strong encouragement and admonition in order to remain faithful in the struggle.

The Vision of Heavenly Worship (4:1—5:14)

This vision sets the tone of the majesty and power of God and the glory of Christ which is foundational to the rest of the book. Such power, majesty, and glory inspires worship from all of creation (the angels, the living creatures, and the elders; see 5:11). In chapter 5 a scroll is introduced with seven seals, and no one anywhere is able to open the seals, which actually is an opening of the revelation given by God.

But the Lion-Lamb is able to do so. A symbolic description of Jesus Christ, the Lamb has "seven horns and seven eyes, which are the seven spirits of God sent out into all the earth" (5:6). In apocalyptic writing, horns, symbolize power and the number seven indi-

cates completeness, so the Lamb has all power. Since the seven eyes are the seven spirits sent out into all the earth, nothing exists of which the Lamb is not aware; nothing can escape His vision. Through this dramatic imagery, John vividly portrayed Jesus as the one of authority and power. He is the one who can open the scroll's seven seals and give the revelation of God.

The Seven Seals (6:1—8:6)

The first four seals tell of judgments that come upon all of creation. Insofar as the church identifies with the commitments and attitudes of the world, it is included in the judgment. The first four seals give the judgment scene upon earth; the remaining three give a vision of what is going on in heaven. Those martyred in the persecution are pictured as being secure, but longing for the ultimate triumph of God's forces (fifth seal). Opening the sixth seal reveals cataclysmic events in the heavens that portend catastrophe upon evil.

Between the sixth and seventh seal is an interlude. The interlude pictures 144,000 sealed under God's protection. A seal, or a mark on the forehead, was John's way of saying that these belong to God and are under His care. Since apocalyptic writing is symbolic, references to marks are symbolic as well. The number 144,000, a multiple of 12 squared and 1000, which expresses totality, stresses that all of God's people are included. An actual 144,000 is not meant. The interlude affirms God's care and protection for all His people.

An opening of seal seven eventuates in silence in heaven for "about half an hour" (8:1), a brief period of time in apocalyptic work which seems to function as preparation.

Frieze from the altar of the Temple of Domitian at Ephesus. Domitian was emperor from A.D. 81 to 96. *Biblical Illustrator* Photo/David Rogers/Ephesus Museum.

Out of the seventh seal arises the vision of seven angels with seven trumpets, who make ready to blow their trumpets. Even with the emphasis upon judgment within the seals, the reader should see the positive nature of the message. God is at work and will continue to be at work. He will hand His people the ultimate victory, keeping them and ultimately delivering them within that victory.

The Seven Trumpets (8:2—11:19)

The trumpets parallel many of the emphases in the opening of the seven seals. Repeti-

tion and reiteration are a part of John's literary expression of the message he delivered. The first four picture judgment upon humanity, primarily through natural agencies. The last three emphasize judgment upon humanity in a more direct way.

Even in judgment, however, God is pictured as giving opportunity for redemption. For example, only a third of the earth is affected in the first trumpet. Nonetheless, judgment does come upon evil; evil brings with it its own reward, and that reward is destruction. Between the sixth and the seventh trumpet, a rather lengthy interlude ensues (10:1—11:14) after which the seventh trumpet sounds.

Amidst all the troubles and struggles is the glorious message coming at the sound of the seventh trumpet, the affirmation of the sovereignty of Christ "for ever and ever" (11:15). Too, the twenty-four elders worship God and proclaim the justice that comes to all the faithful (11:16–18).

The Seven Visions
(12:1—14:20)

While this section does not have the same unity as depicted in the seals and trumpets, seven different visions make up the content. The visions are: (1) a woman giving birth to a son, 12:1–6; (2) war between Michael and the dragon (Satan), 12:7–12; (3) war between the woman and her child and Satan, 12:13—17; (4) worship of the beast of the sea, 13:1–10; (5) the rule of the beast of the earth, 13:11–18; (6) worship the Lamb by the 144,000, 14:1–5 (an interlude between the sixth and the seventh vision occurs, as did an interlude in the seals and trumpets, 14:6–13); and (7) the harvesting of the earth, 14:14–20. Conflict between good and evil occurs within these events. Throughout, God is victorious over evil in His Son, Jesus Christ.

The Seven Bowls
(15:1—18:24)

Chapter 15 is preparatory to the pouring out of the bowls, which actually occurs in chapter 16. The seven bowls become seven plagues poured out by angels upon the earth. Specifically, the plagues are against the enemies of the church. These bowls parallel much of what has been said already, but an added emphasis of the bowls seems to be the comprehensiveness of the judgment. Out of the judgment depicted by the bowls comes judgment upon Babylon, epitomizing as it does the evil against God. Babylon falls.

God's Certain Victory
(19:1—22:5)

The multitudes, who were invited to share in the marriage supper of the Lamb, know the victory over Babylon and praise God. Then is pictured the victory over the beasts and the assembled nations, the binding of Satan and his ultimate destruction, and the judgment of God from His throne. A new heaven and a new earth come into being, which is pictured in terms of relationship where people are with God and God with His people. No wickedness exists in this place-relationship, and there is no need for any sun or moon because God and the Son are there, and they are the light.

Again, determining how to apply the events in Revelation to time, from chapter 6 onward, is the big difficulty and gives rise to the great differences in serious interpretations. Consider one passage in this section where the issue of time is intense, 20:1–10, in which the millennium or 1000 years occurs. Interpreters fall into three broad categories as regards the time of 1000 years and other events related to that time. The categories are pre-millenialists, postmillenialists, and amillenialists.

Premillenialists believe that Christ will return at the beginning of the 1000 years, or shortly after the beginning, and reign with His followers on earth for 1000 years. Afterward Satan will be released for a while, and eventually his final overthrow will be accomplished. *Postmillenialists* believe that Christ will return at the end of the 1000 years of peace and prosperity upon earth, after which evil finally will be overthrown. Those who are *amillenialists* generally interpret the 1000 years as symbolic in some way, having little relationship to chronological time. One approach is that since 1000 refers to humanity, 1000 refers to the reign of God over a person. If God reigns over a person's life, then Satan is bound to that person; if God does not rule over a person, then Satan is loosed to that person. A number of variations exist under each of these approaches to interpreting the 1000 years in terms of time.

Conclusion (22:6–21)

The conclusion or epilogue to the book contains assurances about the trustworthiness of the message given to John and the promise that the Lord will come soon. The book ends appropriately. "Come, Lord Jesus. The grace of the Lord Jesus be with God's people. Amen" (22:20–21) is a fitting prayer and blessing for the end of the New Testament record.

The Apocalypse is a realistic message. The presence, power, and heart of evil are recognized and described vividly. Also, the superior might, power, and deliverance of God in Christ also are vividly proclaimed. Revelation is a message of hope and victory. Although Christians endure difficult times, ultimately God delivers and completes the victory already begun in Christ.

FOR STUDY AND REVIEW

IDENTIFY:

Apocalypsis
Symbolic
Preterist
Premillenialist
Historical
Postmillenialist
Futurist

Amillenialist

QUESTIONS FOR CONSIDERATION

1. Who were the possible persecutors of John's readers? Which is the most likely persecution?

2. What information may point to a conflict with Gnosticism for the context of Revelation?

3. What is apocalyptic literature? What are the characteristics of apocalyptic writing?

4. What is the message of Revelation?

5. What are the meanings of numbers 1, 2, 3, 4, 6, 7, 10, and 12 as sometimes used in apocalyptic material?

FOR FURTHER READING:

Kümmel, W. G. *Introduction to the New Testament,* translated by H. C. McKee. Revised and enlarged ed. Nashville: Abingdon Press, 1975: 455–74.

Ladd, George E. "Book of Revelation." *The International Standard Bible Encyclopedia,* volume 4. 171–77.

Newman, Barclay M., Jr. *Rediscovering the Book of Revelation.* Valley Forge: The Judson Press, 1968.

Robbins, Ray Frank. *The Revelation of Jesus Christ.* Nashville: Broadman, 1975.

ENDNOTES

1. See Barclay M. Newman, Jr., *Rediscovering the Book of Revelation* (Valley Forge: The Judson Press, 1968), for a scholarly but highly readable presentation of this approach.

2. C. Milo Connick, *The New Testament: An Introduction to Its History, Literature, and Thought,* 2nd ed. (Encino, Calif.: Dickenson), 416.

Glossary

The terms or concepts below are explained primarily in relationship to usage in this book.

Abraham - The name means "father of a multitude." He was the first Hebrew patriarch and became the father of the Israelites. God made an important covenant with Abraham (Gen. 12:1–3), promising to bless him with a land and a people according to Abraham's response to God's call.

Abram - "Exalted father." The name of Abraham before he became Abraham.

***Agape* (love)** - A love characterized by self-giving to others, especially exemplified in God's self-giving for others in Christ (Rom. 5:8); an unselfish love directed toward others.

Amanuensis - A Greek word designating a secretary, especially one who takes dictation.

Amillennialists - Those who interpret the thousand years of Revelation 20:4–7 as symbolic and as having little relationship to chronological time; the time might be, without indication of length, the time between the death and the return of Christ, for example.

Another Counselor - To His troubled disciples, Jesus promised that God would give them "another Counselor" whom He called "the Spirit of truth." The Counselor was to be the power and authority for the community of Christ.

Apocalypse of Peter - Written probably not later than the second century A.D., this apocalypse contains several visions including a vision of those in torment in the afterlife. It is among those apocryphal writings attributed to New Testament characters such as Simon Peter, Paul, Thomas, and Stephen.

Apocalypse - A Greek word meaning a "revelation," "disclosure," or "manifestation." The word is found in Revelation 1:1 and became the title of the book. Also, the word is used of other writings possessing apocalyptic characteristics.

Apocalyptic - A belief system or way of thought that perceived the struggle of humanity at present or to come as being caught in the struggle of cosmic powers of good and evil. Apocalyptic literature reflects this thought and dramatizes the struggle of using images, visions, numbers, and other expressions to convey a message or messages.

Apocrypha - A term arising from *apocryphal*, meaning "hidden" or "outside." About fifteen apocryphal books of Jewish literature are included in the Old Testaments of the

Roman Catholic, Orthodox, and Anglican churches. The Roman Catholic Church designates these writings as "deuterocanical," literally a "second canon"; they may not have the same priority of importance as the other books of the Old Testament. These books were written between about 200 B.C. and about A.D. 100.

Apostolicity - A term referring to one of the conditions applied by early church leaders to judging a book's fitness for the New Testament canon. A writing possessed apostolicity if an apostle wrote it, or substantially influenced its content, or if it followed apostolic doctrine.

Athanasius - A pivotal figure in formulating views about the doctrines of Christ and other church doctrines. Athanasius (about 296–373) became bishop of Alexandria. His Easter letter of 367 listed a canon of the New Testament, a list corresponding to the canon in our English translations today.

Authoritative - A word used in this text to mean that the Bible is the writing of supreme authority among all the words and writings of this world because it is the truth about God and about humanity. Consequently, the Bible is the authoritative guide for faith and living.

Babylonian Period - A period of time (605–537 B.C.) when Babylonia dominated the nations of the Near East, including Israel. The period begins with Nebuchadnezzar, king of Babylon, and ends with the ascendancy of Persia as the dominant power. A portion of this period is known also as the exilic period because in 587 B.C., the Babylonians forced many of the Israelites away from their homeland to live in the lands of Babylonia.

Canon - The word comes from the Greek word for "reed." The reed was a plant that grew in the Nile. Reeds were used as measuring sticks. Later *canon* came to mean a standard of measurement. Then canon developed to mean an official standard by which other things are measured. In reference to the Old and New Testament books, the collections of books are known as the standard books which form the Old and New Testament; thus they are the Old and New Testament canons.

Canonical criticism - A more recent variation in historical-critical methodology of studying the Scripture, this approach emphasizes that the canon in its final form, the canon as it now is, should be the focus of biblical exegesis or interpretation; the significant aspect of the Old or New Testament texts in interpretation is the canon as it now is, not the historical process by which the text came into being.

Corporate personality - A term referring to group identity and characteristics as compared or contrasted with individual identity and characteristics. Israel and the church are group personalities. For example, the church as the "body of Christ (1 Cor. 12:27) is the corporate personality of Christ.

Covenant - An agreement or contract between two parties in which each pledges to do something for the other. The biblical covenants stress God's commitment and promise to His people and the commitment and responsibility of the people to God.

Criticism - A term referring to the study and evaluation of the historical and literary backgrounds of the Old and New Testament writings. Hence, Old Testament criticism and New Testament criticism refers to historical-critical methodology in studying the documents of the Bible. Historical methodology includes such disciplines as textual, source, form, redaction, and canonical criticism.

Dead Sea Scrolls - The name for the Hebrew and Aramaic manuscripts and fragments of manuscripts discovered in 1947 in caves near the northwest end of the Dead Sea. The collection includes fragments or complete manuscripts of almost every Old Testament book. The scrolls also include noncanonical Jewish writings describing the life, beliefs, and practices of a community of Essene-like Israelites. Many scholars believe that a community, the Qumran, lived near the caves. This community collected and preserved the Old Testament manuscripts and produced its own noncanonical works.

Diatessaron - The name of Tatian's harmony of the Gospels. The name means an "interweaving," thus a weaving of the Four Gospels into a single account.

Discourse - A term referring to an extended teaching of Jesus about a certain subject or subjects. Matthew 5–7 is a discourse of Jesus.

Docetism - From the Greek word *dokeo,* which means "to seem." Docetism is a modern term given to a Gnostic-like view of Jesus Christ. Docetists taught that Christ was not really human; He only seemed to be human. To docetists anything material, including a human being, was inherently evil.

Ecclesiastical History - Written by Bishop Eusebius of Caesarea (c. 260–c. 340), this work is the main source for the history of Christianity from the end of the apostolic age to about A.D. 330. Eusebius quoted many earlier Christian writers on various subjects that are important for New Testament studies.

Eisegesis - An incorrect approach to interpretation in which interpreters read the text as if their own context and views were those of the author and original readers of the scriptural text. The word implies reading into the text of ideas that are not there.

Epicureanism - A philosophy named after the founder, Epicurus (342–270 B.C.). He believed that the senses should be trusted in determining reality. He taught that pleasure or happiness was the purpose and goal of life.

Epistle of Barnabas - A writing in Greek, dating from around the end of the first century A.D. or the beginning of the second. It belongs to the pseudepigrapha, and treats the relationship of the Old Testament to Jews and Christians and gives instruction to recent converts about living in the way of light as opposed to the way of darkness.

Eschatology, eschatological - A term which came into use in the 1800s and refers to the doctrine of last things. Consequently, eschatology is the part of systematic theology that studies last things. "Last things" carries different ideas according to those treating eschatology, but the destiny of human beings, or nations, or the cosmos is in view sometimes in reference to chronological time and sometimes in reference to the character of time. Included are doctrines about death, resurrection, judgment, and eternal life, and how these ultimate matters impinge upon and relate to individual and collective history now. For example, the expression "last days" (Heb. 1:2) is an eschatological expression meaning the days at the time of the writer of Hebrews viewed as days filled with end-time or end-of-ages reality. The adjective *eschatological* is used to describe a word, concept, or view characterized by last things or end-time views.

Essenes - A Jewish group that separated from the mainstream of Israel. The Essenes believed that Israel had failed to keep the Law. They endeavored to be the true, renewed Israel. Through cultic practices and a strict manner of life, they tried to keep themselves pure and to obey the Law (as they interpreted the Law). Many scholars believe that the Qumran community was an Essene community.

Eusebius - Bishop of Caesarea beginning around AD 315. He was an important leader during the theological controversies in the church of his time. One of his major contributions to Christian history is his *Ecclesiastical History*, a history of Christianity from the apostolic age to the time of Eusebius. He also wrote other works such as *Life of Constantine* and *The Martyrs of Palestine.*

Exegesis - A correct approach to interpretation in which consideration is given first to the context and views of the author and readers of a scriptural text to help direct the views and applications of the interpreter. The basic idea of exegesis is getting out of the text what is there.

Exile, Exilic Period - During the Babylonian Period, the conquerors forced Israelites to leave Israel and live in Babylonian territory. To be away from the homeland was to be in exile. Also called the captivity, the exile covered a period from approximately 586(7) to 538 B.C.

Exodus - This word refers to the deliverance of the Israelites out of their bondage in Egypt and toward the promised land. Moses was their leader. The date of the Exodus has been placed from 2000 to 1270 B.C. Critical

studies, with the aid of archaeological discoveries and records, favor a date between 1300 and 1270 B.C. The date used in this book is 1290 B.C.

Flesh - The word is used in this text to refer to existence in alienation from God (Gal. 5:16–24); the alienation arises out of our humanness when in separation from God. A person in right relationship to God is in an existence of "Spirit."

Form criticism - The discipline of historical-critical methodology of textual analysis concerned with the history of sayings, stories, and narratives in the gospel, including and prior to the writing of the Gospels.

Four-document hypothesis - This hypothesis views the sources behind the synoptic gospels, sources used by the authors, as being four: the Gospel of Mark, "Q" (Quell, a name for about two hundred verses found in Matthew and Luke), "L" (referring to materials that only Luke has), and "M" (referring to materials found only in Matthew).

Gemara - A part of the Talmud along with the Mishna, the Gemara is a commentary on the Mishna.

Glossolalia - The term means "tongues-speaking" and refers to the ecstatic utterance of speaking referred to in 1 Corinthians 14. Similar ecstatic utterance was a phenomenon known before the time of the Christian church.

Gnosticism - A term of modern usage denoting an amorphous philosophy of the first century that became more defined in the second century. Gnosticism taught a dualism in which a good God and a complex of evil powers stood against one another. The dualism manifested itself especially in terms of matter and spirit, matter being evil and spirit being good. The human body composed of matter was evil, but those especially blessed had a divine spark or spirit that could be liberated to make its way back to God by means of the proper knowledge (*gnosis*, Greek for "knowledge"). The philosophical appeal of Gnosticism threatened Christianity in the first and later centuries.

God-fearers - Non-Jewish followers of Jewish faith who would not or could not become proselytes. Therefore, they could not be included into Israel. They admired monotheism and the ethical emphases of Judaism. The God-fearers held some of the main tenets of the Jewish faith.

Gospel, Gospels - The word means "good news." The good news is the content of the Christian revelation, especially is Jesus Christ and His deliverance and salvation for humanity. While all the New Testament proclaims this gospel and what it means for humanity, the word is especially applied to Matthew, Mark, Luke, and John; each is a Gospel and the four together are the Gospels.

Greek Period - The time (331–167 B.C.) of Greek domination of East and West, including Israel, and the spread of the Greek language and culture, a process called Hellenization.

Hanukkah - Jewish feast celebrating the cleansing and rededication of the temple in December of 165 B.C., during the Maccabean Period after the temple had been desecrated by the forces of Antiochus Epiphanes; also called the Feast of Dedication.

Hasidim - Pious Jews who fought with the Maccabees against Antiochus Epiphanes during the Maccabean revolution. Later the Pharisees may have developed from the Hasidim.

Hellenes - Another name by which Greeks are known, after Hellas, the ancient name for Greece.

Hellenization - Also after Hellas, the term refers to the process or movement that promoted and accepted Greek language and culture.

Historical result - Seeking the historical result in interpretation of Scripture is to answer this question: What did the book, chapter, text, or verse mean to the original writer and readers? The purpose of this step in interpretation is to determine as much as possible the context of the text being interpreted as well as how the author and the original readers understood the text.

Homilies - A literary type in the New Testament which is a sermon or sermonic treatment of a subject or subjects. Some New Testament writings are homilies or are like homilies. First John, although possessing characteristics of a letter, is as much a sermon as it is a letter.

Hope - Hope in the New Testament is a promise possessing certain fulfillment. Hope is not a vague wish or wishful thinking; it is an unrealized reality. The eternal life promised to Christians is a "hope."

"In Christ" - A phrase of Paul which also takes the form of "in Him" or "in Christ Jesus," Paul uses the expression in basically three ways. It is mystical in meaning, such as we are in Christ and Christ is in us. It is an eschatological expression, which is to say that to be in Christ is to be in the eschatological age of existence determined by Jesus Christ. It sometimes means "in church;" to be "in Christ" is also to be "in church."

Immanuel - Jesus was to be called "Immanuel" (Matt. 1:23), meaning "God with us."

Inerrant - Some interpreters prefer the word inerrant meaning "without error" as the word which best affirms the errorlessness of the Bible in the autographs (the original copies, or author's copies). The concept of errorlessness usually is qualified in some way to take into consideration the authors' historical and cultural situation and their purpose in writing what they wrote. That the word evokes considerable theological discussion is evident in the kinds of inerrancy which different interpreters advocate. For example, naive, absolute, balanced, limited, and functional inerrancy represent varying views of the concept of inerrancy.

Infallible - Infallible is a word interpreters use to affirm the trustworthiness of the Bible. In its broadest sense, the word means that the Bible, properly interpreted, understood, and applied, will not fail to lead people to the truth about God, Christ, salvation, the world, and life.

Inspired - Most Christians believe the Bible is inspired. The word *inspiration* comes from a Latin word meaning "to breathe in." The Greek word behind the English word is "God-breathed." God inspired the authors in the writing of the biblical revelation.

Interbiblical Period - Dating from about 400 B.C. to about A.D. 135, this period in the history of Israel and the church includes years of Persian, Greek, and Roman domination. The Interbiblical Period is the time between the last part of the Old Testament and the writings of the New Testament. Also referred to as Intertestamental Period.

Irenaeus - An early church leader, or church father, who lived from approximately A.D. 130 to 200, he was bishop of Lyons and a theologian who countered early Gnosticism. In the process of his writings, Irenaeus gives us bits of information about the New Testament writers as well as quotes from the New Testament.

Israel - The name Israel is used in the following ways: (1) as the new name for Jacob (Gen. 32:28); (2) as the name for God's people, sometimes as a national political identity and sometimes as the people who belonged to God; and (3) as the name for the Northern Kingdom,which existed from around 922 to 721 B.C.

Jesus - The name for God's Son and a name expressing His purpose, "for he will save his people from their sins" (Matt. 1:20). The Hebrew form of Jesus is *Joshua,* which means "God is salvation" or "God saves."

Judah - The name of one of Jacob's, or Israel's, twelve sons. His tribe became large and influential. After the division of the kingdom of Israel in 922 B.C., the Southern Kingdom became known as Judah because most of its people were of the tribe of Judah.

Judaizers - Jewish Christians who considered themselves loyal to the law and to Christ because they believed both were necessary to be a part of the people of God. To be saved into the people of God a person had to come through the keeping of the law. Judaizers were probably exclusively Jews and not proselytes.

Justified - A person who is justified is made right before God, or is declared not guilty by God, on the basis of that person's faith in Jesus Christ for the righteousness of salvation.

Kingdom of God, kingdom of heaven - Some devout Jews thought it respectful to God to avoid pronouncing His name unless necessary to do so, so they used other words in the place of the name, such as "heaven." Therefore, kingdom of God and kingdom of heaven are the same expression; a non-Jew would be more likely to say "kingdom of God." The kingdom of God is not a geographical or a political entity, though these may be included. The kingdom is especially God's rule over the world and over His people.

Koine **Greek** - The Greek dialect that was the common language of the people; the common or vernacular Greek language spread through Alexander the Great's conquest and through Hellenization. *Koine* Greek is the language of the New Testament texts from which come our English translations.

Lord's Supper - The Lord's Supper, also called the Eucharist and Communion, is the meal of the New Covenant relationship that God has with His people as the Passover was the meal of the Old Covenant relationship with His people. The bread and cup, elements of the supper, point to God's self-giving in Jesus Christ for the salvation of humanity (Mark 14:12–26). As always, God's covenant is a covenant of relationship: He relates to humanity in and through Jesus Christ and humanity relates to Him in and through Jesus Christ.

Maccabean Period - The period (167–63 B.C.) in which Mattathias, his family, and other Jews rebelled against Antiochus Epiphanes IV, who had tried to force them to accept Greek religion and culture. The Maccabean rebellion began with an elderly priest named Mattathias and his five sons. The first son, who became the leader after his father's death, was Judas the Maccabee ("hammer") from whom the period takes its name. The Jews gained religious freedom once again in 165 B.C., and by about 143 B.C. gained political freedom for the first time since their return from exile.

Marcion - Marcion, who died around A.D. 160, rejected the Old Testament and the Old Testament God. He considered Christ from a Gnostic point of view. He was excommunicated from the church at Rome for his beliefs.

Marcion's Canon - A list of New Testament books developed by Marcion, a Roman Christian who rejected the Old Testament as Scripture. His canon included only Luke's Gospel and ten letters of Paul. Marcion may have edited Luke's Gospel to remove Old Testament influences.

Messiah - The Hebrew word for "anointed." Many Israelites expected a specially anointed one whom God would send to be the leader and deliverer of Israel. The New Testament proclaims Jesus as the fulfillment of that expectation. Consequently, He is Jesus "Christ." *Christ* is the Greek rendering of the Hebrew word, *Messiah.*

Messianic secret - An interpretative idea applied to Mark's Gospel by William Wrede in his book, *The Messianic Secret,* written in 1901 (reprint edition, London: J. Clarke, 1971). Jesus commanded His followers to keep silence about His identity as Messiah. Wrede noted that these commands were especially common in Mark's Gospel and argued that the author of Mark had theological purpose in writing. According to Wrede, Mark stressed keeping Jesus' messiahship secret in order to explain why many people did not recognize who Jesus was in His earthly ministry.

Mishna - A written compilation of the oral law passed down through the interpretations and applications of rabbis. The word *Mishna* is from the Hebrew word for "to repeat." The Mishna makes up part of the Talmud.

Muratorian Canon - The canon or collection of Christian writings used by the church at Rome by at least A.D. 170. It may have been a response to Marcion's Canon. Included were the four Gospels, Acts, two and perhaps three letters of John, thirteen epistles of Paul, Jude, and Revelation.

North Galatian Hypothesis (or Territory Hypothesis) - This is the hypothesis of some scholars that the Book of Galatians was addressed to churches in the territory of Galatia rather than to churches in the province of Galatia.

Oral transmission - At first the apostles and other disciples communicated the events and teachings of Jesus by the spoken word. Communication by the written word did not begin until later. While some written materials existed before, the first of the twenty-seven books we have in the New Testament probably was not written until A.D. 50 (1 Thess.).

Origen - An early leader of the church (c. 185–254), Origen's writings survive mostly in translations and quotes by other writers. His discussions about the Bible and theology constitute early witness to the issues in the church during his lifetime, such as to the state of the New Testament canon.

Papias - Papias was bishop of Hierapolis in Asia Minor. He lived from approximately A.D. 60 to 130, and his writings survive only in the quotations preserved in the writings of Irenaeus and Eusebius. According to the quotations, Papias said that Mark wrote down the teachings and actions of the Lord as he interpreted them from Simon Peter and that Matthew composed "oracles" in Hebrew, which some scholars think may point to a gospel in Hebrew prior to the Gospel of Matthew in Greek.

Parousia - Translated from the Greek word which means "coming," "arrival," or "presence." This word refers to the coming again or "second coming" of Christ.

Paschal lamb, Passover - The Greek word *pascha* is "passover," for the Jewish festival of Passover. The Passover festival celebrated the event when death passed over the homes which had the blood of a sacrificial lamb upon the doorposts. After this event Pharaoh released the people, allowing them to leave Egypt (Ex. 12). The sacrificial lamb, therefore, became associated with the deliverance of Israel from Egyptian slavery to freedom. The Passover meal was the meal of the old covenant. In 1 Corinthians 5:7, Paul calls Christ the "paschal lamb." The Lord's Supper, the meal of the New Covenant, reminds us of the sacrificial Christ who is the means to humanity's deliverance from slavery to freedom from the power of sin and death.

Pentateuch - The work means "five scrolls" and is the first and most important division of the Hebrew Bible, which includes Genesis, Exodus, Leviticus, Numbers, and Deuteronomy. The five books are also referred to as the "Torah," or "Law".

Persian Period - The period (538–331 B.C.) in which Persia became the dominant power over nations, including Israel. Also known as the post-exilic period, in about 539 King Cyrus allowed the Israelites to return to the homeland. Many of the Israelites did so and began to rebuild their nation.

Pharisees - A well-known Jewish group, perhaps deriving from the Hasidim, the "pious ones" joined with Mattathias and his sons when they rebelled against Antiochus Epiphanes. The Pharisees devoted themselves to interpreting and applying the law. The synagogue was the institution closely associated with the Pharisees. They believed in the resurrection and in angels.

Platonism - Plato (427-347 B.C.) proposed two dimensions of reality, a world of change or becoming and a world of forms or ideas which is also the world of changeless prototypes or patterns. This world in which we live is the world of change, and it is an imperfect copy or expression of the real world, the world of forms or ideas. The dimension behind this dimension cannot be reached by the senses, so one must depend upon reason.

Polycarp - Polycarp was an early Christian martyr who lived from about A.D. 69 to 155. He was bishop of Smyrna. His "Epistle to the Philippians," or "Epistle of Polycarp," gives important testimony to the New Testament. Irenaeus was under the ministry of Polycarp when Irenaeus was a young man.

Post-exilic period - The period when many Israelites returned to their homeland from captivity under Babylonia. The post-exilic period occurs within the Persian period (538–331 B.C.).

Postmillennialists - Postmillennialists, after the millennium, or thousand years, believe that Christ will return at the end of a thousand years years of peace and prosperity upon earth, when evil finally will be destroyed (see Rev. 20:1–10).

Practical result - The result sought in the process of interpretation which may be achieved by answering the following questions: What does this text mean to me? What am I going to do about it?

Premillennialists - Premillennialists believe that Christ will return and set up rule on earth resulting in the millennium, the thousand years when Satan will be bound, bringing peace for believers on earth. After the one thousand years Satan will be released for a period of time; then Satan and all his forces will be defeated (see Rev. 20:1–10).

promised land - The land of Canaan (Palestine, Israel) promised to Abraham and his descendants. In this land Jesus lived, died, and was resurrected. Also called the Land of Promise.

Prophecy - The inspired message of God delivered by His prophets or preachers. Prophecy may have a predictive element, but its primary function is to serve as God's message to a given situation in the time of the prophet or preacher.

Proselytes - Non-Jews who, by a prescribed process, adopted the Jewish faith and committed themselves to be Israelites by keeping the law, observing the rituals, and being loyal to Israel.

Pseudepigrapha - Writings attributed to an author rather than the real author, especially Jewish writings not included in Old Testament or the Apocrypha. These Pseudepigrapha were written between 200 B.C. and A.D. 200. The Roman Catholic Church calls these works the Apocrypha.

Quell - A German word which means "source," sometimes symbolized by the letter *Q*. In New Testament studies, *Q* stands for about two hundred verses found in Matthew and Luke but not in Mark. Q is considered one of the sources that Matthew and Luke used in writing their respective Gospels.

Qumran - A community living between 150 B.C. and A.D. 68 near the caves where the Dead Sea Scrolls were later discovered. The community is named for its location near the stream (or *wadi*) named Qumran.

Redaction criticism - Each of the Gospel writers used the same materials in different ways and even included different materials. Each approached and arranged materials differently. The choice, use, and arrangement of materials was driven by the purpose of each of the gospel writers. They "redacted" or edited the materials in order to achieve their purposes. Redaction critics are concerned with the how and why of this editorializing process as they seek the purpose and purposes of the respective authors in their work.

Roman Period - Rome became the dominant power among nations in West and East. The period in which they dominated the land of Israel is the Roman Period and lasted from 63 B.C. to A.D. 135, when the nation of Israel ceased to exist with any significant degree of political identity.

Sadducees - The ruling, aristocratic group among the Jews. The Torah (the first five books of the Old Testament) was their only Bible. The rest of the writings were commentary on the Torah. They did not believe in an afterlife nor in angels. Their institutional center was the temple, and they possessed significant political influence at times with the Romans.

Salvation history - A term used to discuss history from the viewpoint of God's saving work or history as evidence of God's saving work.

Samaritans - Originally, the Samaritans were simply those Hebrews of the ten tribes of Israel, so called because their capital was Samaria. After the destruction of the Northern Kingdom, however, some of those left behind by the Assyrians intermarried with non-Jews. Later Jews referred to the offspring of these mixed marriages as *Samaritans*. Also, there were those Samaritans who had their edition of the first five books of the Old Testament and who had a temple at Mount Gerezim.

Sanhedrin - The supreme ruling council among the Jews in New Testament times. Its origins are uncertain, but it arose in post-exilic times. It ruled in cases of civil and religious matters in Israel, always subject in its rulings to the political power in control over them.

Sarx - A transliterated Greek word meaning "flesh." Paul used the term theologically to indicate a state of existence apart from God characterized by manifestations of evil in life (Gal. 5:16–21).

Scripture - The term by which Christians refer to the Old Testament and New Testament as sacred literature.

Septuagint (LXX) - The Greek translation of the Old Testament and most books of the Apocrypha. It was the Bible for many New Testament Christians as the New Testament itself took shape. The term means "seventy," and the translation is so named because of the legend that seventy (later estimates said seventy-two) translators worked on translation. Designated by the Roman numerals LXX (70), the Septuagint developed over a long period beginning from around 250 B.C. It originated among Jews in Egypt and is sometimes referred to as the Egyptian canon.

Shepherd of Hermas - An apocalyptic writing from the second century, the work is attributed to a prophet named Hermas. One of its chief features is that it teaches a second chance for baptized Christians who repent of their sins. Some of its teachings are strange, such as the belief that the apostles, after their deaths, preached to and baptized the dead.

Sicarii - The term means "dagger men." It refers to the most radical among the Jewish nationalists, very hostile to Rome, who assassinated their opponents and advocated radical violence to achieve their goal of Jewish independence.

Sign - A supernatural act pointing to something inwardly and outwardly true. The Gospel of John uses the word to refer to the miraculous acts of Jesus which point to the reality that He is the Messiah.

Simple biblicism - A designation which refers to those who approach the Bible, not in simplemindedness, but simply saying that they believe the Bible to be true. They are aware of some of the theological issues of inspiration and interpretation, but they have found that the Bible corroborates their experience, needs, and beliefs and leads them to the truth about themselves and God.

Source criticism - This historical-critical method seeks to determine the sources behind New Testament writings, primarily the Gospels. The literary relationship between the Gospels of Matthew, Mark, and Luke is a concern for source criticism. Did one of the three use the other two? Did two use the other as a source? What other sources did they use? Source critics attempt to answer these questions about other books of the Bible as well.

South Galatian Hypothesis (or Province Hypothesis) - Some interpreters believe that the Letter to the Galatians addressed churches in the Roman province of Galatia (primarily southern Asia Minor) rather than churches in the territory of Galatia in northern Asia Minor.

Stoicism - The name "stoic" derived from the place where the adherents met, a *stoa* or porch, in Athens. Zeno of Cyprus (336–263 B.C.) was the founder. Stoics believed that divine reason pervaded the whole material world and that humanity's goals should be to live in cooperation with that divine reason.

Synagogue - The meeting place of Jewish communities where worship and instruction take place. Also, it serves as a place for the Jewish community to meet for other matters, such as making decisions about community life.

Synoptic, Synoptic Gospels - The Greek word *synopsis* is behind this word and means "seeing together" or "viewing together." Matthew, Mark, and Luke are the synoptic Gospels because they view Jesus and His ministry from a similar perspective.

Talmud - A collection composed of the Mishna (transmitted oral teachings of the rabbis) and the Gemara (the commentary on the Mishna). The Talmud is something of a written history of what the teachers did and said about the laws and by-laws to the Law.

Tatian - A defender of the authenticity of Christianity, born around A.D. 120 in Syria. In about 150 or 160 Tatian compiled the four Gospels into a continuous account. The name of this edition is the *Diatessaron*, which means an "interweaving."

Textual criticism - The historical-critical method of study which seeks to determine the best text when bringing together several manuscript copies of a single writing.

The Southern Kingdom - The kingdom of Judah after the division of the United Kingdom into Israel (Northern Kingdom) and Judah. The capital of Judah was Jerusalem.

The Great Galilean Ministry - The title often given to the period in Jesus' ministry in Galilee that occupied a major portion of His public ministry.

The Northern Kingdom - Upon the division of the United Kingdom in 922 B.C., the Northern Kingdom became known as Israel and the Southern Kingdom as Judah. Samaria later became Israel's capital and remained so until the fall of Israel in 721 B.C.

Torah - The word meaning "teaching" or "instruction." The term was used variously: for the first five books of the Old Testament, for the "Law of Moses," and generally for God's revelation and work with His people.

Two-Document Hypothesis - This hypothesis proposes that Matthew and Luke have two source documents at their base—Mark and *Q*.

Universal result - In the process of interpretation, this is the result achieved by asking the following question of the text: What does this text say that is true for all time, not just true for its historical context?

Via Egnatia - The vital highway that linked the East with Rome.

"We" sections - At points the narrator of Acts shifts to the first personal pronoun (we) from the third personal pronoun (they). This suggests that he was present when the events recorded in the "we" sections happened. Study of who was present at the events in the "we" section helps to determine authorship.

Zealots - Revolutionary Jews who may have taken on distinctiveness as a group by A.D. 66, when they inspired the Jewish rebellion against Rome. Zealots advocated armed rebellion and even considered it unlawful to pay taxes to Rome.

Index